W9-COS-376

Public Television for Sale

Critical Studies in Communication
and in the Cultural Industries
Herbert I. Schiller, *Series Editor*

Public Television for Sale

Media, the Market,
and the Public Sphere

William Hoynes

Westview Press

Boulder • San Francisco • Oxford

Critical Studies in Communication and in the Cultural Industries

Copyright © 1994 by Westview Press, Inc.

Published in 1994 in the United States of America by Westview Press, Inc., 5500 Central Avenue, Boulder, Colorado 80301-2877, and in the United Kingdom by Westview Press, 36 Lonsdale Road, Summertown, Oxford OX2 7EW

Library of Congress Cataloging-in-Publication Data
Hoynes, William.
    Public television for sale : media, the market, and the public sphere / William Hoynes.
        p.   cm. — (Critical studies in communication and in the cultural industries)
    Includes bibliographical references and index.
    ISBN 0-8133-1828-9 — ISBN 0-8133-1829-7 (pbk.)
    1. Public television—United States.   I. Title.   II. Series.
HE8700.79.U6H69   1994
384.55'0973—dc20   93-27344
                                                                              CIP

Printed and bound in the United States of America

The paper used in this publication meets the requirements
of the American National Standard for Permanence of Paper
for Printed Library Materials Z39.48-1984.

10   9   8   7   6   5   4   3   2   1

For Deirdre and Benjamin

Contents

Tables and Figures

Acknowledgments

My generation grew up with such public television programs as *Sesame Street* and the *Electric Company,* so it may not be surprising that I would end up writing a book about public television. But I never intended to study, certainly never intended to write a book about, public television. The decision to write a book, I have found, can be as much the result of chance or opportunity as of any long-standing interest. This book is the outcome of my experiences in the Department of Sociology at Boston College, my evolving interest in the mass media as a site of political contest, and the lack of an established body of literature about an institution, public television, that had long been a part of my life. Throughout the years of researching and writing this book, I had a great deal of support. There are several individuals whom I would like to thank.

I am particularly grateful to William A. Gamson, with whom I studied at Boston College for several years. It was his work on the intersection between social movements and the mass media that initially piqued my interest in studying the media, and it was his contact that led me to Westview Press. In between these two developments, Bill Gamson provided invaluable support in my early teaching ventures, helped me to conceptualize several earlier projects, and offered useful comments as well as needed encouragement at every stage of this project. The members of the Media Research and Action Project (MRAP), organized by Bill Gamson, have also been an indispensable resource. Many of the ideas in this book were sharpened in discussions with this group, which has included Kevin Carragee, David Croteau, Janice Fine, Sharon Kurtz, David Meyer, Mary Murphy, Charlotte Ryan, Ted Sasson, Cassie Schwerner, and David Stuart. I am grateful for the criticism and support this group has provided over the years, and I look forward to continuing my work with MRAP.

I also want to thank Charlie Derber, who was perhaps my most trenchant critic during the process of drafting this manuscript. On several occasions, Charlie provided detailed comments on the manuscript, each time pushing me to sharpen my argument and clarify my thinking. I am grateful both for his substantive criticisms and for his ongoing support. Several other individuals were particularly helpful. Kevin Carragee, Jim Ennis, and Eve Spangler all provided useful suggestions in the latter stages of the project. Ted Sasson read two early chapters and encouraged me to keep writing. Mary Murphy and Patty Bergin transcribed most of the interviews and made insightful comments along the way. Ben Sessions at Tufts University and Marilyn Kennepohl at Vassar College provided valuable research assistance. My colleagues at Fairness & Accuracy In Reporting (FAIR), including Hollie Ainbinder, Jeff Cohen, Kim Deterline, Tiffany Devitt, Janine Jackson, Martin Lee, Jim Naureckas, and Steve Rendall, gave their support. As I prepared the final draft, David Meyer helped me think through problems and meticulously critiqued the first chapter. I also appreciate the support of my editor at Westview, Gordon Massman, as well as Westview's anonymous reviewer, whose thorough comments were of great help in writing the final draft.

Three other individuals are worth singling out for their ongoing assistance. David Croteau, Sharon Kurtz, and Charlotte Ryan have, for many years, served as an intellectual, political, and moral support network. All three provided me with detailed comments on a previous draft of this book, and each of them spent the time to help me overcome the obstacles I encountered as I wrote. Beyond their assistance, David, Sharon, and Charlotte continue to serve as sources of intellectual nourishment and personal friendship for which I am deeply grateful.

This book would not have been possible without the cooperation of the individuals I interviewed at WGBH. I want to thank all twenty-five of my informants, and particularly the two individuals who helped to arrange the early interviews. I hope that my informants see parts of their collective experience reflected in this book. Thanks also go to the Graduate School of Arts and Sciences at Boston College for its financial support for the 1990–1991 academic year and to the Department of Sociology at Vassar College for providing me with a research assistant during the 1992–1993 academic year.

Finally, I am deeply grateful to Deirdre Burns for her steadfast encouragement. Deirdre has provided me with the emotional support I needed to complete this book. She was also the primary breadwinner during my graduate school years, allowing me to focus on my research and teaching. And she has always challenged me intellectually and politically. Her careful reading of several earlier drafts of this book improved it immeasurably. For many years, Deirdre has been a true partner, in the fullest sense; my expression of thanks in these acknowledgments can never capture the depth of my gratitude.

William Hoynes

CHAPTER ONE

■

Public Television: The Historical and Political Context

Since its inception, American television has been organized by the principles of the free market. Although early regulatory statements suggested that television airwaves are a kind of public utility, and although federal government licenses are necessary to operate a broadcast outlet, television in the United States always has been fundamentally a private industry. In this regard, the United States stands in marked contrast to Europe, where television has been perceived as a scarce public resource, too important to be left simply to market forces. By the 1960s, concerns about the relationship between television, the market, and the quality of public life surfaced in the United States. Critics argued that commercial television's reliance on advertiser revenue and its need to attract a mass audience made it structurally incapable of serving the broader cultural, informational, and educational functions of a democratic mass communication system. In this view, the market orientation of American television was seen as its principal constraint. Rather than fundamentally restructuring the commercial television industry, reformers created a new institution, public television, to help fulfill the communication needs of a democratic citizenry.

In this book, I examine that system of public television, now represented by the Corporation for Public Broadcasting (CPB), the Public Broadcasting Service (PBS), and local public television stations. When a national public television system was first proposed by the Carnegie Commission on Educational Television in its January 1967 report, it was designed as a uniquely American institution, one that would be supported, but not controlled, by the federal government. The Carnegie Commission argued that the new system had a crucial role to play in a democratic society and urged the federal government to act immediately to establish a national public television entity.

Shifting Political Pressures: From Johnson to Reagan

In November 1967 President Lyndon Johnson signed the Public Broadcasting Act, which created the Corporation for Public Broadcasting and set the stage for the development of the current system of public broadcasting in the United States. The Public Broadcasting Act, which was first discussed in Congress only nine months before its passage, was one of the final pieces of Johnson's Great Society program—indeed, the only piece of communications legislation that was part of the Great Society. The rapidity with which it moved through the legislative process—now almost unheard of—reflected the firm consensus that the United States needed a healthy, federally funded, noncommercial television system. In the twenty-five years since the passage of the Public Broadcasting Act, the structure of public television has evolved, adapting both to the continuing growth of the public television system and, more dramatically, to changing political pressures.

The history of public broadcasting has been well told elsewhere,[1] and I do not intend to review all of the details. However, in order to understand the current state of public television and the dilemmas and contradictions it now faces, we need to begin with a brief historical overview. Because external political pressure has played such an important role in public television's history, we should be particularly concerned with the changing political climate and how public broadcasters have responded to it.

Since its earliest days, there has been a slow but steady privatization of public television. This trend is partially a result of the fact that fear of political control by the federal government has always outweighed fear of commercialization in public television circles. This attitude should not be surprising, because it reflects the broader political culture in the United States, in which intervention by "big government" in any arena of community life is immediately suspect.[2] Fears of state involvement, however, were not based simply on abstract popular notions. The formative experiences of many public broadcasters gave them good reason to watch out for government intervention, particularly from the White House.[3]

Rather than model American public television after state television in Europe, the designers of the system sought to avoid state control and suggested an administrative and financial structure to prevent it. The Public Broadcasting Act, however, only set up an administrative structure (CPB),[4] leaving the financing to the federal government's regular appropriations process. As a result, the funding of public broadcasting—even when money is authorized on a three-year basis, two years in advance, as it has been since the late 1970s—has always been a politically charged issue, with partisan debates about "bias" and "objectivity" a regular feature of the funding process.

Early proponents suggested that the only way to prevent such a politicization of the funding process was to provide stable, long-term funding for public television.[5] Although President Johnson indicated in 1967 that a long-range funding plan would be worked out in the coming year, his ultimate withdrawal from the 1968 presidential race left public broadcasting without such a plan. The election of Richard Nixon brought new problems for the fledgling public television system. From Nixon's perspective, particularly as the Vietnam War continued to drag on, public television was a home for liberal journalists who produced biased news and public affairs programs with the help of federal funds.

By 1970, the Nixon administration was unhappy with the broadcasting of such documentaries as *Banks and the Poor*,[6] which critically examined banking practices that exacerbated poverty in urban areas and "closed with a list of 133 senators and congressmen with banking holdings or serving as directors of banks—while the Battle Hymn of the Republic played in the background" (Stone, 1985: 29). As such, the White House made plans to rein in public television. Federal funding was the weak link in the plan to insulate public television from political pressures, so the administration focused its strategy on the appropriation of money for CPB. On June 30, 1972, President Nixon vetoed CPB's authorization bill, arguing that public television had become too centralized and was becoming a "fourth network." In criticizing CPB and the supposed centralization of the system, the administration had hoped to capitalize on the confusion about the evolving relationship between CPB, PBS, and the local stations. In retrospect, it seems clear that Nixon's call for a return to "the bedrock of localism," as the administration put it, was a cover for the more political problems the administration had with the system—particularly with several members of the CPB board, who were perceived as too liberal and unwilling to work with the administration, and with CPB's relationship to National Educational Television (NET), one of the principal programmers for the young public television system and producer of *Banks and the Poor*. However, as Witherspoon and Kovitz (1987) suggested, the Nixon administration was concerned about the consequences of directly attacking public affairs programs. Its goal of changing the makeup of the CPB board and steering public television away from the production of nationally distributed public affairs programs could be accomplished by focusing on the role of CPB instead of on the particular programs. Such a strategy was intended to shield the White House from the argument that it was interfering politically with public television or that it intended any form of "censorship." To a great extent, the strategy worked: Over the next two months, the chairman, president, and director of television for CPB resigned. At the end of August, after these resignations had been accepted, Nixon signed a bill authorizing public broadcasting funding for 1973.

The political struggle between Nixon and CPB had three important, and lasting, consequences. First, it showed that public broadcasting was vulnerable to political pressure, particularly from the White House. Its vulnerability came from a predictable source: the fact that the federal government had to regularly approve its funding. Second, it meant that public television had to establish mechanisms to protect itself, as much as possible, from the political pressures it was likely to face in the future. This necessity led to the development of a new, decentralized method for distributing production funds, the Station Program Cooperative (SPC), which would be a central component of the public television programming process from 1974 to 1990.[7] The creation of the SPC was one sign of a broader trend to diffuse the potential targets of political pressure by shifting programming decisions away from CPB. Third, the public television system realized that it needed to look for additional sources of revenue, particularly from the private sector, in order to reduce its dependence on the highly politicized federal appropriations process. Specifically, the Nixon veto led public television producers to turn their attention to corporate underwriting, initially from major oil companies, as a new source of program financing.

These three consequences—vulnerability to presidential political pressure, a reorganization of the relationship between local stations and the national public television system, and the reliance on corporate underwriting dollars— can be seen as a set of recurring issues in the history of public television. The 1972 Nixon veto set the tone, and provided a framework, for the ongoing political contest about the need for, and structure of, the public television system.

In contrast to the Nixon years,[8] Carter's presidency was relatively quiet for public television, which continued to grow. Congressional Democrats had traditionally been supporters of public television (and, for the most part, continue to be), and the lack of tension between public television and the Democratic administration served as a temporary respite from political pressure. When Ronald Reagan became president in 1981, however, public television faced renewed political and economic pressures from the White House. On one level, the hostility to public television was philosophical: The Reagan White House supported wide-ranging deregulation, and it frowned upon a host of federally funded programs. As a result, federally funded public television was, to say the least, not a favored institution in the Reagan administration. On another level the hostility was more partisan, as the old claim of a liberal bias in public television, last heard from the Nixon administration, was once again in the news. Such philosophical differences and partisan political charges did have material consequences. The Reagan administration pushed forward funding reductions for public television through the 1981 Public Broadcasting Amendments Act, and federal funding of public television was under siege again.

The reduction of federal support and the simultaneous deregulation of commercial television were not the only signs of a renewed emphasis on the market orientation of the television industry. In 1984 the Federal Communications Commission (FCC) broadened its guidelines for the identification of corporate underwriter support on public television programs, allowing commercial-like announcements at the beginning and end of programs. Rather than simply allowing "advertising" on public television, the new regulations, labeled "enhanced underwriting," permitted "logos or slogans that identify—but do not promote or compare—locations, value-neutral descriptions of a product line or service, trade names, and product or service listings" (Witherspoon and Kovitz, 1987: 56). Not only was the commercial television industry becoming less regulated and therefore less accountable to any measure of the public interest beyond audience ratings, public television itself was—as a result of federal funding cuts and new underwriting codes—becoming more commercial.

The Privatization of Public Television

In the spring of 1992, public television became the subject of national discussion once again. It made newspaper headlines, aroused a great deal of attention on Capitol Hill, and even was the subject of campaign advertisements by one Republican presidential candidate. The attention was not, however, due to the release of another highly acclaimed documentary, such as *Vietnam: A Television History* or *The Civil War,* both of which had catapulted PBS into the national spotlight in previous years. On the contrary, the attention in the first half of 1992 was neither triggered by a particular PBS program nor encouraged by public television executives. It represented, to be sure, the most powerful threat to the survival of a public television system since the 1972 Nixon veto: the growing movement toward the privatization of public institutions.

The process of privatization, as such, does not occur spontaneously, any more than the initial creation of the public sector did. Nor is it simply the product of a particular *zeitgeist,* such as the market fetishism emerging in the post–cold war era in the United States. Privatization must be understood as part of the larger ongoing contest over how societies are to be organized, the social relations of both production and consumption. Occurring at a time in which the collapse of the Soviet Union is taken as the ultimate victory of capitalism—and in which the economic and moral superiority of the free market is celebrated uncritically—the call for privatization must be seen as the work of those social strata, led by corporate America, that have historically had little need for a public sector and will, not surprisingly, benefit most directly from privatization. Although the erosion of the public sector seems to take on a life of its own in a recessionary economic climate—particularly when such an economic climate is combined with a growing perception that some people are "dependent" upon the public sector and others are not[9]—we must avoid the tendency to forget the actual human agency, in the form of organized political activity, that is the driving force behind movements toward privatization.

This is the context in which public television made headlines in early 1992. At a time when the survival of the National Endowment for the Arts (NEA) appeared in jeopardy and the commitment to public education seemed to be wavering, public television, much to the dismay of its principals, momentarily took center stage in the debate over the future of the public sector. The proximate source of the widespread attention was the organized attack on public television by a coalition of conservative organizations, led by the Heritage Foundation, at a time when Congress was to consider the reauthorization of funding for public broadcasting. The substance of the attack was not new, although its increased vigor gave the impression of being something different. The outcome, at least in the short run, was also reminiscent of previous debates, as a Democrat-controlled Congress passed the reauthorization bill but attached tighter strings. Perhaps the only truly new aspect of this contest was the post–cold war political climate that celebrated the market in a quasireligious manner, a climate in which the privatization of public television seemed to have become a viable option.

The 1992 debate about public television, much like those that occurred under Nixon and Reagan, illuminates a great deal about the historical tensions, both economic and political, inherent in the public television system in the United States. Since this book is about the current state of public television—indeed, the very meaning of the term "public" television—the story of the 1992 conservative attack and its consequences is a particularly useful place to begin.

1992: Renewed Attack on Public Television

The conservative attack on PBS came from two apparently contradictory directions. Any contradiction, however, was superficial; it is more useful to see the two strategies as complementary. Laurence Jarvik, the Bradley Resident Scholar at the Heritage Foundation, was the principal representative of one strategy; David Horowitz of the Committee for Media Integrity was the public face of the second strategy. Jarvik's January 1992 report, "Making Public Television Public," was distributed by the Heritage Foundation and quoted widely in the mass media; in it, contrary to the title of the report, he argued for the wholesale *privatization* of public television. The rationale for such an argument was twofold: 1) television, in principle, should be a private enterprise, and 2) the particular institutions that make up the public television system had outlived their usefulness. As such, Jarvik's plan for making public television public was to sell the Corporation for Public Broadcasting to the private sector. Ultimately, Jarvik (1992a: 12) argued that "privatization provides the means to clean up the public television mess by creating incentives for excellence, efficiency and accountability. It is time to privatize public television.[10]"

Horowitz, rather than argue for the total privatization of public television, focused his attack on the politics of public television programming. Horowitz's claims of a systematic left-wing bias in public television, based on anecdotal evidence and made in a vituperative tone, made for good newspaper copy and lively talk show debates. His call for Congress to reassert political control over public broadcasting by ensuring "objectivity" and "balance" on public television found support among conservatives in the U.S. Senate. Ultimately, Horowitz's assertions of left-wing bias, perhaps more than Jarvik's call for the privatization of public television, framed the congressional debate about public television in the months to follow.

The two positions—one calling for the government to take a more active role in regulating the political content of public television, the other suggesting the complete privatization of public television—may appear antithetical. However, as Jarvik's heavy reliance on Horowitz's argument makes clear, they are two sides of the same coin. What they share is a desire to impose new constraints—in one case political, in the other, economic—on a public television system that has been at least partially removed from such regulation in the past. Moreover, increased state intervention is the centerpiece of an intermediate strategy, one that accepts the short-term existence of public television; the call for privatization is part of a longer-term strategy to eliminate public broadcasting altogether. We can see a similar phenomenon with the attack on the NEA in the early 1990s, where the reassertion of political control may be the first step toward total dissolution.

The combined argument for further state control of public television and total privatization, then, highlights the principal questions for the future of public television: What is the relationship between a *public* television system and both market and state? What, indeed, does it mean to be a *public* institution at a time of rapid privatization? These are ultimately the questions that animate this study of public television.

These questions, however, are too broad to provide a suitable starting point for our investigation of public television. They are more abstract questions than those directly addressed by the conservative critique. In the final chapter of this book, I will return specifically to the theoretical realm and address the broader questions about the nature of a public television system. Presently, however, it will be useful to review the conservative argument in some detail, for it provides context important for the understanding of the current system.

Behind the Conservative Critique

The conservative critique—as articulated by both Jarvik and Horowitz and later developed by columnist George Will[11]—rests on two central assumptions about the nature of mass communications systems in general and the makeup of public television in particular. First, the conservatives assume that the forces of the economic market will provide for a mass media with a representative marketplace of ideas. Put more bluntly, they believe that the quality of ideas should be measured by the demand they generate among an audience of media consumers. In the case of television, those programs able to attract an audience (and, presumably, the advertisers interested in selling goods to that audience) will find a home on the schedule. Those programs that cannot attract a sizeable enough audience, the logic continues, have no business cluttering up the television schedule. Government support for public television, therefore, violates a central premise, for the system lacks a market mechanism to determine the necessity of a particular program. (Related to this first assumption is the argument, made most clearly by George Will, that without any kind of market accountability, public television has become a taxpayer-supported luxury for a tiny elite.)

A second assumption is that the television market in the United States has been burst open by the development of new technologies, particularly cable television, so that noncommercial television is no longer necessary. Without the artificial constraints posed by the limited broadcast spectrum—which allowed for only three or four channels in most areas prior to the development of cable—the market will provide for all of the needs of television viewers. Noncommercial television, perhaps necessary when competition was limited, is therefore obsolete.

These two assumptions—media should be organized on market principles, and new technologies have "freed" the television market and made public television obsolete—are the driving force behind the conservative call for privatization. They are presented not as propositions to be analyzed and debated but as inarguable observations about how the world works. They represent a particular worldview, an ideology that reveres the market and distrusts institutions organized on nonmarket principles. Such an ideology has become so commonplace in the 1980s, and in the post–cold war era in general, that it may no longer seem to be ideological at all. It begins to be seen as simple "common sense." This is, in fact, part of the appeal of the conservative attack on public television: Common sense provides powerful ideological cover.

For our purposes, however, such "common sense" assumptions should serve as flags to issues that cannot simply be taken for granted. They highlight the issues upon which the future of public television rests. It may not be overstating the case at all to suggest that the contest to have one's assumptions accepted as truth, not ideology, will be central in the broader struggle over the privatization of public television. Although we will return to a discussion of the market and the new technologies in the final chapter, it will be useful here to briefly examine the premises behind the conservative critique.

The first assumption—that the market is the most democratic basis upon which to structure a media system—is, in many ways, a peculiarly American position. Other advanced industrial countries have never accepted the premise that television should simply be organized as a commercial industry. Rather than being considered a guarantor of a vibrant idea market, the economic market has been seen by many analysts as the principal threat. Entman (1989) argues that there is a "contradiction between the logic of the economic market and the logic of the market place of ideas," suggesting that we should be wary of the conservative assumption. Entman concludes that "the first step to lasting improvements in journalism is isolating some outlets from the economic market altogether," precisely the opposite of the conservative argument for restoring market forces. For the moment, we should take note of the fact that the conservative assumption—often presented without question in media accounts of the attack on public television—is, at minimum, far from an accepted truth. It is, in fact, a topic on which there has been great debate.[12] In Chapter 2, we will return to this question in greater detail, examining the scholarly literature on this debate.

The second assumption—that cable television has opened up the television market, making public television obsolete—is more complex. Its most straightforward claim is that there is a greater volume of programming available to American television viewers. If the number of channels has increased by a factor of five, ten, or twenty in the past decade, then (or so the argument implies) there has been an equivalent expansion in diversity of programming. Such expanded diversity, it is claimed, now satisfies virtually all known taste segments of the viewing population, leaving no reason for the existence of public television, which was created specifically to add diversity to the commercial television system.

The observation about increased volume is undoubtedly true, but the assertion of a corresponding increase in diversity is dubious. The simple equation of volume with diversity may not seem problematic. However, the expanded number of channels still must face the same economic constraints as the smaller number. Neuman (1991) observed that although new communications technologies provide enormous potential for increased diversity, "commercial market forces and deeply ingrained media habits pull back hard in the other direction." The result is a "pattern of common-denominator and politically centrist political communication. The new media will not change this in the main." Neuman's analysis suggests that, in fact, the rise of new media technologies does not make noncommercial media obsolete. On the contrary, new technologies that are developed for commercial purposes may make noncommercial media even more important; they may serve as an oasis for the use of these technologies in an environment partially insulated from the market. Again, the conservative assumption is an issue on which there is an ongoing debate.

What have we learned by looking at the underlying assumptions of the conservative critique of public television? First, we have seen that the apparently "common sense" truths upon which the conservative argument rests are ideological constructions rather than simple facts. (They are connected to a broader set of assumptions that conservative economists make about the superiority of market-based institutions.) Second, and perhaps more important for scholarly purposes, we have seen that the unquestioned assumptions of the conservatives are actually central issues in the debate about the future of public institutions in general and public television in particular. Any discussion about public television or communications policy as a whole will have to take up these very points—the market orientation of mass media and the impact of new communications technologies. Ultimately, the analysis of public television becomes more than a technical or economic question; it becomes a normative question, for we end up talking about the kind of media system our country should have. The normative nature of the discussion can be obfuscated by the use of "common sense" assumptions presented as simple fact. This kind of intellectual sleight-of-hand, common to advocates of various political stripes, is not the only way that highly normative discussions can be recast. Social science, with its reliance on the scientific method, is capable of playing a similar role. As such, it should not be surprising that Jarvik's call for privatization was cast as "scholarship" on public television or that conservative critics pointed to the findings of empirical research by the Center for Media and Public Affairs.[13] In essence, the conservatives tried to have it both ways: Both "scholarly research" and "common sense" supported their positions.

The recent debate about public television, as well as most previous discussions, has been filled with arguments about the supposed partisan nature of the programming. Some have argued that public television is "too liberal"; others have suggested that it is "too conservative." As a result, the discussion has focused on narrow questions of "bias" and "objectivity." These questions are ultimately problematic, for they serve to obscure the broader questions about the reasons for creating a public television system, the structural arrangements necessary to maintain one, and the constraints imposed on public television by both internal and external forces. By focusing on the product and ignoring the process, the "bias paradigm" tells us little about the causes of supposed shortcomings, nor can it provide a theoretically informed analysis of how to move public television forward or, for that matter, where it should go. If the bias paradigm is in decline, as Hacket (1984) has so persuasively argued, no alternative framework has emerged in the ongoing debate about the politics of public television.

This book is a sociological study of public television. It is an effort to grapple with the fundamental contradictions in the system today, to understand how it works, and to envision its future. This is, of course, a project with normative (and increasingly political) undertones. I make no apologies for the

normative nature of the discussion to follow. Any serious discussion of contemporary issues—especially those focusing on social organization and public
policy—must have a normative component (whether it is articulated or not).
As a result, I make my own assumptions clear in Chapters 2 and 3, I explore
the intellectual roots of these assumptions, and I provide evidence to support
my argument throughout the text. Journalists and pundits may, for purely
structural reasons, lack the time or space to present more than the bare bones
of their argument, and lobbyists and advocates make a living off of the certainty with which they express their positions, but academics are in the position of having the time, space, and political freedom to examine their subjects
without taking shortcuts.

The ongoing debate about public television—filled with the charges and
countercharges of those who lack the time or inclination to actually study the
subject—must begin with an examination of some of the fundamentals of our
public broadcasting system. In the following section, I present a brief
overview of the various organizations that make up the system, summarize the
evolution of public television funding, and examine the makeup of the public
television audience. This material will provide a useful background for subsequent chapters.

Public Television Fundamentals

Public TV Organizations

As public television folklore would have it, the lifeblood of the system is the
local station.[14] Although this axiom may understate the degree to which centralized sources of both funding and programming have driven the growth of
public television, the importance of local stations, particularly for viewers,
cannot be overstated. Local stations give public television an identity, and
they provide the public face for the national system. (This role is quite the opposite from that of local network affiliates, whose identity is built, to a great
degree, upon affiliation with the national network.) Before the Corporation
for Public Broadcasting was created, local "educational" stations provided
the backbone for what would later become the national public television system. The Carnegie Commission, as part of its research for its 1967 report, vis-
ited 92 of these educational stations and contacted all 124 such stations in the
United States. The public television system, the commission believed, would
be built by interconnecting the already-existing educational stations. Local
stations, then, predated the existence of a national public television system,
and the creation of CPB facilitated the dramatic proliferation of public television stations in the following years.

Figure 1.1 shows the growth in the number of public television stations between 1955 and 1991.[15] It highlights the sharp growth in the period immediately following 1967, when CPB was created and federal funds were commit-

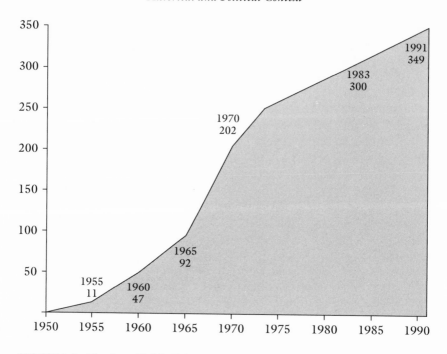

FIGURE 1.1   Number of Public Television Stations, 1950–1991
Source: Corporation for Public Broadcasting; Carey, 1989.

ted. By 1991, there were 349 local public television stations, almost triple the number in operation when the Public Broadcasting Act was passed twenty-five years earlier. The 349 stations, covering 98 percent of American households, were operated by four different types of organizations: nonprofit community organizations, colleges or universities, state government agencies or commissions, and local government authorities. Figure 1.2 shows the distribution of stations among these four types of organizations and indicates that the majority of stations were run by community organizations and state governments. Many of the state government stations were "linked into statewide multistation networks that air a single program schedule in common" (CPB, 1992: 6). As a result, the 349 stations broadcast a total of 196 distinct program schedules. It is difficult to make generalizations about the local stations, for many have their own schedules, each has its own management, and each has its own unique relationship with local viewers. Suffice it to say that these local stations, whose interests often differ from each other's and from those of the national system, serve as the structural framework for the system.

Beyond the local stations, the two central players in public television are CPB and PBS. As previously indicated, the Public Broadcasting Act called for the establishment of the CPB, a nonprofit corporation, not an "agency or es-

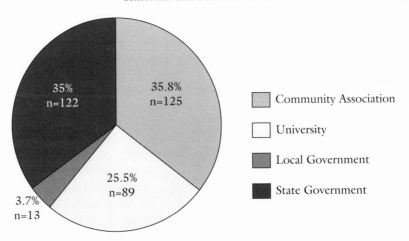

Figure 1.2   Type of Organization Running Public Television Stations, 1991
Source: Corporation for Public Broadcasting.

tablishment of the United States government." The act specifically authorized CPB to

(A)   facilitate the full development of educational broadcasting in which
       programs of high quality, obtained from diverse sources, will be
       made available to noncommercial educational television or radio
       broadcast stations, with strict adherence to objectivity and balance in
       all programs or series of a controversial nature;
(B)   assist in the establishment and development of one or more systems
       of interconnection to be used for the distribution of educational
       television or radio programs so that all noncommercial educational
       television or radio broadcast stations that wish to may broadcast the
       programs at times chosen by the stations;
(C)   assist in the establishment and development of one or more systems
       of noncommercial educational television or radio broadcast stations
       throughout the United States;
(D)   carry out its purpose and functions and engage in its activities in
       ways that will most effectively assure the maximum freedom of the
       noncommercial educational television or radio broadcast systems
       and local stations from interference with or control of program con-
       tent or other activities (Public Broadcasting Act of 1967, PL
       90-129).

The clearest tasks for the fledgling CPB after its formation in 1968 were to
provide support for program production; to facilitate the "interconnection"
of public television stations, which had hitherto shared programs infre-
quently, and only by mail; and to serve as a kind of "heat shield," protecting

public stations from political pressure. CPB was not to produce programming on its own, nor was it to operate the system it was authorized to create. As a result, it was necessary to create another organization, independent of CPB, to operate the interconnection. For this purpose, local stations and CPB created PBS in November 1969.[16]

More than two decades later, the basic structure of public television has changed little: Local stations, CPB, and PBS are the principal players. The specific roles of the two national organizations are clearer now than they were in the early 1970s. CPB uses federal funds to support the production of national programming and to assist in the development of local public television stations. More than half of CPB's support goes directly to local stations in the form of community service grants. PBS purchases programming for the stations, distributes it via satellite, and provides marketing and other support services to the stations. PBS is owned by its member stations, which provide most of its financial backing. It is a complex relationship: CPB provides funding for both PBS and local stations; local stations, in turn, finance PBS.

The final piece of the public television puzzle is the production of programming. Most stations produce some of their own programming; however, local programming only covers a small percentage of the broadcast schedule. Public television stations obtain programs from a wide range of sources: Some stations broadcast old sitcom reruns, others show classic movies, and most air a wide range of material produced specifically for public television and distributed by PBS. This programming comes from independent producers, foreign broadcast outlets such as the BBC, and "producing" stations, among other sources. A small number of stations serve as production centers; the dominant ones are WNET/New York, WGBH/Boston, WETA/Washington, WTTW/Chicago, and KCET/Los Angeles. Regular public television viewers are likely to be familiar with these call letters, since these stations are the producers of a large amount of the prime time schedule.

Of course, not all of the various organizations that fund, produce, distribute, and broadcast public television programs have the same interests, nor do they necessarily serve the same constituency. Large producing stations may have quite different interests than stations that do little of their own production. It is clear, for example, that the major producing stations command many more resources than the bulk of local broadcast stations. Moreover, since local station managers serve very specific audiences of local viewers, there is no guarantee that all public television constituencies have the same interests or tastes. For example, stations in major urban areas—who are, not coincidentally, the producing stations—may have different program needs than stations in smaller, more rural areas. Finally, it is not at all clear that the national organizations—PBS and CPB—have the same interests as the local stations or, for that matter, the program suppliers. It is impressive that these various organizations, with different and sometimes conflicting priorities, have

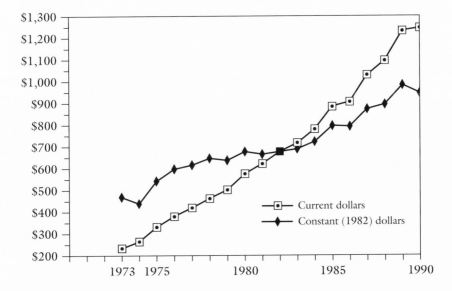

FIGURE 1.3   Public Television Income, 1973–1990 (in millions of dollars)
Source: Corporation for Public Broadcasting.

been able to negotiate a common, if shifting, agenda that allows public television to continue to function.

Public TV Income

Along with expansion in the number of local stations, another sign of public television's growth is the dramatic increase in its total income over the past two decades. Figure 1.3 shows the rise in total public television income, in both constant and current dollars, between 1973 and 1990. The total dollar amount grew steadily, and the relative importance of various sources of income changed over the years. Figure 1.4 compares the percentage contribution of three major income sources—the federal government, businesses, and subscribers—between 1973 and 1990.

Whereas the federal government's portion of public television's total income dropped from a high of 28.9 percent in 1976 to 16.2 percent in 1990,[17] the importance of business and subscriber support increased dramatically. In 1990 business provided 16.8 percent of public television's total income, the result of a steady increase from the 4 percent contribution in 1973. Subscribers in 1990 provided 21.9 percent of total income, up from a contribution of 7.2 percent in 1973. Chapter 5 addresses the issue of public television's funding in more detail and discusses the consequences of the changing sources of revenue. At this point, we should take note of the fact that public television, as a system, has grown steadily for two decades and that the character of its funding has changed at the same time that the financial resources of the system

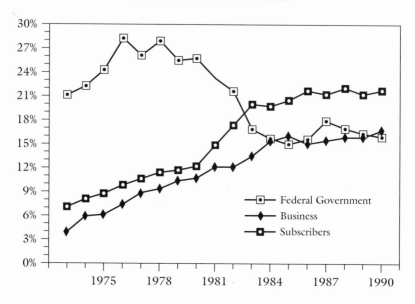

FIGURE 1.4   Sources of Public Television Income, 1973–1990 (as a percentage of total)
Source: Corporation for Public Broadcasting.

have increased. We should also note that different sources of income bring their own particular constraints; with changing sources of income, it is likely that we will also find changing constraints.

Public TV Viewers

Although the number of stations and the total income of public television continued to grow through the 1970s and 1980s, public television executives could only hope that the size of the audience would hold its own. At a time when network television ratings were dropping dramatically as cable television continued to spread and the VCR became a standard household item, public television fought to maintain its audience.[18] Figure 1.5 shows the daytime, prime time, and post–prime time ratings for winter quarters in the years 1988 to 1992. Although daytime and post–prime time ratings remained stable, prime time ratings dropped slowly but steadily. This trend, as we will see in Chapter 6, is of considerable concern to public television executives

More important than the sheer size of the audience[19] is its demographic composition. Public television today faces conflicting pressures on this issue. On the one hand, it must pitch its programming to potential corporate underwriters, and one of public television's strong suits from this perspective is the "upscale" nature of the audience. On the other hand, public television executives are sensitive to the charge that the audience is simply made up of "elite" individuals. They point out that a wide range of the American public watches

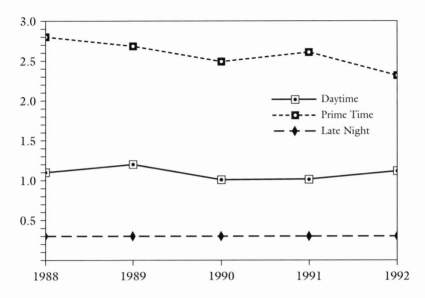

FIGURE 1.5   Public Television Rating Trends, 1988–1992
Source: PBS Research.

public television. In fact, the charges of elitism are so ingrained in the minds of those in the public television system that a 1986 PBS publication began by asking, "Who watches public television? A small, select audience? Only the well to-do? Quite the contrary. Public television has grown to become what its founders intended, a truly *public* television service" (PBS, 1986: 1; emphasis in original). As a public institution, then, public television is conscious of the need to do more than serve an upscale audience.

The principal difficulty, of course, is that the audience for public television is not uniform: It changes from program to program and, undoubtedly, from one locality to the next. This variability makes generalizations of the kind that we frequently hear—public television has an elite audience, or public television has a diverse audience—incomplete at best. Rather than providing unequivocal support for one side or the other in this debate, the evidence seems to suggest that, in fact, both claims have some merit.

Public television does serve a large, and clearly diverse, audience. The "four-week cume" measures the percentage of television households that tune in to public television at least once during a four-week period (traditionally in March); in March 1992, 80.8 percent of TV households in the United States tuned in to public television. The prime time figure was 59.2 percent. Figure 1.6 shows the growth in the "cume ratings" from 1978 to 1992. This data is only a first step, but it does provide one very simple insight: A large percentage of the American public finds something worth watching, at least oc-

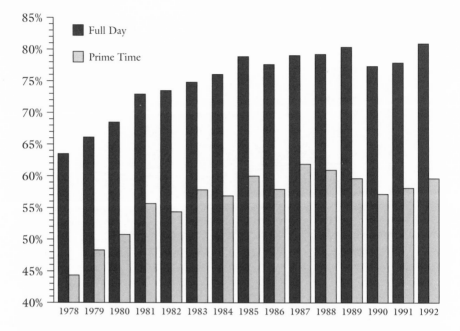

FIGURE 1.6   Percentage of U.S. Television Households Turning on Public Television,
1978–1992
Source: PBS Research.

casionally, on public television. Public television's assertion that it serves a
wide range of the public, then, certainly has some merit. It is not, however,
the whole story.

We can learn more about the public television audience by examining its
demographic makeup. A variety of prime time programs, including the *American Experience, Frontline,* and *Nova,* have audiences disproportionately composed of white, college-educated, high-income families.[20] Several other public affairs programs, including the *MacNeil/Lehrer NewsHour, Wall Street
Week,* and *Washington Week in Review,* show similar trends. Whereas 23 percent of U.S. television household heads are college graduates, the percentage
of the viewers for these six programs who are college graduates ranged from
32 percent to 40 percent. And whereas 19 percent of TV households have an
annual income above $60,000, the comparable figure for the audience for
these six programs ranges from 26 percent to 31 percent.

We should, however, be careful not to jump to quick conclusions here.
Even the programs that can boast about their "upscale demos," as the jargon
goes, have wide-ranging audiences. For example, 17 percent of *Frontline*'s
viewers do not have a high school degree, and 24 percent have a family income of less than $20,000. For the *MacNeil/Lehrer NewsHour,* the figures are

similar: 16 percent of the viewers have not completed high school and 29 percent have a family income of less than $20,000. Although such figures are below the U.S. television household averages (22 percent do not have a high school degree and 31 percent have a family income of less than $20,000), they still suggest that large numbers of people who are not part of the upscale audience watch these programs. Moreover, several programs—such as *Big Band Ballroom Dancing*, *Nature*, and *Victory Garden*—have audiences that more closely reflect the U.S. population.[21]

What are we to make of all of this data? It seems clear that the public television audience is not some easily describable, uniform mass. More likely, it is constantly changing, composed of a series of different audiences for different time blocks and different programs. We can say with some confidence, however, that it is diverse but has a tendency to overrepresent those in upscale demographic groups, particularly for the prime time schedule. Does this tendency make it a narrow, elite audience? Or does this make it a wide-ranging and largely representative audience? Ultimately, it seems, one could make a case for either of these interpretations. However, the answers we assign to these questions—or, for that matter, that official PBS publications or outside critics provide—are of little consequence. What is more important are the *meanings* attached to the actual and perceived makeup of the public television audience. In order to focus on these meanings, it is necessary to examine how those who produce public television programs perceive the audience, how they respond to this perceived audience, and the subsequent constraints that the audience places on program production. We will return to these issues in Chapter 6.

Plan for the Book

Now that the context, both historical and political, has been set and the principal organizational characters have been introduced, we are prepared to move ahead. In the following chapters, I will take a close look at various aspects of our public television system and argue that the continuing intrusion of the market is the single most important constraint on public television. The funding of public television is increasingly influenced by market forces; the perception of the public as an audience suggests a market-oriented ideology; and the lack of a clear alternative mission serves to reinforce these market forces. The use of the market as a central organizing theme, however, should not be misunderstood as an argument that an explanation of public television can be reduced to a crude market model. Other factors, including a strong professional culture and subtle organizational imperatives, are important influences on public television. Although I emphasize the impact of the market, it is not presented as an exclusive determinant. As such, there are several points in the text where both market and nonmarket factors are discussed. As we will see, these forces often push public television in a similar direction.

In Chapter 2, I review the theoretical literature on the relationship between mass media and the market, emphasizing the importance of corporate ownership, advertising, and the new horizontally integrated media empires. I examine the primary market mechanism in commercial television—ratings—and argue that these are far from the embodiment of a democratic process. The chapter closes with an examination of the public nature of broadcasting and a review of the main tenets of the model of European public service broadcasting.

In Chapter 3, I analyze three early articulations of a vision for public television, including the report of the Carnegie Commission, as a means for developing an "ideal type" of public television. This ideal type becomes a heuristic device throughout the book, helping to highlight tensions and contradictions in the development of public television. Chapter 3 briefly reviews the recent scholarly literature on public television, which is relatively scant, and suggests that its primary focus on the content of programming leaves a wide range of questions untouched. The chapter closes with a short outline of the research methods used in this study.

Chapter 4 provides a case study comparing the principal nightly news program on PBS, the *MacNeil/Lehrer NewsHour,* with one hour of ABC News (*World News Tonight* and *Nightline*) over a six-month period. I find that *MacNeil/Lehrer* covers a wider range of stories than ABC but is no more diverse in the perspectives it features. I argue that reliance on corporate underwriters may provide a partial explanation but suggest that the norms of professional journalism are central to why *MacNeil/Lehrer* relies on the same narrow set of analysts as ABC News. I close the chapter by suggesting that research needs to move beyond content studies and examine public television from the inside.

In Chapters 5 through 7, I make use of in-depth interviews with producers of national PBS programming to examine the internal workings of public television. Chapter 5 analyzes the funding process as the primary market mechanism at public television. I argue that funding scarcity inhibits risk taking and that funding serves as a subtle drive on programming. I discuss the influence of major corporate funding and find that corporations have little interest in underwriting controversial programs and are attracted to PBS by the perception (cultivated by PBS) that it has an upscale audience. I also suggest that the need to attract contributions from high-income viewers further pushes public television in the direction of narrow programming choices and conclude that the funding market, although different from the advertising market in commercial television, exerts significant pressures on public television.

Chapter 6 explores the relationship between public television and the public, suggesting that it is in many ways similar to the relationship between commercial broadcasters and the public. Although ratings pressures are considerably less severe in public television, I find that the public is perceived by producers principally as a market for public television programming. As such, there is no room for an active public, only for a passive audience. With growing competition from cable television, ratings pressures have only increased. Rather than rethink the role of the public and stress a more participatory orientation, public television continues to pursue a market television model that stresses the need for increased program promotion.

Chapter 7 examines the mission that drives those who produce public television programming and finds little agreement on the purpose of public television. To the degree that any shared mission exists, it is signaled by criticism of commercial television instead of by affirmation of public television. Rather than describing a mission that provides a counterweight to the market forces discussed in the previous chapters, I find that the lack of any clear mission permits resource considerations to play a central role in the decisionmaking process in public television.

In Chapter 8, I return to a theoretical discussion of the relationship between media and democracy and suggest a role for public television in this equation. In particular, I argue that public television needs to be further insulated from market forces, and I present five principles of a nonmarket, nonstate public television system. I close by suggesting why, increasingly as we approach the twenty-first century, we need to once again rethink the structure and role of public institutions.

The year 1992 was one in which public television was the subject of much debate. When I began this investigation, however, there was little discussion in the mass media or on Capitol Hill about public television. That, in fact, was one of the reasons for undertaking such a project. Public television's recent appearances in the headlines, however, only highlight the fact that even recent work has paid little attention to a central contradiction: Our public television system has increasingly become attuned to the forces of the market. Although scholars and critics have explored the constraints imposed by market forces on commercial media, there has been little or no attempt to understand their impact on public television, an ostensibly noncommercial form of media. Such an investigation is long overdue, for it has serious implications for the relationship between television and democracy.

Ultimately, this book is about the relationship between media and democracy and the kind of media system needed by a democratic society. This is a theme that will run through the book and to which I will return most specifically in the final chapter. As such, this analysis of public television implicitly evaluates the degree to which public television as it currently exists meets these needs.

I would be remiss if I did not begin by indicating that, from my perspective, PBS offers some of the best programming on television today. From its children's programs to its historical documentaries and Bill Moyers's specials, PBS often provides insightful and challenging television. On any given night there is a good chance that PBS is broadcasting the most interesting programs on free television. However, it is too easy to simply compare PBS programming with that of the networks, note the differences, and be thankful for the existence of public television. The point is not to rank television structures in terms of some measure of "quality" of programming, just as it is not—for the social scientist, at least—to rank television by the size of the audience. The challenge, as far as I am concerned, is to understand both the possibilities and the constraints on different media structures in order that we might create the most democratic broadcast system possible. In other words, were I a television critic I would have much praise for individual programs on PBS; comparing them to network program offerings would make me that much more likely to recommend that viewers pay close attention to PBS. The role of the sociologist, however, is different from that of the television critic. This study is a critical evaluation of our public television system, its relationship to both the market and the state, and its ability to serve the needs of a democratic citizenry. Although the constraints imposed by both market and state are severe, I remain convinced that public television can play a positive role in reinvigorating democratic public life in the United States.

Notes

1. See Witherspoon and Kovitz (1987) for the "official" history of public broadcasting, a concise report paid for by CPB and distributed by the public broadcasting trade publication *Current*. Rowland (1986) provides a revisionist account of the history of public broadcasting. The 1979 Report of the Carnegie Commission on the Future of Public Broadcasting (known as Carnegie II) also provides a useful early history of public broadcasting. Stone's (1985) analysis of Nixon's relationship to public television includes a detailed history of the years between 1969 and 1974.

2. A large body of recent scholarship has examined the centrality of "individualism" in American political culture and a corresponding fear of large state structures. See Gans (1988), Bellah et al. (1985; 1991), and Reinarman (1987) for discussion of these themes.

3. See Stone (1985) for an analysis of the Nixon administration's efforts to pressure public television. Lashley (1992) argues that "executive turnover has profoundly influenced the strategic behavior of public television. Because performance preferences change with each administration, the organizational structure and strategic behavior of this public organization have been adjusted accordingly" (p. 64).

4. We should recognize, however, that even the administrative structure is not totally insulated from the federal government: The president appoints the CPB board.

5. As we will see in Chapter 3, the initial proposal by the Carnegie Commission recommended that an excise tax on the sale of television sets, to be placed in a trust fund specifically for the use of public television, would remove the possibility of politicizing the funding process. Witherspoon and Kovitz note that the idea was a political non-

starter: "Legislators dislike excise taxes because they are hard to control; economists dislike them because there may not be connection between the amount of money raised and the amount needed" (1987: 14). A more cynical reading is that legislators opposed the excise tax precisely because it would have created a federally funded public television system that was, at the same time, financially autonomous of the federal government.

6. See Witherspoon and Kovitz (1987) and Stone (1985) for discussions of the reaction to this particular documentary.

7. Under the SPC, local stations, which received most of CPB's money through community service grants, would decide which programs to support through a complex process of voting. See Reeves and Hoffer (1976) and Campbell and Campbell (1978) for a more thorough description of the SPC. Reeves and Hoffer also provide a content analysis of the SPC's first year. They found that "[t]he stations purchased two kinds of proposals: Those that were cheap and those already on the air. The first criterion was understandable; there was little money to spend. The second is difficult to reconcile with the lofty statements made by PBS officials and the Carnegie Commission regarding the necessity of risk-taking by public broadcasters. The SPC ventured and gained little" (p. 562). In 1990 the SPC was abolished and the program funding process was centralized under the leadership of PBS's new programming chief, Jennifer Lawson.

8. In 1974, public television was thrust into the middle of national politics again, as it broadcast live the entire set of Watergate hearings. See Fletcher (1977) for a discussion of the audience for PBS's coverage and Stone (1985) for a discussion of what he calls the "poetic symmetry" of public television's broadcasts of the hearings that brought down its nemesis.

9. See Coontz (1992) for a thoughtful analysis of the myths associated with the discourse on "dependence."

10. See Jarvik (1992a; 1992b) and Horowitz (1991) for fuller versions of their own arguments. A variety of critics have responded directly to the substance of these arguments. See, for example, Daniel (1992), Grossman (1992), Schone (1992), FAIR (1992), and Ouelette (1991) for analysis and criticism of the conservative mobilization against PBS.

11. Will's widely syndicated column helped to popularize the conservative argument. See his columns "Public TV Charades" (*Boston Globe* April 23, 1992) and "$1.1 Billion for Public TV?" (*Washington Post,* May 12, 1992).

12. Of particular interest on this question is Kellner (1990), in which the author develops a "critical, institutional theory" of television. Gitlin (1985) provides a thorough discussion of how market pressures influence the production of prime time network television.

13. See Lichter, Amundson, and Lichter (1992) for a study that argues that PBS programming has a liberal bias. Naureckas (1992) provides a thorough, and very persuasive, critique of the methods used by Lichter et al., pointing out that the study excluded the vast majority of public affairs programming on PBS.

14. Witherspoon and Kovitz (1987: 23) suggest that the first verse of a public broadcasting testament would read, "In the beginning was the station." CPB's 1991 Annual Report, *From Wasteland to Oasis: A Quarter Century of Sterling Programming,* uses virtually the same language: "'In the beginning, there was the station,' a history of public broadcasting in America might appropriately begin" (CPB, 1991: 31).

15. The term "public" television was not used until 1967. Data for prior years reflect the number of what were then termed "educational" stations.

16. See Pepper (1979) and Avery and Pepper (1980) for a discussion of the evolving relationship between CPB and PBS in their early years. It was not until May 1973 that CPB and PBS signed a "partnership agreement" that defined the roles of the two organizations.

17. CPB accounted for 13.5 percent of public television's income in 1990; an additional 2.7 percent came from other federal government agencies, including the Department of Education, the National Endowment for the Arts, and the National Endowment for the Humanities.

18. Auletta (1991) points out that the three-network share of the audience dropped from 92 percent in 1976 to 62 percent in 1991.

19. Although an average rating of 2.3 may seem small, it indicates an average of more than 2 million households tuned in, a large number by the standard of most mass media, particularly newspapers and magazines.

20. This is based on data from Winter Quarter 1992, as distributed by PBS Research. See National Audience Report, produced by PBS Research, July 20, 1992, for more detailed data. PBS research also produced pamphlets in both 1985 and 1986 entitled, "Who Watches Public Television?" (PBS Research, 1985; 1986), both of which have detailed data on the public television audience.

21. The data also indicate that the public television audience is older than the general population. In particular, men and women over fifty years of age make a large part—in many cases 40 to 50 percent—of the audience. This audience is, of course, quite different from that of the networks, who, particularly in the 1992 fall season, focused on attracting young viewers.

CHAPTER TWO

———————————— ∎ ————————————

The Political Economy of Mass Media

For decades, scholars in the United States and Europe have examined the relationship between the mass media and democratic politics. From discussions of media and electoral politics (Nimmo and Combs, 1990; Jamieson, 1984) and the manipulation of media by politicians (Paletz and Entman, 1981; Hertsgaard, 1988) to investigations of the impact of the media on public opinion (Iyengar and Kinder, 1987; Gamson and Modigliani, 1989; Philo, 1990; Lewis, 1991; Neuman et al., 1992) and the relationship between media and collective action (Gitlin, 1980; Ryan, 1991; Gamson, 1992), recent research has paid close attention to the ways that media facilitate and inhibit the development of democratic societies. Although specific research questions have varied, underlying many of these studies is an interest in how the mass media can serve the needs of citizens in a democratic polity. In the past decade there has been a decidedly pessimistic tone to the bulk of this work, with most writers concluding that the current media in the United States serve these needs poorly. It will be helpful to briefly review this body of critical research.

Those emphasizing the importance of mass media for the construction and maintenance of democratic societies have suggested that media can serve democracy by helping to create an open public sphere. Habermas (1989 [1962]), in particular, advances this view. Kellner, describing Habermas's argument, suggests that in the seventeenth and eighteenth centuries "the media composed of the press, journals, and books fostered this public sphere and thus produced at least a potential space for political debate, opposition, and struggle" (1990: 11). In his discussion of public education, Giroux (1988: 32) similarly argues that public spheres—in this case, schools—must be defined as sites where "the dynamics of popular engagement and democratic politics can be cultivated." Such public spheres are meaningful precisely because a well-informed, active citizenry is essential for a healthy democracy.

Numerous critics maintain, however, that the contemporary public sphere does little to cultivate an active citizenry. For example, Habermas suggests that the public sphere was fundamentally altered in the late nineteenth century. According to Kellner, Habermas argues that "the public was transformed from participants in political and cultural debates into consumers of media images and information" (1990: 12; cf. Keane, 1984).[1] Others, following Habermas, argue that although mass media have the potential to serve as a public sphere open to debate and opposition, the public sphere in the United States and Great Britain has been shrinking in recent years. Elliott (1982: 244) writes that "what we are seeing and what we face is a continuation of the shift away from involving people in society as political citizens of nation states towards involving them as consumption units in a corporate world." One of the principal reasons for this change, according to Elliott, is the increasing privatization of information. Herbert Schiller, writing specifically about the United States, advances a similar argument. Discussing the rising corporate influence in the cultural arena, he suggests that "the substantive institutional changes that have occurred in the informational-cultural sphere preclude any kind of independent expression" (1989: 6).

Television plays an unquestionably significant role in the construction of this public sphere. In the 1990s, it is the dominant form of mass media in the United States. More Americans get their news and information from television than from any other medium. Presidential elections throughout the 1980s indicated that political contests are waged primarily on television.[2] And in the wake of the 1991 Gulf War, it appears that television is where wars are now largely fought (cf. Kellner, 1992; Mowlana et al., 1992; Hoynes, 1991). Moreover, with the rise of the Cable News Network (CNN) over the past decade, new communications technologies are making television more than ever an international public sphere. Yet television is not merely a source of information for Americans. It is the principal activity around which we organize our leisure time. Households in the United States have the television set turned on for an average of seven hours per day. Families spend much of their time together viewing prime time television.[3]

Recent research suggests that television falls far short of its promise to contribute to democracy. Kellner (1990: xiii), for example, argues that "television and the media not only have failed in recent years to carry out the democratic function of providing the information necessary to produce an informed citizenry but also have promoted the growth of excessive corporate and state power." Bennett (1988: 9) notes that "the news we are given is not fit for a democracy: it is superficial, narrow, stereotypical, propaganda-laden, of little explanatory value, and not geared for critical debate or citizen action." And Edelman (1988) argues that the news helps to detach individuals from the public world, observing that "news about 'public affairs' encourages the translation of personal concerns into beliefs about a public world people witness as spectators rather than participants." Gamson and his colleagues (1992: 391) conclude their review of recent scholarly literature on the mass media by noting: "Ideally, a media system suitable for a democracy ought to provide its readers with some coherent sense of the broader social forces that affect the conditions of their everyday lives. It is difficult to find anyone who would claim that media discourse in the United States even remotely approaches this ideal."

Rather than dismissing television as mindless entertainment or simply lamenting its contribution to the demise of the public sphere, however, sociologists must subject it to rigorous analysis. It is important to provide more than critique; we need to articulate a vision of how television can contribute to the ongoing work of (re)creating and nourishing a democratic public sphere.

There are several ways that television can do so. Let me briefly suggest some of this potential. First, television can serve as an open marketplace of ideas, accessible to all, in which debates and controversies rage. Rather than providing a predigested view of current events or one that equates "debate" with the views of the two major political parties, television can serve as a forum that allows for a wide-ranging battle of ideas. Second, television has the capability to give us a picture of the broad diversity in contemporary American society. By providing "multiperspectival" programming, to use Gans's (1979) term, television can expose us to the worlds and worldviews of a broad spectrum of people. The experiences and thoughts of people living on the other side of the country or the other side of the world, who we may never have to encounter, can enter our increasingly privatized lives. Third, television has the capacity to bring substantive discussions of local, national, and international issues directly into people's living rooms. Through public affairs programming, the presentation of a wide range of conferences and lectures, and, increasingly, viewer participation programs, the distance between the private world of the home and the public world of politics can be bridged. And fourth, by serving as a kind of watchdog on government, television (and mass media more generally) can help to check government corruption and abuse. In an increasingly complex (and often highly secretive) government bureaucracy, television journalists serving in some sense as representatives of the viewing public can uncover and publicize official misdeeds, providing citizens with the resources they need to act.[4]

These four functions revolve largely around the need for information. In order to be active participants in a democratic society, citizens need information about their world. Since the nation and the world are far too large to comprehend based solely on personal experience, television has become a central transmitter of such information.[5] Ideally, such information would come from a wide range of sources, encompass a wide range of people and events, and reflect more than just the preferences of those with political or economic power. In short, functioning democracies need more than simple information—they need a truly free media, one not constrained by state or private interests.[6]

Media and the Market

For half a century, television in the United States has been dominated by the large commercial networks. In the 1980s, network television became more fully integrated into corporate America,[7] and the concentration of media ownership in a few hands continued to increase dramatically. At the same time, a host of regulations, including the Fairness Doctrine (which required broadcasters to present contrasting views on controversial issues), were abolished by the Reagan administration, making television more reliant on market forces.

Critics concerned about the relationship between television and democracy have suggested that in order to understand why media more generally, and television in particular, serve democracy so poorly, we need to understand the political economy of television. In other words, learning the economic structure of mass media is central to an understanding of media organizations that may be profitable and prestigious, but fall short of the promise to enhance democracy.

At the most general level, such arguments suggest that the for-profit orientation of commercial media organizations permeates all aspects of decisionmaking. Analyses of news media, in particular, have advanced this argument (cf. Entman, 1989; Herman and Chomsky, 1988; Epstein, 1973). Profit pressures provide incentives for news organizations to produce a least-common-denominator version of the news, one that will attract a large audience. At the same time, the for-profit orientation provides severe cost-limiting pressures; as a result, news organizations develop strategies to contain their expenses by, for example, relying on political elites for most information, using resources to cover primarily preplanned, predictable happenings, and focusing on a limited number of major institutions in major cities. Profit pressures may be, as Entman (1989) has suggested, central to understanding why different news organizations produce very similar news.

Critics who advance a political-economic approach often begin with a discussion of the for-profit orientation of the media, but the analysis moves on to several additional issues. Versions of this argument focus primarily on four issues: ownership concentration, the influence of advertising, the development of new global media empires, and the integration of media organizations into the nonmedia corporate sector.

Ownership Concentration

Recent scholarship and criticism pays close attention to the increasing concentration of media ownership. Bagdikian (1990) articulates the most well-known argument about the problems of the "media monopoly," suggesting that a "private ministry of information" has emerged in the past twenty-five years.[8] The third edition of his book reports that "twenty-three corporations control most of the business in daily newspapers, magazines, television, books and motion pictures" (1990: 4) in the United States, down from forty-six in 1983. This trend, he argues, has grave consequences for democracy in the United States. At the most fundamental level, Bagdikian observes, concentrated ownership of media inevitably narrows the range of information and imagery disseminated on a national scale. In short, "contrary to the diversity that comes with a large number of small, diverse, media competitors under true free enterprise, dominant giant firms that command the nature of the business produce an increasingly similar output" (1990: 243).

Bagdikian raises a central question about the relationship between competition and diversity. Although his argument is complex, an underlying premise is that monopoly prevents a wide-ranging, diverse media. In contrast, Entman (1989) suggests that economic competition may produce low-quality, least-common-denominator news. He raises a serious question about any simple equation between economic competition and high quality, diverse news. Bagdikian and others who have examined ownership concentration, however, do not argue that simply restoring competition will produce a higher quality of news, only that reversing the trend toward monopoly is a prerequisite for broader change.

The Influence of Advertising

The power of advertising dollars profoundly affects the free market under which publications and broadcasting outlets operate. Since the sale of advertising provides most or all of the revenue, media outlets compete for the patronage of large advertisers.[9] Therefore, media content is linked not simply to competition between media outlets for viewers but also to the competition to please advertisers. One can imagine that even under genuinely competitive circumstances, the marketplace of ideas would be restricted by the need of publishers and broadcasters to court large advertisers.

Bagdikian argues that advertisers are concerned with more than just the sheer size of an audience. They are also concerned with the "quality" of the audience and the content of the programs and articles that accompany their advertisements. These considerations are likely to become important to producers and editors at mass media outlets that depend on advertising dollars for survival. And those who do not meet advertisers' criteria are not likely to exist for very long. Herman and Chomsky (1988) include the power of advertisers as one of the five filters in their model of the news media. They suggest that large corporate advertisers will have little interest in sponsoring media that target audiences with little buying power or that produce images critical of corporations. More generally, they will shy away from sponsoring material that is disturbing so as not to interfere with the "buying mood." As Jhally (1989: 76) puts it, "programs not only have to deliver large numbers of the 'correct' type of people to advertisers, but they also have to deliver them in the right 'frame of mind.' Programs should be designed to enhance the effectiveness of the ads that are placed within them."

Gitlin, in his study of prime time television, argues that advertisers and the networks have developed a similar vision. In his view, the fact "[t]hat the bulk of major advertisers retain a veto power is important, but no less important is the fact that advertiser power ordinarily comes into play only after the networks make the essential decisions. ... Knowledge of who pays the bills can't be dispelled, even when it doesn't always rise to consciousness. Network executives internalize the desires of advertisers as a whole" (1985: 253). Steinem (1990), in the premier issue of the advertising-free *Ms.* magazine, describes how advertisers demanded a "supportive editorial atmosphere" and "complementary copy" as a condition for buying space in *Ms.* She tells of the "insertion orders" given to advertising salespeople from various manufacturers. Procter & Gamble, for example, ordered that "its products were not to be placed in *any* issue that included *any* material on gun control, abortion, the occult, cults, or the disparagement of religion. Caution was also demanded in any issue covering sex or drugs, even for educational purposes" (italics in original).

Advertising, by providing the principal financial support, plays a crucial role in the production of culture in the United States. Although it does not wholly determine the nature of mass media products, advertising sets limits on the range of expression. In particular, it serves as an important force—both as an external constraint and one that has been internalized by major cultural producers—toward the homogenization of media imagery.

Global Media Empires

The analysis of growing ownership concentration encompasses more than simply the increase in local (or even national) media monopolies. Bagdikian points out that a few large multinational corporations are now global media empires, owning large portfolios of newspapers, magazines, television stations, movie studios, and publishing houses. This sort of ownership concentration affects the kinds of media images that are produced. Control of so many different types of media opens up new possibilities for these empires. Media giants can send the same images, ideas, and personalities to the national and global audience in different forms via different media. The various components of the media empires are used to promote each other and to sell affiliated products. When corporations own both the production houses and distributors of media images, they can guarantee themselves a captive audience for their product. Bagdikian paints a vivid picture of how corporations are taking advantage of their wide-ranging media properties. For example, he suggests the fondest scenario for the new media giants.

> A magazine owned by the company selects or commissions an article that is suitable for later transformation into a television series on a network owned by the company; then it becomes a screenplay for a movie studio owned by the company, with the movie soundtrack sung by a vocalist made popular by feature articles in the company-owned magazines and by constant playing of the soundtrack by company-owned radio stations, after which the songs become popular in a record label owned by the company and so on, with reruns on company cable systems and rentals of its videocassettes all over the world (1990: 243).

This kind of ownership structure, according to Bagdikian, has a significant impact on the media product. It makes mass marketability the central creative concern in all segments of the media empire. The increasingly important need to produce a commercial success for the mass market leads in the direction of product uniformity.

Miller (1990), in a similar argument, suggests that the new media empires have fundamentally changed the film industry, turning motion pictures into just one more piece of the larger marketing pie. Movies are used to sell a wide range of services and to promote other products in the media empire. The blockbuster motion picture *Batman*, for example, became a consumer bonanza with a broad array of spin-off products. The Time-Warner film was promoted by (and helped to promote) other company holdings including *Time* magazine and HBO. Miller (1990: 7) argues that "Hollywood's loss of vision and the new moguls' disdain for cinema reflect an enormous structural change in the movie business: the absorption of the old vertical movie monopoly ... into the (still evolving) 'horizontal' media monopoly that reigns today."

New technologies, which were once identified as democratizing forces, only accentuate this trend toward both horizontal and vertical monopoly. Neuman (1991) argues that there is an enormous potential in new communications technologies for a diverse pluralism and increased participation in public life but concludes that political-economic forces make this widely heralded potential unlikely to be realized. And Gitlin (1985: 332) sums up the situation nicely, arguing that

> the brave new cornucopia is likely to create only minor, marginal chances for diversity of substance—and fewer and fewer as time goes on. ... Conglomeration proceeds apace. Homogeneity at the cultural center is complemented by consumer fragmentation on the margins. Technology opens doors, and oligopoly marches in just behind, slamming them. There can be no technological fix for what is, after all, a social problem.

Corporate Ownership

Herman and Chomsky (1988) point out that the size of the investment necessary to operate a mass media organization necessarily limits its ownership to the wielders of major corporate capital. The fact that a few large corporations dominate the media suggests that media are unlikely to be independent forces in American society. Rather than serving as a public sphere accessible to a range of interests in society, major media have become an integral part of one of those interests: corporate America. Moreover, media empires are not simply a result of the market system—they also serve as cheerleaders for the market system. Now that large corporations, who are major investors in nonmedia sectors, own the major media, their ability to promote corporate interests is greatly enhanced.

Herman and Chomsky (1988) suggest that we need to focus on the combination of ownership concentration, the profit orientation of media owners, and recently relaxed regulations. Loosening of regulations in the 1980s led not only to increased concentration of ownership but also to control of media by nonmedia companies. Now, Herman and Chomsky argue, media owners are part of the mainstream of the corporate community, with which they share similar interests. In this regard, Kellner (1990: 66) notes that "television networks are now entrenched as a central force within the transnational corporate power structure and have served capitalist interests even more directly during the 1980s." As the media business has become increasingly profitable, the bottom line pressures have only increased.

Herbert Schiller, taking the argument one step further, asserts that the media have become the central component of an "organic process by which the corporate 'voice' is generalized across the entire range of cultural expression" (1989: 44). Commercial success has become the primary consideration in the media world, and artists and writers who want access to this world are well aware of the importance of marketability. For Schiller, the cultural limitations have increased because "most imagery and messages, products and services are now corporately fashioned from their origin to their manufacture and dissemination" (p. 44).

New information technologies only increase the corporate advantage, since their high cost limits access. Private wire services, electronic press kits, and private video and computer networks provide corporations with new ways to communicate with each other, journalists, and the public. D. Schiller (1986) concludes that these new technologies give corporations the ability "to restrict access to strategic information about their activities while at the same time gaining unparalleled control over the flow of positive images to the public at large."

Taken together, this literature provides a picture of the context in which the television industry exists: It is an industry owned principally by major corporations whose decisions are driven by the dictates of profit maximization. In either a competitive market or a fundamentally oligopolistic market, bottom-line considerations increasingly rule the process. Whether such bottom-line decisionmaking is consistent with the public interest in an open, diverse, and vigorous public sphere is not at all clear.

Discussions of the political economy of television, as we have seen, are often abstract. Although they provide a firm theoretical basis for understanding the culture industry, they often say little about the day-to-day reality of the television industry.[10] In order to assess the ability of market television to serve democracy, which most argue it does rather poorly, we need to examine the concrete practice by which the market asserts itself in network television: audience ratings.

Ratings and the Market

In order to fully understand the pressures exerted by the market on American television, we have to locate the analysis of ownership patterns and advertising within a discussion of audience ratings and what ratings represent. This is an important theoretical point that is too often neglected. Ratings serve as the primary market mechanism for the television industry, and they are heralded by those in the industry as a fundamentally democratic mechanism. Social scientists should be particularly interested in examining the nature of television ratings, since social science research methods are used for the purposes of audience research to generate these ratings.

The fundamental measure of success in the television market is success in ratings, a statistical mapping of the size and demographics of the audience for each program. Ultimately, the goal of commercial television is, as the now familiar phrase goes, to deliver audiences to advertisers. Television programming needs to be understood fundamentally as an effort to attract large audiences to the television screen, where they can be sold products during the commercial breaks. Most viewers may not consciously understand the importance of commercials, but it is clear that advertising time is the most important time—and ultimately what pays the bills—on commercial television. As an ABC executive puts it: "The network is paying affiliates to carry network commercials, not programs. What we are is a distribution system for Procter & Gamble and other advertisers" (quoted in Auletta, 1991: 301).

Ratings measure the size and "quality" of the audience that an advertiser can assume will watch its ad. In response to advertiser and network demands, audience ratings have shifted from a simple measurement of the size of the audience and now focus on its demographic makeup, particularly age and gender. As a result, measuring techniques have moved from the home diary to the television set meter to the people meter, with a "passive people meter" currently in development.[11] The audience is, in essence, a market of potential consumers. Ratings, particularly the demographics, are central to the process of ad placement, and they are the currency that sets the price of advertising time.

Champions of commercial television and the current system of ratings that measure potential consumer markets argue that ratings are, most fundamentally, a democratic mechanism. They are, according to Beville (1985: 240), "an expression of democracy in action." As Abramson (1990: 262) describes the argument, "[r]atings are the democratic way; the Nielsen or Arbitron services are but polls of the people to find out what they want from television. In fact, ratings are a way of empowering people to have the final say on television programming." Even the promotional material that the families participating in Nielsen research receive suggests that they are partaking in a great democratic act by filling out their viewing chart. A note accompanying the TV viewing diary indicates that "the real reward for making Diary entries is knowing that your TV viewing information will be used in future TV programming." Viewing, then, is seen as a form of "voting," and the ratings are simply a tally of the votes.

Critics of commercial television have not fully responded to the argument that ratings are a fundamentally democratic mechanism. For those who find fault with a television system dominated by the bottom-line consideration of who can sell the biggest, "best quality" audience to major advertisers, it is necessary to first contend with the notion that, in fact, ratings are the democratic mechanism that makes the market work.

Ratings and Democracy

If audience ratings are a kind of "electoral process" whereby audience members choose the programming, is it reasonable to characterize this as a democratic system? If we look at ratings closely, we will see that the notion of ratings as a democratic mechanism is highly simplistic. Although television ratings may provide a useful portrait of the television audience, they have little relationship to a system of democratic decisionmaking. As Hurwitz (1984: 213) notes, "democratic rhetoric and claims of methodological sophistication have inhibited more perspicacious analyses of the underlying processes and patterns of relationship to which audience research has responded and which it has come to embody."

First, it is important to recognize the purpose of ratings: They provide information that is a central component of the negotiation between advertisers and television stations over the price of advertising time. As such, ratings are not some form of disinterested, objective measure of the television audience. Meehan, in her analysis of the historical development of radio and television ratings, argues persuasively that ratings are not the simple result of research. They are tools designed by firms to achieve economic success—control over ratings production. Forms of measurement are selected on the basis of economic goals, not according to the rules of social science. ... The differences between the commodity audience and the public viewership, between manufacturing the commodity audience through ratings and measuring the public taste through social research, cannot be overemphasized (1990: 127).

And Jhally (1990: 112) reminds us that "what appear as seemingly objective data about the audience are in fact a social creation—the result of political and economic factors." Hurwitz makes a similar argument in more theoretical terms, drawing on the tenets of the sociology of knowledge: "Our notions of the broadcast audience ... depend upon what research tells us, but ... this in turn depends upon *who is asking* and *for what purpose*" (1984: 207, italics added). We must begin, then, by understanding that audience ratings are a commodity produced by A. C. Nielsen, which has a virtual monopoly on national television ratings, and sold to broadcasters and advertisers to be used as a price-setting mechanism.

Commentators disagree about the relationship between Nielsen and the two industries—some arguing that the networks control Nielsen, others arguing that the big advertisers control it (cf. Jhally, 1990). Still, audience research, much like other industrial and social scientific research, must be understood in the context in which it is produced. As such, it is problematic to argue that the research that produces television ratings is "neutral" or that it has meaning outside of its use as a price-setting commodity.

Second, critics claim that measures of ratings are not necessarily representative of the entire American public. Gitlin (1985: 52), who largely accepts the Nielsen ratings as a measurement tool, suggests that the most serious shortcoming of ratings is that they undercount blacks, Hispanics, and the poor. He offers two possible reasons to account for this. First, the census data, from which Nielsen draws its sample, undercounts minorities and the poor. Second, less educated people are generally less likely to cooperate in surveys, and the less educated in the United States are still disproportionately minorities and the poor. Meehan (1990: 132) questions the representativeness of the Nielsen sample more directly, suggesting that with new "people meters," "the metered group is not a scientific sample of the viewing public since it is not randomly selected from and not representative of that public."

This criticism is not likely to be distressing to broadcasters or advertisers. Given that ratings provide the key to television advertisement placement, the poor, in particular, are not an audience that is likely to be in substantial demand. In fact, we might better understand the meaning of ratings if we perceive them as measuring the size and demographic composition of *potential consumers* rather than as public preferences of, or voting on, particular television programs. As such, if ratings serve as a democratic mechanism, it is a democracy that is, at the very least, weighted by income.

Third, the audience being measured does not have a wide range of choices. As far as "free" television goes, viewers are selecting from a narrow range of standard-fare television, often with little difference between the programming on the three networks. The public has no systematic role in selecting which programs will make their way from the idea, development, and pilot stages to its television sets. Nor are there mechanisms for the public to suggest, let alone introduce, new programs. To return to the democracy metaphor, it is as if the public is voting in the final round of an election in which it was locked out of the candidate selection process, the campaign, and the primary elections and caucuses.

Furthermore, measuring what programs people have their television sets turned to is a poor semblance of democracy in action. Turning on one's television set is an extremely passive form of participation for even American political theorists to accept as part of a legitimate democratic process. Television viewing may be relaxing, pleasurable, even engaging or challenging; however, it is a far cry from what can be reasonably considered "participation." Rather than using the language of democracy to describe audience ratings, perhaps it is more instructive to turn the relationship on its head. To the extent that the American political process has become increasingly mass mediated, audience ratings may serve as a useful metaphor to describe the future of politics in the United States. Moreover, ratings do not measure why people prefer one program over another, nor do they suggest what kind of programming the public would prefer if given the opportunity to participate more fully in a decision-making process. And as long as overall audiences do not fall too dramatically, there will be no incentive for either broadcasters or advertisers to permit the public to participate more in programming decisions. Ratings, as they currently exist, are functional for the major players in the television industry, serving "as an essential mechanism to maintain equilibrium among ever more integrated institutions" (Hurwitz, 1984: 212).

Fourth, television audience ratings represent a version of democracy that only responds to mass audiences numbering in the millions. At least as far as network television is concerned, there is little or no room for programming that is important or meaningful to small sectors of the public but that cannot garner a mass audience. The outcome of this kind of process is certainly less than democratic, as programming that does not "win" the ratings war quickly disappears into oblivion. Those members of the public who may not have "voted" on the winning side by watching the most highly rated programs have little recourse and no representation on the network schedule.

The rise of cable television may begin to modify this system of programming. Narrowcasting, as opposed to broadcasting, provides the opportunity for targeted programming to prosper as long as there is an identifiable audience. Still, such programming is not free; more important, advertisers will still be reluctant to support programming whose audiences have little potential as consumers. Therefore, even the rise of narrowcasting on cable television is likely to provide little programming targeted at audiences having weak consumer clout, maintaining this television "democracy" weighted by income.

Ultimately, ratings, despite their shortcomings, do provide a substantive measure of what the American audience is watching. But it is problematic to suggest that this measurement is somehow the equivalent of a democratic process, in which the television industry responds to the preferences of the public. More problematic is the equation of an audience of potential consumers with a citizenry that participates in a democracy. Despite the utility of ratings for the various players in the television business and the legitimacy that ratings seem to have engendered in American culture, audience ratings are a product of a system in which the viewing public is seen almost exclusively as a market—a market to be sold both the television program and the goods profferred by advertisers, who provide the financial support for the medium.

Following political economy theorists, I have suggested that understanding the economic organization of the television industry is central to understanding the televised product, and I have argued that audience ratings, the principal market mechanism in the television industry, are far from being the democratic wonder cited by many in the television industry. If this is the case, then there is one sector of American television that we have overlooked: noncommercial television. The system of public television in the United States, largely neglected by the growing body of literature on American television, is precisely where we need to refocus attention.

Public television provides a particularly useful setting to analyze the relationship between democracy and the public sphere. And for those interested in developing a system of television that contributes to a more democratic public sphere, public television provides the best hope. In the remainder of this chapter, I will discuss the historical relationship between television in the United States and notions of the public interest and explore the differences between commercial television and public service television on a more theoretical level.

Television and the Public Interest

Is television fundamentally a medium that advances commercial interests by selling goods to consumers? Or is it a medium that contributes to the creation of a healthy public sphere? Put another way, should we understand television as a commercial industry or a public good? Although the former conception clearly emerged as the predominant vision of American television in the postwar years, there has always been an undercurrent that challenges the supremacy of this vision. From the beginning of radio at least until the deregulatory years of the Reagan administration, the notion that media should serve the public interest persisted. Even those who most successfully profited from the commercial orientation of broadcasting had to reaffirm, at least in rhetoric, the public service value of radio and television.

It is particularly important to remember the undercurrent stressing the importance of the public interest when we examine the relationship among those private corporations who make large profits by owning the networks or local stations, the advertisers who supply most of the revenue to run local and national television, and the actual medium that is used to generate these profits. Television is, after all, broadcast over airwaves, which cannot be privately owned. In essence, the space through which television signals are sent belongs to the public, and broadcasters obtain licenses from the federal government to use these public airwaves. This arrangement implies some kind of responsibility on the part of the broadcaster to the public, which is not simply an audience for commercial messages but also the "owner" of the frequencies that broadcasters are licensed to use. Television may currently be organized in the United States as a profit-generating enterprise for private interests, but as a medium it must also be understood as a public good. Although the U.S. government has never played the kind of active role in broadcasting that governments have in Europe—where states have maintained a high degree of control over or placed strict regulations on private broadcasters—it is important to recognize that American television was initially conceptualized as a fundamentally public medium.

In the 1920s, radio was understood to be a public concern and was likened to other public utilities. Herbert Hoover noted in 1925 that radio communication had "to be considered primarily from the standpoint of public interest to the same extent and upon the same principles as our other public utilities" (quoted in Hood, 1986: 56). Hood has explained how scarcity, or the limited nature of the radio (and later television) spectrum, combined with the notion that radio was a public utility, formed the basis for the first attempt at comprehensive broadcast legislation in the United States, the Radio Act of 1927. The same spirit informed the Communications Act of 1934 (amended several times since, including the 1967 Public Broadcasting Act), which regulates broadcasting today.

The Radio Act of 1927 made clear that those licensed to use radio waves were required to serve the "public interest, convenience, or necessity." Although the act was vague about the meaning of the public interest, the Federal Radio Commission (FRC) clarified its position in a 1928 statement. The statement indicated that radio was not a private good, and it contrasted the benefits radio brings to advertisers and the public. As such, it noted that "broadcasters are not given these great privileges by the United States Government for the primary benefit of advertisers. Such benefit as is derived by advertisers must be incidental and entirely secondary to the interest of the public." The statement closed by noting that "the emphasis must be first and foremost on the interest, the convenience, and the necessity of the listening public, and not on the interest, convenience, or necessity of the individual broadcaster or advertiser" (2 FRC Annual Report 166 [1928], in Kahn, 1978, pp. 49–55).

The history of the FRC and its successor, the Federal Communications Commission (FCC),[12] is filled with similar statements about the public nature of broadcasting. The FRC's 1929 Great Lakes Statement indicated that "broadcasting stations are licensed to serve the public and not for the purpose of furthering the private or selfish interests of individuals or groups of individuals." The FCC's 1946 statement on "Public Service Responsibility of Broadcast Licensees," commonly known as the "Blue Book" because of the color of the statement's cover, reiterated the importance of serving the public and attempted to specify the meaning of the phrase "public interest, convenience, and necessity." Its definition focused on "four major issues currently involved in the application of the 'public interest' standard to program service policy; namely, (A) the carrying of sustaining programs, (B) the carrying of local live programs, (C) the carrying of programs devoted to public discussion, and (D) the elimination of commercial advertising excesses." It is notable that the Blue Book indicated that sustaining programs, or programs without commercial sponsorship, played "an integral and irreplaceable part in the American system of broadcasting" by, among other things, serving "significant minority tastes and interests" and providing "a field for experiment in new types of programs." And the Blue Book stated firmly that "the public interest clearly requires that an adequate amount of time be made available for the discussion of public issues; and the Commission, in determining whether a station has served the public interest, will take into consideration the amount of time which has been or will be devoted to the discussion of public issues." Ultimately, the FCC's 1952 order reserving 242 television channels across the United States for noncommercial educational use was based on the same understanding of the public nature of the television airwaves.[13]

In 1961, FCC chair Newton Minow's speech to the National Association of Broadcasters, now famous as the "vast wasteland" speech, repeatedly referred to the "public's airwaves." Minow noted that "the squandering of our airwaves is no less important than the lavish waste of any precious natural resource." He urged broadcasters "to put the people's airwaves to the service of the people." In articulating the "fundamental principles" that would guide his role at the FCC, Minow began by pointing out that "the people own the air. They own it as much in prime evening time as they do at 6 o'clock Sunday morning. For every hour that the people give you, you owe them something." Such sentiment was not limited to those associated with the FCC. In his 1967 speech urging the passage of the Public Broadcasting Act, President Johnson insisted that "the public interest be fully served through the public's airwaves."

Of course, the FCC has not always acted in accordance with its own rhetoric on the importance of the public interest.[14] Cole and Oettinger (1978: v) argue that, at least until the mid-1970s, "the FCC had been a tight little world in which commissioners enjoyed many personal contacts with the broadcasters they regulated (and their lawyers and lobbyists) and none at all with the amorphous public whose interest the agency supposedly protected." The FCC's shortcomings, however, are not simply a matter of lack of contact with the public. As Cole and Oettinger explain (1978: 64),

> [b]roadcast regulators face a dilemma. Legally broadcasters are trustees of the airwaves, which belong to the public; broadcasters are also businessmen who have made substantial investments; in a capitalistic society, broadcasters are entitled to profit from these investments. Often commissioners have shown more concern for the broadcasters' economic health than for the service audiences receive.

One of the principal explanations for the FCC's interest in broadcasters' needs, according to several scholars, is the close connection between individual commissioners and the broadcast industry. Traditionally, opposition from the broadcast industry to FCC appointments spells doom for would-be commissioners. Perhaps more important, after serving on the FCC, many commissioners become affiliated with the broadcast industry. Noll, Peck, and McGowan (1973) point out that between 1945 and 1970, almost two-thirds of those commissioners who left the FCC became affiliated with the communications industry. This "revolving door" between the FCC and the industry it is supposed to regulate can have a profound impact on the nature of broadcast regulations. As Cole and Oettinger (1978: 8) note, "[w]ith the prospect of future industry employment, commissioners naturally avoid fouling the nest to which they may fly. Nor are industry representatives reluctant to remind them." The outcome, as Kahn (1978: 512) has suggested, is that regulatory bodies such as the FCC "gradually come to equate the public interest with the private interests they regulate. They eventually nurture, protect, and defend the very industries they were established to control."

Other scholars do not accept the argument that the FCC has simply served the interests of those it is intended to regulate. Baughman (1985), for example, points out that broadcast regulation in the United States has gone through several phases: "Broadcast regulation between 1912 and 1958 typified [the] argument over ineffective trusteeship. Only for a brief period between 1941–46 did the Federal Communications Commission take its tasks seriously. ... Indeed, the FCC by the late fifties had so besmirched itself with conflict-of-interest improprieties that its initials came to stand for "From Crisis to Crisis" (p. 3). However, Baughman argues, between 1958 and 1967 the FCC's ineffectiveness was not a result of its status as a servant to the industry. "It was not a matter of a captive agency but a weak one, crippled, indeed, at the start of the race. Congress and the president could not abide a strong

FCC. ... The commission was a small, toothless dog kept on a very short leash" (1985: 169). Regardless of whether the FCC's inability to successfully protect the "public interest" was due to its close relationship with the broadcast industry or its inherent weakness as a regulatory body, there is widespread agreement that even with commissioners sympathetic to regulation, who were largely missing in the Reagan and Bush years, the FCC has had difficulty living up to its own rhetorical commitment. Nevertheless, the ineffectiveness of the FCC should not blind us to the current of thought throughout this century—a current that rose and fell, but never disappeared—that understood television to be a kind of public utility.

The dominant, and perhaps more dramatic, story of American television is about the growth of the great networks, the huge profitability of local and national television, and the commercial interests that paid for the growth of the medium (cf. Barnouw, 1990; MacDonald, 1990). However, there is another, less well-known chapter in this history. It is not about private fortunes or personal success stories but about the ownership of the radio and television airwaves by the American public. Even as American commercial television was rapidly growing, government regulators continued to reiterate that broadcasting was a public utility. In fact, in the early years of broadcasting, the public was rarely described as an "audience"—as passive consumers to be won. The undercurrent stressing the public nature of broadcasting, even when there was little evidence of it in practice, can be seen as a force that would ultimately lead to the passage of the Public Broadcasting Act of 1967, the subsequent federal funding of public broadcasting, and the dramatic growth of public radio and television over the next twenty-five years.

Public Service Broadcasting

In Europe, the notion of broadcasting as a public utility has been, at least until recently, the dominant perspective.[15] As such, the theoretical elaboration of public service broadcasting has been much more advanced in European countries. In fact, European television has been largely organized along the lines of the public service model.

There is a large body of literature, particularly in England, that identifies the basic tenets of a model of public service broadcasting (McDonnell, 1991; Keane, 1991; Ang, 1991; Scannell, 1989, 1990; Collins et al., 1988; Garnham, 1983, 1986, 1990). Of course, there is not a uniform model upon which all analysts agree; particularly at this time of growth for European private sector broadcasting and rapid technological change, there is debate about the future of public service broadcasting. As Ang (1991: 28) points out, "The idea of 'public service' as such can be and has been interpreted and concretized in a variety of ways in diverse national contexts, manifested in historical particularities in institutional structure and socio-political and ideological grounding." However, there are several components of this model that are widely, if not universally, agreed to be central to public service broadcasting. Let me briefly sketch some of these components.

Scannell argues that public service television has two essential characteristics: "the provision of *mixed* programmes on *national* channels available to all" (1989: 137, italics in original). By providing a wide range of programming—news, public affairs, drama, arts, sports, and so on—that is accessible to the entire nation, public service broadcasting helps to create a more democratic public life. Scannell suggests that "broadcasting ... brings public life into private life, and private life into public life, for pleasure and enjoyment as much as for information and education. The many voices that speak in this domain—the broadcasters themselves, public persons and private people—amount to a universe of discourse" (p. 143). Garnham argues that the strength of the public service model of broadcasting is "the way it a) presupposes and then tries to develop in its practice a set of social relations which are distinctly political rather than economic, and b) at the same time attempts to insulate itself from control by the state as opposed to, and this is often forgotten, political control" (1986: 45). As such, Garnham points out, the public service model regards members of the public as "rational political beings rather than consumers." This view may be, above all else, the central difference between the public service broadcasting and commercial broadcasting models. It may also describe, to a great degree, the differences between American commercial television and European public service television. This is clearly what Ang has in mind when she notes that "public service broadcasting is explicitly conceived as an interventionist institutional practice: it should presumably contribute to the construction of 'quality' citizens rather than merely catering to, and therefore reinforcing and reproducing, the already existing needs and wants of consumers" (1991: 102). As such, public service broadcasting is, in Ang's words, "emphatically opposed to the easy going commercial dictum of 'giving the audience what it wants'" (1991: 28).

In the United States, our highly decentralized system of public television most closely approximates the model articulated by European theorists of public service broadcasting, although it is its own, uniquely American institution. It has never had the same close connection to the state that public service broadcasting has had in Europe. It has always been a marginal component of the American broadcasting picture and never enjoyed the same stability or institutional legitimacy as public television has in Europe. Nevertheless, in its general philosophy and, perhaps more important, its relationship to the market, American public television fits within the general parameters of the public service model.

The remainder of this book examines the current state of American public television and analyzes the degree to which public television serves to promote democratic public life. In an age in which politicians and pundits proclaim that the market has won the final victory, the arguments advanced in this work will cut against the grain of current popular ideology by suggesting that nonmarket television is an essential feature of any democracy. For, as I have suggested in this chapter, a democratic society with active, participating citizens cannot rely solely on the market to transmit the kinds of imagery and information that fundamentally prepare the public for its role in a democracy.

It has been twenty-five years since the term "public television" was coined by the Carnegie Commission, and public television has become a seemingly permanent fixture in American life. Yet even after a quarter-century, the meaning and purpose of our public television system remain unclear. What makes public television different from commercial television? Why does the United States need a public television system? What is the purpose of public television, and what is the public's role in it? Before examining these and other questions, we will take a close look at three early visions of our public television system and use them to construct an ideal-type of American public television to guide our analysis in later chapters. Along the way, we will pause for a brief overview of previous research on U.S. public television, highlighting both the strengths and weaknesses of this body of literature.

Notes

1. The distinction between active participants and consumers has been a central theme in much of the scholarship on the failings of the contemporary public sphere. Several of the essays in Angus and Jhally (1989) discuss this theme.

2. The 1992 presidential election has suggested an expanded role for television in the electoral process. Televised debates and campaign advertisements are now only part of television's larger role, which includes the use of the live television call-in show, particularly CNN's *Larry King, Live,* and the appearance of various candidates on traditionally entertainment-oriented programs such as *Donahue* and *The Arsenio Hall Show,* and on audience-participation segments on MTV.

3. Recent scholarship suggests that analyses of television need to focus specifically on the viewing experience—see Morley's 1986 study of the family context of television viewing and Press's 1991 study of class, gender, and the experience of television viewing. Spigel's 1992 study of the impact of television on family life in the postwar era demonstrates the enormous impact of television on leisure in the United States.

4. See Greider (1992) for a thoughtful discussion of the "betrayal of American democracy" and the media's inability to provide citizens with the proper resources to combat it.

5. See Gamson (1992) for a discussion of the relationship between "experiential knowledge" and media discourse.

6. Murdock (1992: 21) has recently identified a similar set of possibilities for the mass media's contribution to democracy. He notes "three important ways in which the communications system is implicated in the constitution of citizenship. First, in order for people to exercise their full rights as citizens, they must have access to the information, advice, and analysis that will enable them to know what their personal rights are and al-

low them to pursue them effectively. Second, they must have access to the broadest possible range of information, interpretation, and debate on areas that involve public political choices, and they must be able to use communications facilities in order to register criticism and propose alternative courses of action. And third, they must be able to recognise themselves and their aspirations in the range of representations on offer within the central communications sectors and be able to contribute to developing and extending these representations."

7. In the mid-1980s, the three networks changed ownership. NBC was bought by General Electric, ABC by Capital Cities; Loews became the major stockholder of CBS. See Auletta (1991) for a discussion of the takeovers and resulting changes at the three networks. Auletta has a particularly useful discussion of the changes in organizational cultures of the networks after the ownership changes, as well as the increased profit pressures on each of the news divisions.

8. Lee and Solomon (1990), Kellner (1990), Schiller (1989), Herman and Chomsky (1988), Picard et al. (1988), and Powell (1987) provide additional discussions of the concentration of media ownership.

9. This is, of course, particularly important for radio and television broadcasters, who do not receive payment directly from the public, as newspapers and magazines do, from the sale of their product. As a result, virtually the only source of revenue available to broadcasters is that which comes from advertisers.

10. Gitlin (1985) is the exception here. *Inside Prime Time* is one of the few works that both employs a broad political economy perspective and examines the television industry from the perspective of those who write, produce, and schedule the programming. At its best, the work demonstrates how those inside the industry interpret and internalize commercial pressures, the effects of these pressures on individuals within the industry, and the content of programming.

11. Questions have been raised about the reliability of most audience measuring techniques. The most straightforward and reliable measure, represented by the set meter that records the programs a television set is tuned to, does not satisfy advertiser or network demand for knowledge about who is watching the program. The "people meter," which provides data on the specific household members (and, theoretically, visitors) who are watching each program, meets these demands for demographic information. Since it requires the active participation of each household member each time they begin or cease watching television, its reliability is questionable. The proposed "passive people meter" is intended to overcome this shortcoming by developing a computer system that can recognize each household member and determine both who is watching and what the set is tuned to without requiring regular participation by viewers.

12. The Communications Act of 1934 created the FCC, a bipartisan commission whose members would be appointed by the president. The FCC was given broad regulatory powers, but the principal task of the newly created commission was the licensing of radio stations.

13. The order reserving 162 UHF and 80 VHF stations was a watershed moment in the development of what we now call public television. The reservation of spectrum space for educational television came as a result, in part, of organized activity from the educational community, who argued that if space was not reserved for future educational use, there would be no chance for educational television to develop. The first non-

commercial educational television station to receive a license was KUHT in Houston, Texas, in 1953.

14. See Krugman and Reid (1980) for an interesting discussion of the various definitions of the "public interest" among FCC policymakers.

15. A growing body of literature examines the changing nature of broadcasting in Europe. See, for example, Keane (1991) for a discussion of new developments in broadcast policy in Britain; Holtz-Bacha (1991) for analysis of developments in Germany; Slade and Barchak (1989) for a discussion of television policy in Finland; and Syvertsen (1991) for analysis of the situation in Norway.

CHAPTER THREE

—————— ■ ——————

Early Visions
of Public Television

As Chapter 2 demonstrated, critics have long suggested that commercial television faces severe economic constraints. By the middle of the 1960s, a consensus was emerging in the United States that commercial television did not fully serve the public interest as it had originally been charged. Minow's characterization of the medium as a "vast wasteland" was widely accepted. And, as Baughman (1985) showed in his study of the FCC, the ability of regulation to change commercial television was limited.

Rather than restructure, reform, or further regulate the networks, eyes turned to the already existing group of educational stations around the country. By 1966 there were 124 of them operating in the United States, up from 10 such stations only twelve years earlier. Much of the programming was produced by National Educational Television, which was largely supported by the Ford Foundation.[1] Still, the local stations had little formal connection to one another, and programming had to be distributed by mail or messenger, making it virtually impossible for stations across the country to broadcast one program simultaneously. The goals of educational television were limited as well, with a great deal of programming dedicated to instructional purposes. With no semblance of a national presence, educational television did not provide any real alternative to commercial television.

The Carnegie Commission on Educational Television was convened in 1965 to study the financial needs of educational television. Its report, issued in January 1967, called for the establishment of a "public television" in the United States. For our purposes, the story of public television begins with the coining of that term by the commission in 1967. The commission was suggesting that the United States needed a television system that was more than "educational" yet not simply "noncommercial." It would be a system designed specifically to serve the public interest in ways that commercial broadcasters had shown they could not. The report eventually led to the passage of the Public Broadcasting Act of 1967, which created the Corporation for Public Broadcasting.

The Carnegie Commission report, now more than twenty-five years old, continues to serve as the single most important document in the history of public television. Defenders and critics from both inside and outside of public television have cited the report to support a wide range of arguments. Similarly, I want to begin by drawing from the Carnegie Commission report the basic model of public television. Although it is not helpful to engage in an argument based on the original intent of the commission—seeing the report as a kind of public television "constitution"—it will be useful to examine the commission's report, along with other early documents, to try to come to an understanding of the essential components, an ideal-type, of American public television. As such, it will be particularly helpful to examine how this new creature was understood to be *public*—that is, not simply educational or noncommercial.

The Use of Ideal-Types

The analytic utility of the ideal-type has long been understood in academic sociology. Max Weber, the pioneering German sociologist, identified ideal-types as a central methodological tool for his project of interpretative sociology and said they were "of great value for research and of high systematic value for expository purposes when they are used as conceptual instruments for *comparison* with and *measurement* of reality. They are indispensable for this purpose" (Weber, 1949: 97, italics in original). Following Weber, the ideal-type construct has been used in social scientific research throughout the twentieth century.

Weber's ideal-type, according to Gerth and Mills (1946: 59) "refers to the construction of certain elements of reality into a logically precise conception." Giddens (1971: 141–142) described Weber's most well-known use of this analytic strategy: "The characteristics of the 'Calvinist ethic' which Weber analyzes in *The Protestant Ethic* are taken from the writings of various historical figures, and involve those components of Calvinist doctrines which Weber identifies as of particular importance in relation to the formation of the capitalist spirit."

It is important to note, however, that the term "ideal" did not have normative content.[2] Weber did not mean to refer to a desirable type and pointed out that one can construct an ideal-type of highly undesirable behaviors or institutions just as easily as of desirable ones. "Ideal," in this usage, referred to "a pure type in a logical and not an exemplary sense" (Giddens, 1971: 142).

An ideal-type, however, was not considered particularly useful unless applied to a specific research problem. Weber suggested that the very reason for constructing an ideal-type was to use it as a comparative device. As

Abercrombie and his colleagues (1988: 117) put it, "[n]ot all characteristics [of the ideal-type] will be present in the real world, but any particular situation may be understood by comparing it with the ideal-type. ... Ideal-types are therefore hypothetical constructions, formed from real phenomena, which have an explanatory value." Or, in Giddens's words (1971: 142), "the only purpose of constructing [an ideal-type] is to facilitate the analysis of empirical questions." Weber made the point most clearly: "Whatever the content of the ideal-type, ... it has only one function in an empirical investigation. Its function is the comparison with empirical reality in order to establish its divergences or similarities, to describe them with the *most unambiguously intelligible concepts,* and to understand and explain them causally" (Weber, 1949: 43, italics in original).

For our purposes, the utility of the ideal-type for comparative, empirical analysis is the central point. I am delineating an ideal-type of public television specifically for comparative use. Although it does not describe the current state of public television or reflect any past state, the ideal-type articulates the principal theoretical components of a public television system. In highlighting these components, the ideal-type provides an analytical framework for examining and explaining the real-world public television. The ideal-type does not come out of thin air, nor, I might add, simply from the individual preferences of the analyst. Much as Weber's "Calvinist ethic" was extracted from the writings of several Calvinists, in the following sections I extract the basic components of public television in ideal-typical form from three early articulations of public television.

Components of a Public Television System

The Carnegie Commission began its report by indicating that public television "includes all that is of human interest and importance which is not at the moment appropriate or available for support by advertising, and which is not arranged for formal instruction" (1967: 1). The report went on to argue that public television "will be a civilized voice in a civilized community" (p. 18). Public television, in the eyes of the Carnegie Commission, would serve a much larger role than a system devoted solely to education. But what was to make it public?

The Commission did not provide explicit guidelines, but its report and other early works on public television suggested three principal components to a system of public television in the United States: 1) a well-defined mission that emphasizes public television as an alternative to commercial television, stressing, in particular, the diversity of public television programming; 2) a system of stable public funding; and 3) the involvement of various "publics" in all aspects of the enterprise. Using the Carnegie Commission report, along with Robert Blakely's *The People's Instrument: A Philosophy of Programming for Public Television* (1971) and John Macy's *To Irrigate a Wasteland* (1974), I want to elaborate these three components.

Public Television's Mission

One of the more notable aspects of the Carnegie report is the degree to which it was infused with an overwhelming sense of the important mission of the proposed public television system. The most well-known and often-cited expression of this sense is E. B. White's letter to the commission, which was printed in the report. White suggested that public television, as opposed to commercial television,

> should be the visual counterpart of the literary essay, should arouse our dreams, satisfy our hunger for beauty, take us on journeys, enable us to participate in events, present great drama and music, explore the sea and the sky and the woods and the hills. It should be our Lyceum, our Chautauqua, our Minsky's, and our Camelot. It should restate and clarify the social dilemma and the political pickle (p. 13).

The rest of the commission report was less poetic, but it made it clear that the principal reason for inventing the term "public television" was to signify the important mission of this newly proposed system.

And what was this mission to include? Public television, as envisioned in the early years, was to provide an *alternative* to commercial television fare and to reflect the *diversity* of the American public. These two notions—alternativeness and diversity—were fundamentally interconnected. The commission recognized the constraints of commercial television and noted how it "lends itself to uses that increase pressure toward uniformity" (p. 13). If one phrase summed up the commission's charge for public television, it was "excellence in the service of diversity" (p. 14). Later, the report spelled this theme out more fully, suggesting that programming "can help us see America whole, in all its diversity," serve as "a forum for controversy and debate," and "provide a voice for groups in the community that may otherwise be unheard" (p. 92).

Blakely, whose work grew out of the 1969 Conference on Public Television Programming, also stressed the importance of an alternative orientation. He argued (1971: 11) that the United States needs "an adequate alternative and supplementary system of broadcasting" to go along with commercial broadcasting. He suggested the need for a system of public broadcasting "that has a different *purpose*, that performs different *functions*, that pursues different *objectives* and that serves the American people as different *clienteles*" (p. 34, italics in original). Again, as with the Carnegie Commission report, the notion of alternativeness was joined with the notion of diversity.

Macy, the first president of the Corporation for Public Broadcasting, stressed the same central points. He noted that "[p]ublic broadcasting was intended to be a supplementary or alternate service that did not duplicate commercial offerings. But more important, public broadcasting has a special concern for the public's interests and needs" (1974: 40). And, as opposed to commercial television and its search for the mass audience, public television needed to commit itself to diversity—in both the content of programming and the makeup of the audience (pp. 116, 137).

Over the past two decades, the specific mission of public television has been often contested, beginning with early questions about the role of purely instructional television within a public television system. One of the most vociferous challenges to public television's mission was the Nixon administration's attempt to pressure CPB to abandon the production of public affairs programming. For our purposes, however, the ideal-type of public television is driven by a mission to provide an alternative service to the public through the diversity of its programming and its audience. Any close reading of the early work on public television (as well as much of the more recent work) should make this point abundantly clear.

Public Television Funding

Most institutions that we call public, or refer to as part of the public sector, are defined as "public" because of the source of their funding or ownership. A public company is owned by a public made up of stockholders. Organizations in the public sector are funded through either federal, state, or local government. The Carnegie Commission's proposal for the creation of public television had as one of its principal recommendations a structure of public funding.

The commission, however, was concerned about political interference in this new system of public television. Rather than recommending direct government funding through the regular appropriations process, the commission advised that a private, nonprofit corporation be created to "receive and disburse governmental and private funds in order to extend and improve public television programming" (p. 36). In fact, the Corporation for Public Television (changed to the Corporation for Public Broadcasting, to include public radio, when the Public Broadcasting Act was written) was deemed so central to the establishment of public television by the commission that it "would be most reluctant to recommend other parts of its plan unless the corporate entity is brought into being" (p. 36).

The corporation was necessary to maintain the independence of this public system: The commission wanted to create a system that was publicly funded but not government-run. Its members envisioned a system of television that would serve the public interest, not simply the interest of those who controlled the federal purse strings. As the commission put it, "[t]here is at once involved the relation between freedom of expression, intimately and necessarily a concern of public television, and federal support" (p. 37).

Despite the commission's concerns about the potential political pressures associated with federal support (or the appearance of such), the report made clear that "federal funds ... must be the mainstay of the system" (p. 73). In fact, the commission's proposal for the first four years of the corporation's funding included a budget with more than 90 percent of the revenue coming from federal government sources. It is clear that public television and federal funding were intimately connected in the commission's eyes.

The federal money on which the new system would rely, however, was not to be appropriated through ordinary procedures. To ensure the independence of public television, the commission recommended that the corporation be funded from a federal excise tax on the sale of television sets to be "made available to the Corporation through a trust fund" (p. 68). As we will see later, the corporation was created, but the notion of an excise tax was rejected by Congress. Despite this rejection, the idea of major federal support for public television remained intact. Macy referred to assured and insulated long-range financing as a "magic but illusive" goal (p. 79). And although President Nixon's 1972 veto of CPB's authorization bill convinced Macy that it was necessary to draw upon a variety of funding sources (and led to his resignation as CPB president), he still maintained that "it is entirely appropriate and necessary that federal funds be a part of a total financing plan" (p. 111).

Ultimately, the need for long-range funding with no strings attached has been, and continues to be, something on which the public television community can agree. Whether or not the federal government was seen as the principal source or one of several significant sources, the early visions certainly included a major role for public funding in public television. For the Carnegie Commission, in particular, part of the "public" in public television was the source of the system's funding.

Public Participation in Public Television

The third principal component of public television is public participation in the system. Whereas commercial television regards the audience as a mass of potential consumers to be delivered to advertisers, the early proponents of public television envisioned a much different relationship between the system and the viewers. In this vision, the public was not some undifferentiated mass but rather a diverse set of citizens with wide-ranging experiences, interests, and needs. A system of public television could, it was thought, work with the public to help bring the technology of television "into the full service of man [sic], so that its power to move image and sound is consistently coupled with a power to move mind and spirit" (Carnegie Commission, p. 13).

The Carnegie Commission highlighted the important role public television could play in local communities and stressed the responsibility that the system and local stations must exercise toward the public. The commission noted that "public television in particular is dependent for its well-being upon an identification with the community it serves" (p. 34). It suggested that programming on public television "can deepen a sense of community in local life. … It should bring into the home meetings, now generally untelevised, where major public decisions are hammered out, and occasions where people of the community express their hopes, their protests, their enthusiasms, and their will" (p. 92).

Implicit in the commission's emphasis on the community are three points about the relationship between public television and the public: 1) there is no generic public, but rather a wide range of publics, all of which are within public television's constituency; 2) public television cannot operate in a vacuum, without involvement from the various communities in the United States; and 3) public television can play a role in making people more active citizens by helping to open the gates to political participation.

Blakely focused even more explicitly on the importance of connecting the new system to the public. The title of his work, *The People's Instrument,* indicated the importance Blakely attached to public involvement in public television. Drawing on the commission's vision, Blakely suggested that "the basic need and opportunity … is for the American people to use telecommunications to create a new sense of community" (p. 9). The development of a public television system provided a new opportunity to fulfill this need.

Blakely also stressed that public television needed to have a different relationship to the public than other mass media had. In fact, he explicitly contrasted the historical use of mass communications with the need for a system of public communication. "While the public broadcasting system uses the media of mass communications, its purposes, functions, and objectives are to provide *publics* with a flexible, two-way instrument of communication—from, by and with the people, not just to them" (pp. 40–41, italics in original). Public television was to be more than simply another network that broadcast different programs. Blakely argued that it should not even be seen as an institution "that tries to do good things *for* and *to* the American people, but an *instrument that the people use* to communicate with one another" (p. 48, italics in original).

One principal purpose of public television (and what made it such an important phenomenon in the early 1970s) was to "provide means for participation in the making of public decisions and the solutions of problems" (p. 91). Throughout his work, Blakely suggested that public television can play an important role in broadening democratic participation. He noted that public television can "be an instrument by which the people can participate in the making of decisions and can cooperate in actions that they agree upon" (p.

58); that "the people should be encouraged and enabled to use the system as an instrument to accomplish their many purposes, both public and private" (p. 78); and that public television could help "to create new forms and procedures of self-government appropriate to our highly institutionalized society" (p. 93). In short, public television was to bolster democracy, to help make Americans more active and knowledgeable citizens.

Macy also acknowledged the importance of community building and the need to see public television as an agent of increased political participation. But his work focused more on the internal mechanisms of the new system and the need to build a relationship between public television and the public. He suggested that "dominance by the public is an imperative in this system's development, not just as a slogan but as a conscious planning and operating objective. That public should be viewed as individuals and groups with interests, desires, and needs that can be effectively approached through the delivery of program services in sight and sound by electronic means" (p. 116). At the same time, Macy noted, reviewing the earliest years of the system, that the "public itself, the 'public' in public broadcasting, has been forgotten more often than remembered" (p. 116). In stressing the importance of the public for public television, Macy referred not to an audience but to the "citizen viewer."

Macy argued, more explicitly than either the Carnegie Commission or Blakely, that greater citizen involvement was needed for the system to be more fully "public." Macy specifically identified the "ascertainment of community needs" as an essential part of public broadcasting, as opposed to some bureaucratic imposition. As such he recommended that "on-air public hearings, mini-town meetings, structured canvasses of major community groups, man-in-the-street interviews, and 'stockholder' mailings with proxy questionnaires" (p. 127) all be considered means for involving the public. Ultimately, Macy argued, the early years of public television indicated that public involvement was one of the imperatives for the future of public television in order to "secure for the public the benefits of television" (p. 141).

Let me briefly review the components of the ideal-typical public television system. The three essential elements of a system of public television are a mission to produce a diverse alternative to commercial television; substantial public funding; and public involvement. Each of these three components contrasts significantly with commercial television, in which the purpose is principally to increase profits, programming is funded by advertising, and the public is seen as a mass audience of potential consumers. Certainly there are individuals in commercial television, most likely in the news divisions, who may be mission-oriented or who may have a different view of the public. Here, however, we are examining commercial television as an institution; its institutional mission and relationship to the public are in sharp contrast to the ideal-type of public television.

Previous Research on Public Television

Given the centrality of these three components to the early vision for a public television, it should not be surprising to find that previous research on public television focused largely on the same three themes: the nature of funding, the role of the public, and public television's mission. Shortly, I will provide a brief overview of this literature and its implications for this study. First, however, it is worth noting that the recent scholarly literature on public television is scant. Ivers and Clift (1989: 7) refer to the 1980s as the "decade of quiet" with respect to scholarship on public television. They report that "no independently published books focusing on public broadcasting [were] published during the decade of the 1980s."[3] And they note that since the *Public Telecommunications Review* (formerly the *Educational Broadcasting Review*) ceased publication in 1980, the number of scholarly papers and publications on public broadcasting decreased dramatically—from over 600 in this journal alone in the 1970s to only 60 papers in *all* publications in the 1980s.

Explaining the Paucity of Research on Public TV

Ivers and Clift contend that "many of our academic colleagues have dismissed public broadcasting as a viable research topic due to an attitude of indifference regarding its current form and function" (1989: 20). They suggest that such apathy "may indeed be contributing to the 'crumbling' of that element of the public sphere called public broadcasting" (p. 23).

The vast sociological literature on the news beginning in the 1970s raised important questions about the social organization of media, the political economy of the mass media, and the relationship between media and democracy. The unique position of public television makes it an important subject for furthering our understanding of these issues. And the changes in television ownership in the 1980s, along with the increasing privatization of television in Europe in the 1980s, suggest that research into the nature of public television in the United States is long overdue.

As we enter the 1990s, however, television critics, rather than academics, continue to be the principal chroniclers of the development of public television in the United States. Even as media research has grown as its own field of study, public television has been more of an afterthought, a subject that may raise an interesting question or illuminate developments in commercial television but not a focus of study in its own right. How, then, can we explain the absence of sustained scholarly work on public television?

I want to suggest three reasons that may have contributed to this general lack of attention. First, and most obvious, is the fact that public television has a very small audience in comparison to network television and therefore is perceived to have a much smaller political and cultural impact. Public television may merit brief discussion or a passing reference, but as a relatively minor piece of the mass media, it has been peripheral to the study of American television. By neglecting public television, however, researchers have helped to legitimize its marginal position. Rather than simply accepting that public television will always be a relatively insignificant component of the mass media, research needs to begin to raise questions about its role, paying particular attention to its future potential.

Second, public television, with its focus on cultural and intellectual programming, is likely to appeal precisely to people with, to use Bourdieu's (1984) term, the "cultural capital" of university professors. Because the programming on public television is generally more refined and less simplistic than most programming on commercial television, scholars are more likely to watch and enjoy it than to analyze it critically. As such, scholars have spent considerable time and energy analyzing and critiquing commercial television and comparably little time examining public television.

Third, media research in the United States has generally started with the assumption that media are driven (or constrained) by market forces. In particular, research on television has focused on the economic factors that serve to organize the commercial television industry. In such discussions there has been little room for analysis of public television and its very different relationship to these economic forces. It is precisely on such terrain, however, that we need to set our discussion of public television, for public television exists within the larger context of a market system and has itself become increasingly integrated into that system. As such, the relationship between public television and the market, a relationship that most research implicitly denies, can illuminate a great deal about the way public television works.

Keeping in mind the paucity of scholarly research on American public television, particularly in comparison to the number of studies of commercial television in the United States or public service broadcasting in Europe, we will briefly look at the body of literature that does exist.

Research on Funding

The literature on the funding of public television has centered primarily on the impact of major corporate contributions. As early as 1971, Les Brown warned about the privatization of public television. Noting that fundraising in the private sector was increasing, Brown indicated that private funding could "make a myth of 'public' television" (1971: 339). Others pointed to the early 1970s as the beginning of the privatization of public television. Barnouw (1978) highlighted the 1972 Nixon veto as the beginning of a funding crisis for public television. He noted that the oil crisis in the early 1970s led to record profits for the major oil companies and presented them with a public relations problem at the same time. Barnouw suggested that it "was the sort of combination—an image problem plus a glut of money—that had given birth to du Pont's *Cavalcade of America* and Alcoa's *See It Now.* This time public television was the beneficiary" (1978: 66).

As a result of the infusion of resources from major oil companies, Barnouw argued, "cultural" programming, rather than potentially controversial public affairs programming, "became the dominant feature of prime time" (1978: 147). In a similar vein, Kellner noted that the "de facto economic control of public broadcasting by big oil companies inspired critics to mock the 'Petroleum Broadcasting System'" (1990: 202).

Other work highlighted the overall impact of private funding on public television. Lee and Solomon remarked that PBS should be understood as the "Pro-Business Service" (1990: 84–92), citing the increased corporate support for public television in the 1980s. Westin, who produced programs for both commercial and public television, noted that money is "the key to understanding public television" (1982: 251) and said that concerns about sponsor interference are more acute in public television than at the networks.

More recently, Aufderheide (1989: 16) asserted that private interests rule public television, writing that "the key thing to understand is that the corporate and foundation funding sets the agenda for what public TV puts on the screen."[4] Other work examined the motivations of corporations for funding public television. Aufderheide (1991: 176) argued that "corporations use public television for 'ambush marketing'—influencing upscale consumers who are suspicious of advertising."[5] Ermann's 1978 research on the "operative goals" of corporate contributions to PBS examined the issue more closely. Comparing tax rates for contributing and noncontributing corporations between 1972 and 1976, Ermann found that "PBS contributions are not explained in terms of a propensity to contribute to social overhead" (p. 508). On the contrary, Ermann argued, his findings "suggest that PBS contributions may be related to the need for milieu control" (p. 510) in the form of good public relations.

What do all of these studies tell us? First, it is worth noting that little of this work is based on in-depth empirical research. Given that much of this research comes in the form of brief sections of writings otherwise devoted to commercial television, this shortcoming should not be surprising. What is surprising, however, is how little the literature actually tells us about the process by which funder influence is wielded. Garnham (1978: 53) may indeed be correct that "[i]t is the quantity of the funding and the nature of the financing source that is the most fundamental determining constraint on a broadcasting structure." But even if we take this statement as axiomatic, it is still necessary to specify how the quantity and nature of financing influence programming in different broadcasting structures. Although there is broad agreement about the dangers associated with major corporate funding of public television, research has yet to explain the underlying processes at work in the relationship between funders and the public television system. This is the principal shortcoming of the existing literature on public television funding. In Chapter 5, I begin to answer these largely ignored questions and suggest why and how funding is such a key variable.

Research on the Public

A significant body of literature examines the makeup of the PBS audience. In Chapter 1 I summarized recent data from Nielsen and PBS on the demographic makeup of the audience and will not repeat it here. Others, however, have made use of different analytical frameworks to describe the public television audience.

Frank and Greenberg (1982) produced the most extensive analysis of the PBS audience. Following their 1980 work, *The Public's Use of Television*, Frank and Greenberg were commissioned by the Corporation for Public Broadcasting to examine the audiences for public television. They suggested that research needs to move beyond simple demographics and apply an "interest-based audience segmentation scheme." Based on their fourteen interest segments, they argued that

> only two segments, accounting for 17% of the U.S. population age 13 and over, demonstrate an unambiguous attraction to abstract, culturally upscale material. … With the exception of these two segments, one observes extremely modest levels of PTV [public television] viewing and finds program viewing patterns that reflect more limited interests in subject matter not driven by the generalized attraction to abstract, culturally upscale material. Excellence embedded in this type of programming has a limited potential, in and of itself, to attract voluntary viewing (p. 215).

Ultimately, Frank and Greenberg urged programmers in public television to make use of an interest-based scheme for strategic planning, with an eye toward broadening both the type of programming and the audience.[6] In another effort to reconceptualize the nature of the public television audience, Lashley (1992) suggested that any analysis must be "program-dependent" instead of a description of the overall audience. Moreover, she argued that "viewer checkwriters as well as the general audience use public television as a secondary source of programming … to augment the commercial, cable, and independent television menus" (p. 109).

Another line of research moved beyond the audiences for programs, analyzing the role of the public in public television. Wenner (1975: 45) found that "the level of citizen involvement in public television is discouragingly low. What is even more discouraging is the low level of awareness that citizen involvement is an important consideration in the operation of a public television station." Rowland similarly characterized public involvement in public television as a "myth": "noncommercial broadcasting publics have been and remain unaware of their rights and potentialities in the formulation of policy for the control and funding of the enterprise" (1976: 113). And he made the important point that increased research about audience desires is not the same as increased participation in programming and policymaking. Ten years later, in his reinterpretation of the history of public broadcasting, Rowland suggested that "the notion of the 'public' introduced difficult questions about governance, access, and accountability which public broadcasters were slow to recognize as legitimate" (1986: 261).

Questions about public involvement did not come only from outside critics. CPB's Task Force on Public Participation in Public Broadcasting reported similar findings in its 1978 report. The report stated that "each public broadcasting entity, including the Corporation for Public Broadcasting, must more aggressively involve the public in all phases of the operation of this nation's public broadcasting system" (p. 33). It stressed that "[i]t shall be the *affirmative obligation* of public broadcasting stations and other public broadcasting entities to *encourage* and *seek participation* from the general public, and the various sub-publics to maximize the interaction between the broadcasting system and the public" (p. 44, italics in original). The 1979 report of the Carnegie Commission on the Future of Public Broadcasting, known as Carnegie II, also stressed the need for more public accountability. Along with making other recommendations calling for the structural reorganization of public broadcasting, Carnegie II called for stations to

> provide serious opportunities for individuals to participate in and understand the system. Mechanisms for public participation in station planning and development should be continued and strengthened. These include greater commitment to equal employment opportunity, broadened access by minorities, public involvement in station governance, more complete financial disclosure, and community ascertainment (1979: 19).

These recommendations, however, were met with what Rowland (1986) has described as a "deafening silence."

One structural change in the relationship between public television stations and the public was the provision in the Telecommunications Financing Act of 1978 mandating all public broadcasting stations who receive federal funds to establish community advisory boards.[7] However, no recent research has systematically examined the importance of these boards or public participation more generally. Nor has recent work followed up on Rowland's point that we need "to examine the suggestion that at its root, the vision carried around in the heads of many public broadcasters remains one of largely undifferentiated audience collectivities" (1976, p. 112).

Ultimately, the literature on the role of the *public* in public television has focused more on the nature of the *audience* for public television. Although previous work has raised important questions, it has not gone very far—particularly in recent years—toward explaining either the causes or implications of the connections, or lack thereof, between public television and various publics. In short, citizens' role in public television as both participants and constituents needs to be more fully examined. I will return to this point more specifically in Chapter 6.

Research on Public Television's Mission

Over the years, a variety of writers have discussed the mission of public television. Despite different assessments of the exact nature of that mission, there is a general consensus that public television has exhibited a confused sense of its identity. Branscomb (1976) noted the "crisis of identity" in public broadcasting; in the same volume, Millard (1976: 185) lamented public broadcasting's "chronic inability to name its own mission." Rowland's (1980: 141) analysis of the federal government's role in public broadcasting pointed out the long-term existence of the confusion about public broadcasting's purpose: "There never has been and there understandably may never exist any single, official view of what ought to be the purposes, character, and degree of independence of public broadcasting."

More recently, Katz suggested that "the largest and most persistent problem ... that the system has had to face is its lack of a clear role or identity" (1989: 198). Westin (1982) argued that public television's purpose was not defined sharply enough and suggested that public television had lost its direction. His hope for the future of public television included its defining for itself a more narrow mandate. And Stavitsky (1988) suggested that for public television to succeed it must have a more clearly articulated "rhetorical vision."

Two recent works have provided more theoretically grounded discussions of the problems associated with the mission of public television. In her discussion of the 1988 creation of the Independent Television Service (ITVS), which was established to provide financial support for independent producers to expand the diversity and innovativeness of PBS programming, Aufderheide (1991) argued that the the process that created the ITVS signalled a "crisis of mission."[8] She asserted that "the public television bureaucracy today—and it is a formidable one—is committed to a broadcasting service, not to a public project executed through broadcasting. Its aspirations are more similar to those of, say, commercial stations ... than they are to the ideal of using mass communication as a tool of public life" (1991: 170–171). Lashley's (1992) organizational analysis of CPB blamed the crisis of mission on the structure of the system: "Over time, resource dependence and political vulnerability erode the public organization's discretion and autonomy such that this loss generally culminates in goal dilution" (1992: 12).

Other authors started with the assumption that public television is committed to serving a diverse public and conducted empirical studies of PBS programming and the demographic composition of PBS employees. Various studies have painted a bleak picture of public television's commitment to diversity, understood here (and by many other authors) as a central focus of its mission. Reeves and Hoffer (1976) analyzed the first Station Program Cooperative (SPC), the mechanism by which local stations purchased national programs and, therefore, allocated CPB funds, from 1974 to 1990. They found that stations purchased programs that were cheap and well known and concluded that the procedure is "inherently biased against innovation, against risk-taking, and against minorities. These biases will probably remain no matter how much money is poured into the cooperative" (1976: 563).

Isber and Cantor's (1975) content analysis of public television programming found that only 15 percent of participants on adult programs were women and that only 9 percent of these programs had a female announcer/narrator. Cantor (1978: 88) concluded that public television's presentation of women is no more diverse than commercial television's: "In fact, it is less so. A few high status, well-educated women appear but they are not representative of women's position in our highly differentiated and complex society. Ultimately, one must conclude, both commercial and public television disseminate the same message about women, although the two types of television differ in their structure and purposes."

Matelski (1985) conducted a similar study several years later to assess the progress in public television. She found that male participants still outnumbered female participants by at least two to one and that women very rarely served as narrators. Matelski concluded that although progress has been made since Isber and Cantor's report, "[p]rogramming alone is evidence enough to support the claim that the male roles are, in fact, more numerous than female roles. But, not only are male roles in a disproportionately high percentage; they are also disproportionately strong" (1985: 150).

Another study examined the class character of PBS's prime time programming. The study found that twice as many programming hours focused on the "business and social elite" than on all other social strata combined and that "programming about workers represents less than one half of 1% of the total PBS programming hours, and in the years studied, more than two thirds of the miniscule amount of programming about workers was about British, rather than American workers" (CUNY, 1990: 1). Aufderheide also reported the results of a 1987 indexing of subjects on PBS current affairs programs: "Under 'Business' there are 169 references. 'Labor' gets 29, almost all within business-oriented shows such as *The Business File* and *Adam Smith's Money World*" (1988: 12). Lashley's (1992: 109) was the most recent study to suggest a lack of programming diversity, arguing, in particular, that "[t]he percentage of children's programming produced and aired has decreased. There have been fewer programs for senior citizens. Programs produced by or about minorities have also declined."

Other studies have examined the participation of minorities in public broadcasting. The CPB Task Force on Minorities in Public Broadcasting released a highly critical report in November 1979. However, when little action was taken to respond to the report, the task force dissolved itself in April 1980, noting that "the continued unwillingness of and apparent refusal of public broadcasting entities to effectively address corrective actions to historical discrimination and racism within the industry, constitutes a blatant disregard for the principles of justice and public broadcasting's legislative mandates" (quoted in Berkman, 1980: 186).

More recently, Dates (1990: 303), in an extensive review of African-American participation in public television, wrote that the system "has consistently failed to address the concerns of African American groups." Dates also indicated that "[d]uring the 1980's some progress was made ... as measured by programming and employee levels." As a result, Dates suggested that in the late 1980s, "African American consumers and television practitioners alike, without dwelling on the negative elements that in the past had prevented their full participation, began to throw their support and interest into public television, hopeful that opportunities would increase to the degree they could eventually become full-fledged participants" (p. 338; see also Williams, 1985). Similarly, Lashley's analysis of employment diversity in public television found that "public television stations are compliant with the congressional mandate for employment diversity overall, but managers exercise considerable latitude. Most stations employ significantly more women than minorities in managerial positions. Moreover, many stations employ no minority persons as managers or officials, and little, if any, pressure is exerted to bring them into compliance" (1992: 109).[9]

This wide-ranging body of literature indicates that public television does, indeed, face a crisis of mission. On the one hand, there is confusion about the identity of public television; on the other, the widely recognized goal of diversity—in terms of programming, audience, and employment—has met with only partial success.

Despite the important contributions of this work, none of it has analyzed the issue of mission from inside public television. Such questions as how those who make the programs see this mission or how this vision (or lack thereof) may influence the content of the programming have not been systematically addressed. Much like the literature on the funding process, the literature on the mission of public television is useful in framing the issues and in suggesting some of the shortcomings of the system. However, the interpretation of the mission of public television—the meanings attached to it—by those who actually make the programming, and the incentives and constraints imposed by these interpretations, have been entirely ignored by this literature. These are the questions that I take up more specifically in Chapter 7.

Moving Forward

In the previous sections, I have argued that the principal shortcoming of the existing literature on public television is its focus on the product. That is, it focuses primarily on the output produced by public television and only peripherally on how and why it is produced. Clearly, product-oriented research provides fewer methodological difficulties than process-oriented research. Samples are identified and collected, coding schemes are developed, and content analysis yields hard, quantitative data for the testing and refining of hypotheses. Although such product-oriented research continues to provide useful data on public television, it must be seen as only one part of a larger research agenda. I will also provide an output study in the next chapter, a case study of the *MacNeil/Lehrer NewsHour*. Rather than being considered an end point, however, this will only serve as a starting point for my investigation.

Powell and Friedkin's (1983, 1986) and Lashley's (1992) organizational analyses of public television programming were important additions to a literature dominated by output-oriented research. Powell and Friedkin's work is particularly useful for both its methodological and substantive contribution. Drawing on interviews and fieldwork at two public television stations, Powell and Friedkin explored the ways that funding sources and organizational routines constrain the production of programming. They were particularly interested in how station personnel interpret and respond to these financial and organizational constraints. The analysis was set specifically within the context of a public television system that, in contrast to commercial television, had imprecise goals and vague criteria for decisionmaking. At the substantive level, this work implied that our ability to understand content analyses of public television can be greatly enhanced by research focusing on the social and organizational forces that shape program content, and perhaps more important, the meanings production personnel attach to these forces. By reorienting research along these lines, we move from the arena of describing content to that of explaining what shapes that content. Powell and Friedkin's useful methodological framework highlighted the importance of qualitative research, particularly in-depth interviews, as a means for understanding how public television works.

A Note on Method

A more detailed discussion of the research design for this study appears in the Methodological Appendix. Before moving on, however, a brief overview of the research methods used in the upcoming chapters is in order. Chapter 4 presents a comparison of PBS's *MacNeil/Lehrer NewsHour* and two ABC News programs over a six-month period in 1989. I make use of the principles of content analysis to examine the topics covered and the guests appearing on three programs—*MacNeil/Lehrer, Nightline,* and *World News Tonight.* The chapter also draws upon more in-depth qualitative analysis in comparing the coverage by *MacNeil/Lehrer* and *Nightline* of four major stories during the six-month period.

In Chapters 5 through 7 my data are a series of in-depth interviews with twenty-five people who worked at Boston's WGBH in the production of national public television programming. Since the early years of public television, WGBH has been among the largest producers of national programming for PBS, and it has gained a reputation for the quality of its documentaries. It is currently the major supplier of public television's prime time lineup, producing, among others, *Frontline, Nova, American Experience, Masterpiece Theater,* and *Mystery.* WGBH is also known as the producer of many of PBS's major multipart historical documentaries, including *Vietnam: A Television History* and *Inside Gorbachev's Soviet Union.* Its station manager in the 1960s, Hartford Gunn, was the first president of PBS, and WGBH continues to be one of the most powerful players within the national public television system. This research, following the example of Powell and Friedkin, sets out to illuminate the constraints under which public television programs are produced in order that we might better understand how the system works, where it is headed, and the dilemmas that public television is likely to face in the years ahead.

Notes

1. See Lashner (1976, 1977) for a discussion of the role of foundations in public broadcasting. The 1977 article focuses specifically on the role of the Ford Foundation.

2. Weber is adamant about this point. He argues that "the *elementary duty of scientific self-control* and the only way to avoid serious and foolish blunders requires a sharp, precise distinction between the logically *comparative* analysis of reality by ideal-*types* in the logical sense and the *value-judgement* of reality *on the basis of ideals.* An 'ideal type' in our sense, to repeat once more, has no connection at all with *value-judgements,* and it has nothing to do with any type of perfection other than a purely *logical* one. There are ideal types of brothels as well as of religions" (1949: 99, italics in original). See Burger (1976) for a thorough discussion of Weber's use of the ideal-type construct.

3. I did find one such book, Stone's (1985) study, *Nixon and the Politics of Public Television.* Also, *Current,* the weekly trade newspaper of public broadcasting, published a short volume, *The History of Public Broadcasting* (Witherspoon and Kovitz, 1987). CPB paid for the research, writing, and editing of this work.

4. Two recent journalistic accounts make a similar argument. Wicklein (1986) and Emerson (1989), both writing in the *Columbia Journalism Review,* argued that private funders have too much power in the public television system. Wicklein (1986: 33) suggested that "at best, the funding system established by Congress encourages timidity in

programming; at worst, it invites political and commercial interference." And Emerson (1989: 26), writing three years later during the controversy over the broadcasting of the documentary about Palestinians of the *intifada, Days of Rage,* noted that some believe "PBS's dependence on corporate contributions has made the service willing to do almost anything to accommodate the funders."

5. Rapping (1987) and Schiller (1989) both noted that corporate underwriters use public television for public relations purposes and as a means of targeting upscale consumers.

6. Contrary to this advice, as we saw in Chapter 1, PBS continues to make extensive use of more traditional demographic data in its audience research.

7. Pearce and Rosener (1985) discussed these community advisory boards; however, their conclusions focused on their larger model of advisory board performance and said little about the makeup or impact of citizen advisory boards for public television.

8. Ivers's (1989) unpublished paper also focused on the creation of ITVS but located the discussion in a different context. For Ivers, "The independent production service can be viewed as a case study for a series of larger questions, each dealing with all forms of access to the public broadcasting system. Who should have access to the public broadcasting system? Which 'publics' will the public broadcasting system serve? What is to be the 'public' role in public broadcasting" (p. 33)?

9. Although Lashley's book was published in 1992, the data used for the analysis of employment diversity is from FY 1977 to FY 1979. She did not discuss the possibility that employment patterns have changed since 1979.

CHAPTER FOUR

■

The Content of Public Television: A Case Study of the *MacNeil/Lehrer NewsHour*

Since the initial release of the Carnegie Commission report in 1967, supporters of noncommercial television have argued that news and public affairs programming are essential components of a public television system. When the
Nixon administration attempted to redirect public television away from public affairs programming through political pressure and the veto of a funding
bill, the public broadcasting community reaffirmed its commitment to examining current issues and events through a range of both national and local programming. In the 1990s, with the news divisions at the three major television
networks bearing the brunt of increased economic pressures, public television's commitment to the production of public affairs programming became
even more important.

Auletta (1991) painted a vivid picture of the clash between the old-guard
network journalists and the new cost-conscious network owners in the late
1980s. He suggested that the new owners, particularly NBC's parent corporation, General Electric, had doubts about the argument that network news
should be removed from the profit considerations faced by all other aspects of
the corporation and did not easily accept the argument that news should be
viewed as a "public trust." At the same time, the new owners (most notably
CBS's Laurence Tisch) were astounded by the combination of rising costs and
declining audiences. As a result, each of the three network news divisions
faced significant cost cutting in the second half of the 1980s, and the once
widely held notion that news should be insulated from the pressure to make
profits no longer held. By the mid-1980s, the networks could no longer rely
on entertainment and sports programming to make the kind of profit that
would offset losses by the news divisions. The economics of network television, combined with a new corporate culture that frowned upon financial

losses in even the most prestigious component of the corporation, lead both to cost cutting in the news divisions and the further erosion of the line between news and entertainment. As Auletta summed up one of the major consequences of the changing ownership of television networks:

> Although the weakening of the walls that traditionally stood between News and the rest of the company began before the new owners arrived, that process was now surely accelerated. Increasingly the networks pressured their local stations to promote network entertainment shows and stars on its newscasts, thus tarnishing the independence a newscast needs to retain the trust of viewers. ... News re-creations knocked down the walls, as did most docudramas. ... The new owners speeded the trend to hold news to the same ratings standard as entertainment shows. If a news documentary or special couldn't approximate the desired Nielsen numbers, it usually got the hook (1991: 564–565).

By the late 1980s there was a great opportunity for the public television system, removed from many of the pressures associated with commercial television, to provide more substantive news and public affairs programming. If one surveys the regular PBS schedule, it is clear that the long-standing commitment to this type of programming has continued into the 1990s.

The flagship program for PBS in the realm of news and public affairs is undoubtedly the *MacNeil/Lehrer NewsHour*. After premiering in 1976 as the thirty-minute *MacNeil/Lehrer Report*,[1] the *NewsHour* now occupies more time—five hours a week—than any other public affairs program on the public television schedule. According to journalist James Traub (1985), this time commitment, an hour each weeknight, led one PBS source to label the *NewsHour* "an 800-pound gorilla." The *NewsHour* is important to PBS for reasons beyond its simple visibility on the evening schedule. It is highly regarded by politicians and journalists and has gained a reputation for the quality of its reporting. Its two hosts, Robert MacNeil and Jim Lehrer, are both highly regarded in the journalistic community and, perhaps more important, have been central players in public television since the conflicts between public television and the Nixon administration. Moreover, the program is regularly broadcast by more than 300 of the 349 public stations in the United States, making it one of the most widely carried programs in the system.

The significance of the *NewsHour* is heightened by the shortcomings of the remaining public affairs programs on public television. One important shortcoming is the dearth of local news programs on public television stations. In 1990, for example, New York's highly regarded *Eleventh Hour* was discontinued, and in 1991 Boston's prestigious *Ten O'Clock News* was cancelled. In both cases, budgetary considerations were cited as the primary factor. Despite campaigns by community groups to save the two programs, neither was restored to the local lineup. By 1992, only a handful of PBS stations produced a local evening news broadcast, making *MacNeil/Lehrer* the only daily news program on the vast majority of public television stations.

Another problem is that public television's regular public affairs programs provide a narrow view of the world. *Adam Smith's Money World, Wall $treet Week,* and *Nightly Business Report* provide financial information for the corporate community. And *Firing Line, The McLaughlin Group,* and *One on One* provide discussion of current political issues with decidedly conservative hosts—William Buckley and John McLaughlin of the *National Review.* Moreover, the one PBS program devoted specifically to the African-American community is hosted by Republican Tony Brown. In Chapter 5, which focuses on the funding of public television, I will return to these programs and examine why they are so visible on the PBS schedule.

With little or no local news and a narrow range of public affairs programming, the *MacNeil/Lehrer NewsHour* is clearly public television's standard bearer. As such, *MacNeil/Lehrer* is a particularly useful program to study, for it plays such an important role in defining our public television system.[2]

By the 1980s, *MacNeil/Lehrer* had earned a reputation as the best nightly news program in the country; it was widely heralded for both the breadth and depth of its reporting. In 1982, for example, *Time* magazine's Thomas Griffith called the thirty-minute report "TV's best discussion of public affairs." And *NewsHour* correspondent Charlayne Hunter-Gault's 1984 *Vogue* article labeled *MacNeil/Lehrer* "TV's finest hour." By 1991, the *NewsHour,* according to the program's "fact sheet," had been "singled out by a Gallup Poll as the most believed news program on American television and has been further recognized by five Emmys and five Peabody Awards."

Much of this praise suggests that *MacNeil/Lehrer* is superior to other television news programs. The implicit, and sometimes explicit, suggestion that *MacNeil/Lehrer* is a "better" news program—more in-depth, more serious, less "fluffy"—carries with it an explanation for *why* the *NewsHour* is better. The fact that *MacNeil/Lehrer* is on public television is central to this explanation. As a PBS program, the *NewsHour* does not face the daily pressures associated with ratings and profits that its counterparts on the networks face. As a result, so the argument goes, the *NewsHour* does not have to produce news to attract or entertain an audience, only news to inform its viewers. Furthermore, the absence of commercials allows the *NewsHour* significantly more time: roughly fifty-seven minutes of its hour as opposed to the networks' twenty-two minutes of their half-hour. Ultimately, then, the fact that *MacNeil/Lehrer* is on noncommercial television helps explain why it can be more in-depth and less flashy than the network newscasts that have little time, must compete for a large audience, and have to constantly watch the bottom line. Scholars and critics might add the pressures associated with the need to attract sponsors to the list of constraints imposed on network news; *MacNeil/Lehrer*'s partial removal from these pressures is thus another reason it apparently differs from the network news.

It should be evident to anyone who has regularly watched both the *NewsHour* and network news that there are significant differences. The argument that *MacNeil/Lehrer* is the "best" news program suggests that these readily visible differences reflect a qualitative difference in news content. However, empirical research has neither tested such propositions nor specified the nature of the difference in content. This chapter makes use of empirical research to examine these propositions through a comparative study of *MacNeil/Lehrer* and ABC News programs.

Comparing ABC and PBS

The following comparison between *MacNeil/Lehrer* and ABC News will examine the differences, if any, between the content of public television news, which is partially removed from commercial pressures, and the news on commercial television. I have selected ABC News for two reasons. First, ABC had the most commercial as well as the most critical success with its news in the late 1980s. *World News Tonight* was the late-1980s ratings leader, and anchor Peter Jennings was often singled out for high praise. Second, ABC broadcasts *Nightline,* the late-night single-issue supplement to the evening news. *Nightline* is *MacNeil/Lehrer*'s major competitor for the label as the most prestigious news program on television today. *World News Tonight* and *Nightline* combined are a nice match with *MacNeil/Lehrer,* particularly if one is familiar with the history of *MacNeil/Lehrer.* As a thirty-minute show, *MacNeil/Lehrer* focused on a single story each night. After *Nightline*'s success with this same format, *MacNeil/Lehrer* expanded to its current *NewsHour* structure—a short news update, followed by in-depth coverage of (usually) three stories each night. As such, the *NewsHour* has turned into a kind of cross between the evening news and an in-depth, single-issue news program.

More difficult than identifying the appropriate programs to compare, however, is the task of defining the framework for comparison. There are a wide range of dimensions upon which such a comparison can rest. Our task is to define discrete questions that we can formulate as hypotheses that will provide answers to the broader question about the relationship between commercial and public television news. Since both the scholarly literature and public television's own goals focus on the issue of content diversity, it will be useful to frame our hypotheses around this issue. At the theoretical level, as Chapter 2 indicated, scholarly analysis of mass media has found that commercial pressures lead to homogeneity of content. The implication, then, is that insulation from the economic market should allow for a broader range of expression, for increased diversity. On a substantive level, as Chapter 3 explained, diversity in content has always been a central goal for public television. The initial report of the Carnegie Commission, in fact, noted the "pressure toward uniformity" from commercial television and stated the hope that public television could "resist that pressure" and serve diversity. In short, there are both theoretical and practical reasons to believe that the differences between *MacNeil/Lehrer* and ABC's news shows revolve around the issue of diversity.

Having identified the framework for comparison—the relative diversity in content of the two news outlets—we need to operationalize the concept and formulate hypotheses. Previous research suggests that diversity of news coverage has two principal components: the range of stories covered and the range of perspectives featured. At the level of story range, critics have argued that commercial news organizations "work within a competitive bind that encourages them to offer virtually the same news" (Gans, 1979: 289). Television news at each of the networks consists largely of predictable, often preplanned, visually oriented events. As for the range of perspectives, Gans (1979) argues that news should seek to provide a wide range of perspectives on issues and events. Gans notes, however, that economic, organizational, and professional factors lead major media outlets away from a multiperspectival approach. Entman (1989: 18) further specifies the importance of economic forces, arguing that "economic competition encourages news organizations to minimize costs and generate growing profits. The least expensive way to satisfy a mass audience is to rely upon legitimate political elites for most information."[3]

Our comparison, then, will focus on these two dimensions: the range of stories covered by *MacNeil/Lehrer* and the ABC program that covers multiple stories each night, *World News Tonight;* and the range of perspectives represented by the guests featured on *MacNeil/Lehrer* and ABC's program that provides discussions and debates, *Nightline.*

To summarize, we begin with the general hypothesis that news on public television will exhibit certain differences from network news. Removed from commercial pressures—profits and high ratings—as well as the pressures associated with advertising and corporate ownership, the *MacNeil/Lehrer NewsHour* is expected to be more diverse, both in the topics it chooses to cover and in the voices it uses to interpret events, than ABC News's shows. These expectations are bolstered by the fact that *MacNeil/Lehrer* not only is ostensibly removed from commercial considerations but also is part of a television system whose express purpose is to provide a diverse forum. More specifically, we will test the following two hypotheses:

Hypothesis One: *MacNeil/Lehrer* will cover a more diverse set of stories than ABC's *World News Tonight.* In particular, the *NewsHour* will be more likely to examine issues that are not tied to breaking events and stories that are less visually oriented.

Hypothesis Two: The guests used in interviews and discussions on
MacNeil/Lehrer will represent a wider range of perspectives than the
guests featured on *Nightline*.

In this chapter, I compare the two news outlets over a six-month period in
1989, beginning with the first Monday in February (February 6 through August 4).[4] A detailed discussion of the research design for this chapter is in the
Methodological Appendix, but a brief overview is in order here. All weekday
programs over the six month period are included in the analysis, for a total of
130 editions of each of the three programs. The analysis is divided into three
sections: The first section tests Hypothesis One, and the second and third sections test Hypothesis Two. Stories on each of the three programs have been
coded on two dimensions of story topic.[5] These codes serve as the principal
data for the first section, the comparison between *MacNeil/Lehrer* and *World
News Tonight*. Similarly, all guests appearing on discussion and interview segments on either *MacNeil/Lehrer* or *Nightline* have been coded on a variety of
dimensions, including race, gender, nationality, occupational status, and institutional affiliation. These codes serve as the data for the second section, the
quantitative comparison of guest diversity on *MacNeil/Lehrer* and *Nightline*.
The third section provides a more detailed analysis of the two guest lists and
uses qualitative analysis to further examine Hypothesis Two by comparing
coverage by *MacNeil/Lehrer* and *Nightline* of four major story topics of the
sample period.

Before I report results of this research, let me briefly indicate some of the
ways in which the *MacNeil/Lehrer NewsHour* clearly differs from network
news. First—and this may be very significant for viewers as well as for journalists—there are no commercial interruptions. Second, the program's one-hour
format makes it unique among national evening news programs. The
NewsHour's time budget must be the envy of other television journalists, and
its focus on a limited number of stories each night means that reports are regularly allotted up to ten minutes—almost half of an entire network news
broadcast. As a result, the *NewsHour* does not rely as heavily on short sound
bites as do the networks. Third, the program is less flashy and generally es-
chews the catchy slogans, upbeat theme music, and dramatic visuals favored
by the networks. In short, there is a much different look and feel to *MacNeil/
Lehrer* than there is to the network evening news. In the following pages, we
will determine whether these stylistic differences lead to news with a fundamentally different content.

Stories on *MacNeil/Lehrer* and *World News Tonight*

In this section, the analysis focuses on the degree to which *MacNeil/Lehrer*'s
choice of stories overlaps with *World News Tonight*'s. This study covers 130

TABLE 4.1 Topic of Lead Stories: *MacNeil/Lehrer NewsHour* and *World News Tonight*, 2/6/89–8/4/89

	International Political	Domestic Political	Economic	Social	Culture	Other	Total
PBS	31.0%	43.7%	8.5%	11.3%	1.4%	4.2%	
only	n=22	n=31	n=6	n=8	n=1	n=3	n=71
ABC	50.7%	28.2%	8.5%	5.6%	1.4%	5.6%	
only	n=36	n=20	n=6	n=4	n=1	n=4	n=71

editions of the two evening news programs. *MacNeil/Lehrer* and *World News Tonight* had the same lead story on 45 percent of the days examined (59 programs). The figures are very similar for overlap on all stories aired. *MacNeil/Lehrer* covered a total of 412 stories in the six month period. Forty-five percent of these (186 stories) were also covered by *World News Tonight* on the same night. These figures illustrate substantial overlap. Still, more than half of *MacNeil/Lehrer*'s stories were not covered by ABC on the same night.

I further analyzed the stories on the two programs by creating three story categories. *Overlap* stories are those that were covered by both programs on the same night; *PBS Only* stories are those covered by *MacNeil/Lehrer* but not by ABC on the same night; and *ABC Only* stories are those covered by ABC but not *MacNeil/Lehrer* on the same night. For lead stories, *Overlap Leads* are those that led both programs on the same night; *PBS Only Leads* are those that led *MacNeil/Lehrer* but not ABC on the same night (regardless of whether ABC covered the story later in the broadcast); and *ABC Only Leads* are those stories that led ABC but not *MacNeil/Lehrer* on the same night. By removing the Overlap stories (those covered by both programs) and comparing the stories that were only covered by one of the two programs on a given night (or led only one of the two programs), we will be able to determine whether there is a substantial difference in story selection between *MacNeil/Lehrer* and ABC.

As Table 4.1 shows, ABC Only Leads were much more likely than PBS Only Leads to focus on international issues (51 percent to 31 percent), and PBS Only Leads were more likely than ABC Only Leads to focus on domestic political issues (44 percent to 28 percent). Table 4.2 indicates that a similar pattern is evident when we analyze all stories. ABC Only stories were more than twice as likely as PBS Only stories to examine international issues (38 percent to 16 percent), whereas PBS Only stories were more likely than ABC Only stories to examine domestic political issues (29 percent to 20 percent). Moreover, PBS Only stories focused more frequently on economic issues (11.5 percent to 7 percent) and social issues (24 percent to 20 percent) than did ABC Only stories.

The overwhelming number of ABC Only international stories can be partly accounted for by the network's on-location news broadcasts from around the

TABLE 4.2   Topic of All Stories:[a] *MacNeil/Lehrer NewsHour* and *World News Tonight*, 2/6/89–8/4/89

	International Political	Domestic Political	Economic	Social	Culture	Other	Total
PBS only	15.9% n=36	29.2% n=66	11.5% n=26	23.9% n=54	8.8% n=20	10.6% n=24	n=226
ABC only	38.1% n=259	19.9% n=135	7.2% n=49	20.3% n=138	7.7% n=52	6.8% n=46	n=679

[a]Excludes stories from brief *MacNeil/Lehrer news update segment* and *World News Tonight* stories shorter than one minute.

globe, as ABC followed President Bush on his trips to Japan, England, and Eastern Europe in 1989. ABC's access to greater resources may explain why its stories were much more focused on international issues than *MacNeil/Lehrer*'s. However, the choice to follow the president abroad must be understood not as some immutable law of broadcast news but as a specific decision by ABC News about what to cover. In this regard, there are substantial differences between ABC News stories and *MacNeil/Lehrer* stories.

What can we say about the stories covered by *MacNeil/Lehrer* that were not covered by ABC on the same day? They were more heavily weighted toward domestic political issues, economic issues, and social issues than ABC's. This difference reflects the fact that *MacNeil/Lehrer* often examined stories that were less than breaking news. The background to the HUD scandal, the question of ethics in government, the changing international economy, and the reasons for drug abuse are the kinds of domestic political, economic, and social stories that *MacNeil/Lehrer* featured regularly rather than focusing on the president's travel agenda.

It is worth noting that more than a quarter of the PBS Only stories were multipart series ("Talking Drugs," "High-Tech Frontier," and "Considering the Cabinet," for example) and video essays. Neither of these story forms is necessarily connected to a breaking event (only 8 percent of multipart series and video essays were Overlap stories). As such, the series provided an in-depth examination of enduring issues facing American society. And the video essays provided for a more personal and sometimes quirky look at topics ranging from the newest styles and popular trends to change in the Soviet Union and the quality of American leadership. Of course, we should not overstate the case. *World News Tonight* also has a regular feature, "American Agenda," that looks at less immediate stories, but it appears with less frequency than *MacNeil/Lehrer*'s essays and series.

These data make clear that the points of overlap between *MacNeil/Lehrer* and ABC are on traditional, event-oriented, "hard news" reporting. Both programs generally cover a similar set of breaking political stories. Even on similar stories, however, *MacNeil/Lehrer*'s format allows it to provide more

TABLE 4.3 Occupational Status of U.S. Guests: *MacNeil/Lehrer NewsHour* and *Nightline,* 2/6/89–8/4/89

	Government Official	Profes- sional	Corporate Representative	Labor Representative	Public Interest	Other	Total
MacNeil/	46.2%	37.8%	5.2%	0.8%	5.2%	4.8%	
Lehrer	n=232	n=190	n=26	n=4	n=26	n=24	n=502
Nightline	34.3%	39.1%	4.7%	0.7%	9.1%	12.1%	
	n=102	n=116	n=14	n=2	n=27	n=36	n=297

in-depth analysis than any of the networks. But *MacNeil/Lehrer* also spends considerable time examining political, economic, and social developments that are not pegged to a particular late-breaking event. Regular coverage of these kinds of less-traditional stories serves to differentiate *MacNeil/Lehrer* from its counterpart at ABC.

Guests on *MacNeil/Lehrer* and *Nightline*

This section examines the range of guests appearing on the *NewsHour* and *Nightline.* By itself, the demographic makeup of these programs' guest lists does not guarantee a diversity of perspectives. However, as Gans (1979) has pointed out, demographic diversity is one important sign of substantive diversity, because where people exist in national and social hierarchies often affects how they view the world.

Both *MacNeil/Lehrer* and *Nightline* have disproportionate numbers of white males on their guest lists. For *MacNeil/Lehrer,* 90 percent of the U.S. guests were white and 87 percent were male. *Nightline* was only slightly broader in this regard: 89 percent were white and 82 percent were male.[6] On programs about international politics, the numbers were even more stark: 94 percent of the *NewsHour*'s U.S. guests were white and 94 percent were male, whereas 96 percent of *Nightline*'s U.S. guests were white and 90 percent were male. During discussions about foreign policy, women and people of color from the United States were virtual nonparticipants.

Coverage of domestic politics was more representative. Twenty-one percent of the U.S. guests on *MacNeil/Lehrer* were women, as against 26 percent of *Nightline*'s U.S. guests. Many of the women appeared on programs about abortion. Both programs featured wide-ranging discussions of the abortion debate, involving activists on both sides of the issue, along with journalists and legal and medical experts.

On the whole, as Table 4.3 shows, *MacNeil/Lehrer*'s guest list was populated heavily by government officials. A total of 46 percent of the *NewsHour*'s U.S. guests were current or former government officials. Another 38 percent were professionals (primarily academics, doctors, and lawyers), and 5 percent were corporate representatives. In contrast, only 6 percent represented either public interest, labor, or racial/ethnic organizations. On programs about international politics, the *NewsHour* relied more heavily on official perspectives; two-thirds of the *NewsHour*'s U.S. guests on discussions of international issues were current or former government officials.

Nightline made use of a similar set of guests, but it showed somewhat more diversity than did *MacNeil/Lehrer* (see Table 4.3). Thirty-four percent of its U.S. guests were government officials, 39 percent professionals, and 5 percent corporate representatives. On *Nightline*, 10 percent of the guests represented public interest, labor, or racial/ethnic organizations.

Each guest was also coded for institutional affiliation. On *MacNeil/Lehrer*, two conservative Washington think tanks stood out: the American Enterprise Institute (AEI) and the Center for Strategic and International Studies (CSIS). AEI fellows appeared six times and CSIS fellows eight times in this six-month period. In general, AEI provided the resident experts for discussions of domestic political issues and CSIS for foreign policy issues.

Although AEI and CSIS fellows were introduced as nonpartisan experts, it is clear that both institutes are strong conservative voices. Himmelstein (1990) has pointed out their major corporate funding and argued persuasively that AEI and CSIS, among other conservative think tanks, are not neutral research organizations but in fact have been central players in promoting a conservative agenda at the highest levels of the U.S. government. In contrast to the voices from AEI and CSIS, fellows from more progressive think tanks were rarely included. In fact, representatives of well-known think tanks such as the Institute for Policy Studies and the World Policy Institute did not appear once on *MacNeil/Lehrer* in the six-month period. *Nightline* did not rely as heavily on the same particular think tanks, although AEI fellows appeared three times and a CSIS fellow appeared once during the six months.

It is clear that a similar set of guests appear on both *MacNeil/Lehrer* and *Nightline*. In both cases, it is a relatively narrow range of voices. If anything, in fact, *Nightline* presents a slightly wider range of perspectives than *MacNeil/ Lehrer*. In the next section, case studies of four major issues will examine more thoroughly the similarities and differences between the guest lists of *MacNeil/Lehrer* and *Nightline*.

Issue Analysis:
China, Environment, Economy, Central America

China

The student-led occupation of Tiananmen Square was the major story of the summer of 1989, and both *MacNeil/Lehrer* and *Nightline* gave it a great deal of air time. Both programs did an impressive job of keeping abreast of events, with daily updates on breaking news. But analysis of the history, motivations, and consequences of the student movement and the government response was severely limited.

MacNeil/Lehrer broadcast eighteen segments that focused on China during this study, with a total of thirty-seven guests. Seventy-three percent of these guests were from the United States, the remainder from China. In all, 61 percent of the guests were white and 39 percent were Asian, the latter including both Chinese citizens and Chinese-Americans. Eighty-nine percent of the guests were men—despite the fact that the news media were heralding the important leadership role played by female students in China.

The occupational breakdown of the guest list was broader than for other international issues. Thirty percent of the guests were government officials, 46 percent professionals (mainly academics and journalists), and 14 percent public interest activists. These activists were all Chinese students who either were living in the United States during the hostilities or fled to the United States shortly after.

Nightline's coverage of China was even more extensive than *MacNeil/Lehrer*'s: China was *Nightline*'s story ten nights in a row in early June. During the period studied, there were nineteen programs on China, with forty-nine guests. Fifty-three percent of the guests were from the United States, and the remainder included foreign journalists, Chinese dissidents, and Chinese student activists. Fifty-one percent of the guests were white, 49 percent of Asian descent.

Nightline's coverage of China was significantly different from its coverage of other international issues, as only one-tenth of the guests were government officials, whereas 20 percent were public interest activists, all Chinese student leaders. It was refreshing to see *Nightline* pay so much attention to "unofficial" views of events. It is curious that neither *Nightline* nor *MacNeil/Lehrer* paid as much attention to unofficial views in coverage of other events.

Both *MacNeil/Lehrer* and *Nightline* covered the story in China much as television news covers natural disasters, with a premium on getting the latest information, reporting the casualties, and providing video footage. But *MacNeil/Lehrer* and *Nightline* are capable of providing more than just the drama of nightly news. Both programs purport to offer in-depth analysis of events. Yet neither program seriously examined the history leading up to the 1989 student activism, the reasons for the unrest, or the demands of the students. MacNeil, Lehrer, and *Nightline* host Ted Koppel regularly asserted that the Chinese students were leading a "prodemocracy" movement, but they rarely explored the meaning of this label. It was as if "prodemocracy" was somehow self-explanatory. And far from being a straightforward mobilization against "communism," the student movement came, in part, in response to the problems associated with free market experiments. Yet *MacNeil/Lehrer* and *Nightline* failed to explore such issues.

Ultimately, viewers of the *NewsHour* and *Nightline* may have been left with a good sense of what was happening in China but not why it was happening or what the long-term effects of the student movement might be. Analytical coverage of events such as those in China is supposed to differentiate *MacNeil/Lehrer* and *Nightline* from the evening news, yet this kind of reporting was largely missing from both programs.

The Environment

The destruction of the environment is arguably one of the most significant issues facing humanity at the end of the twentieth century. *Nightline*'s Ted Koppel has called the threat to the ozone layer "perhaps the most imminent danger now confronting this planet" (3/7/89).

After decades of ignoring warnings from environmental activists and scientists, the national media have recently begun to pay more attention to growing ecological devastation. In 1990, for example, PBS broadcast *Race To Save the Planet*, a series about various current environmental issues. Despite the growing interest in this subject, the environment still poses two major difficulties for the news media. First, it is rarely a "breaking" story; the dangers and developments affecting the environment evolve gradually over a period of time. There is not always a convenient "peg" on which to hang an environmental story. The exception proves the rule: The dramatic Exxon oil spill in Alaska in March 1989 provided journalists with a compelling story line, an individual villain, and engaging visuals. Nearly half the environmental stories aired during the study period focused on this spill. Second, environmentalists know that in order to fully assess the issue of ecological destruction, one has to "follow the money." For journalists this approach can pose problems. Tracing environmental damage back to the corporate and industrial organizations that benefit from weak environmental protection laws might result in pressure from corporate owners or advertisers. Even when environmental stories are covered, the role of corporate polluters is often obscured. As Ralph Nader has noted, "Look at all the stories on the destruction of the Amazon rain forest. Do you ever see the names of any multinational corporations mentioned?"[7] *MacNeil/Lehrer*'s July 4, 1989, story on Brazil's Amazon rain forest was no exception: No corporations were mentioned.

MacNeil/Lehrer broadcast sixteen environment-related stories during this six-month period. Besides the Exxon *Valdez* spill, subjects included President Bush's clean air proposal, other oil spills, environmental/safety problems at nuclear weapons facilities, the search for nuclear waste sites, driftnet fishing, the food additive Alar, Brazil's rain forest, and a proposed dam outside Denver.

A total of seventeen guests—all white, American males—appeared on *MacNeil/Lehrer*'s environmental segments. If viewers expected to find representatives of environmental groups on programs about the environment, they would have been disappointed: Only one such representative appeared. Instead, government and corporate figures dominated *MacNeil/Lehrer*'s guest list for environmental stories. More than half of the guests were government officials, and almost one-third were corporate representatives.

MacNeil/Lehrer's inattention to environmentalists is highlighted by the sole case in which an environmentalist actually made an appearance. On March 16, 1989, Al Meyeroff of the Natural Resources Defense Council (NRDC) appeared on *MacNeil/Lehrer* to discuss NRDC's report on the dangers of Alar. However, since NRDC was the source of the Alar story, it would have been virtually impossible for *MacNeil/Lehrer* to cover it without including an NRDC representative. Such was not the case for most environmental stories; tellingly, no other environmentalists were guests on the show.

When *MacNeil/Lehrer* looked at the government's plan to clean up environmental and safety problems at major nuclear weapons plants (8/2/89), it invited Energy Secretary James Watkins for a "Newsmaker" interview—alone, with no dissenting voices. When *MacNeil/Lehrer* examined President Bush's proposals for cleaner air (6/12/89), it invited the Environmental Protection Agency's William Reilly—again without including any critical voices.

Without critical voices, many of the *NewsHour*'s environmental programs presented extremely limited perspectives on events, sometimes with corporate and government voices supporting each other. *MacNeil/Lehrer* featured the Alaska oil spill on four consecutive programs and had three later follow-ups during the six-month study period. The first program featured Exxon's Alaska coordinator, Don Cornett, and Alaska governor Steve Cowper. Cornett assured the audience (wrongly, it turned out) that, with chemical dispersants, Exxon would "handle a great deal of the spill before it ever touches the shoreline of Prince William Sound" and argued that "people tend to forget that oil is biodegradable." For his part, Governor Cowper expressed concern at the lack of preparedness by the oil company but felt that this spill should not interfere with future expansion of oil drilling in the Arctic. He concluded, "By and large the Trans-Alaska Pipeline is a very effective way to get oil from one place to another. It's clean from an engineering standpoint and while there have been some relatively minor incidents, I think that they're acceptable." No environmentalists were present to challenge such assertions.

Although the scale of the oil spill could not be overlooked, government experts and corporate representatives presented a largely reassuring view of the impact of the accident. Exxon chairman Lawrence Rawl was featured on *MacNeil/Lehrer*'s fourth story on the spill (3/30/89). He apologized for the spill but downplayed its impact on the oil industry. Rawl's appearance was "balanced" by Governor Cowper who, although critical of the oil company consortium responsible for cleanup plans, argued that "the chairman of the board of Exxon, I think, has been too heavy on his own company. ... Obviously Exxon's skipper caused this accident, but after it took place, I think that Exxon did a good job under the circumstances. I really do."

Nightline featured six programs on environmental issues with a total of fifteen guests. All the guests were white, and only two were women. All but one guest (Margaret Thatcher) were U.S. citizens. Sixty percent of the guests were government officials, and 13 percent were corporate representatives. *Nightline* included two environmentalists—Wilderness Society president George Frampton (future of oil spills) and Janet Hathaway of the NRDC (health effects of pesticides).

As it did on *MacNeil/Lehrer*, the Exxon oil spill dominated *Nightline*'s coverage of the environment. *Nightline*'s three programs on the spill, spread over a four-month period, had a decidedly more skeptical tone than *MacNeil/Lehrer*'s. Its first program featured a spokesperson for the Alaska Department of Environmental Conservation, the agency conducting on-site coordination of the oil-spill cleanup; the mayor of Valdez; and a fisherman, Jim Brown. The inclusion of Brown was a rare case where the perspective of someone affected by events was presented (*MacNeil/Lehrer* also invited a fisherman to take part in one of its discussions of the oil spill, on 3/29/89). It is worth noting that Exxon, which had sent a representative to appear on *MacNeil/Lehrer* on the same day, turned down *Nightline*'s invitation to have a spokesperson appear. The same thing occurred on July 25, when Exxon turned down *Nightline*'s invitation but sent its president, Lee Raymond, to appear on *MacNeil/Lehrer* two days later.

Although Koppel did ask tough questions about the bungled cleanup operation, both programs relied heavily on government and corporate experts for commentary and analysis. And in a taped introduction to one program, ABC's Roger Caras said: "The torn hull of the Exxon Valdez is the greatest environmental 'I told you so' in history." Yet notably absent from any of the Exxon oil spill programs were representatives from environmental groups that had long warned about just such an accident.

Neither *MacNeil/Lehrer* nor *Nightline* presented wide-ranging discussions of the environment. Both programs showed little interest in the views of the individuals and groups who have long struggled to bring attention to this problem. There are numerous respected and well-known environmental organizations in the United States with knowledgeable representatives who could be valuable assets in illuminating the complex issues surrounding environmental degradation and protection. Neither *MacNeil/Lehrer* nor *Nightline* provided regular access to these potentially critical perspectives.

The Economy

Perhaps the most striking feature of economic coverage on both *MacNeil/Lehrer* and *Nightline* was its narrow focus. Both programs concentrated more on Washington budget debates than on economic trends in particular industries or the labor force. Consequently, much of the "economic" reporting on the *NewsHour* and *Nightline* was really about Washington political debates. In this section, the discussion is limited to programs that actually focused on economic issues—whether in particular industries, the United States as a whole, or the international economy.

MacNeil/Lehrer broadcast thirty-five segments on economic issues, with a total of forty-two guests. Only four of the guests were women: two appeared on a program about the "mommy track," the separate corporate career track for women who plan to have children. Economic coverage on *MacNeil/Lehrer* was characterized by a heavy reliance on government spokespersons. Government officials made up 41 percent of the guests, and corporate representatives accounted for another 29 percent. Only 10 percent of the guests were labor representatives.

The most heavily covered economic issue during the six-month period was the Eastern Airlines strike and subsequent bankruptcy filing. *MacNeil/Lehrer* did five stories on this topic. It was during this coverage that all four appearances by labor leaders took place. The strike provided for a dramatic conflict with two clearly demarcated sides: union and management. *MacNeil/Lehrer* made a strong effort to include the union's opinions to balance those of Eastern Airlines executives.

However, this was the only time during the study period that the views of workers or their representatives were ever considered in *MacNeil/Lehrer*'s economic coverage. No labor or consumer rights representatives appeared on *MacNeil/Lehrer*'s other fourteen economic stories that featured guests. When the program did a story on the U.S. government's suit to seize control of the Teamsters, no union or rank-and-file representatives were on the show. The only guest was a reporter from the Long Island paper, *Newsday*. In addition, a week-long series that examined the economic implications of the "High-Tech Frontier" did not have any labor or consumer representatives as guests.

A regular viewer of *MacNeil/Lehrer* might think that there are no longer workers in the U.S. economy: Primarily government officials, corporate representatives, and "experts" populated the *NewsHour*'s economic reporting. The budget deficit and the savings and loan bailout were covered extensively by *MacNeil/Lehrer*, but without the perspective of a single consumer rights advocate. The economic conditions of the workers who make up the vast majority of the U.S. economy were rarely considered. For example, the Pittston coal strike that began in April 1989 and lasted through the end of the six-month study period was not featured on *MacNeil/Lehrer* or *Nightline*.

Nightline's economic coverage was less frequent, with only four programs and a total of twelve guests in the six-month period. Two women appeared, both on a program about the "mommy track." One-third of the guests were government officials and one-third were corporate representatives. Seventeen percent were labor representatives.

Nightline's four economic programs examined the indictment of junk bond king Michael Milken, the implications of the crash of United Flight 811 for the airline industry, the debate over Felice Schwartz's article on the "mommy track," and the bankruptcy of Eastern Airlines. Prompted by dramatic, individual events, these are the kind of stories covered on the evening news.

Typically missing from both *MacNeil/Lehrer* and *Nightline* was analytical coverage of economic trends. The one exception was *MacNeil/Lehrer*'s series on the "High-Tech Frontier," which attempted to analyze an issue that did not easily lend itself to short news formulas. Also generally missing from both programs' economic coverage were women (except on programs about "women's" issues), people of color, consumer rights advocates, and labor representatives. Just as the media tend to equate the nation with the federal government (cf. Gans, 1979), both *MacNeil/Lehrer* and *Nightline* seem to equate the economy with corporate America, to the exclusion of workers and consumers who do the bulk of the earning and spending.

Central America

Seven *MacNeil/Lehrer* programs featured segments on Central America: two on the election in El Salvador, two on aid to the Nicaraguan contras, and three on the Panamanian election. All twenty-two guests were men, and all of the U.S. guests were white. Most interesting is the fact that 100 percent of the guests were current or former government officials from the United States or elsewhere. Furthermore, all of the foreign government officials were from nations friendly to the United States—there were no voices from the Nicaraguan government or Manuel Noriega's Panamanian government.

MacNeil/Lehrer's coverage of Central America presented essentially one perspective on this complex region without even attempting to include opposing positions. Democrats and Republicans may have disagreed on the specific tactics of U.S. policy, but they rarely disagreed on the goals of that policy or on the intentions of the U.S. government. And friendly foreign government spokespeople seeking U.S. support were not likely to fundamentally disagree with U.S. officials.

What makes this kind of coverage curious is that the U.S. government's (often bipartisan) policies toward Central America were vigorously condemned by a significant part of the international community and by large sectors of the U.S. population, especially in the religious community, the labor movement, and academia. Yet as far as *MacNeil/Lehrer* was concerned, these critical perspectives did not exist.

MacNeil/Lehrer's coverage of Nicaragua and the contras featured appearances by two U.S. congressmen, Secretary of State James Baker (whom Lehrer "congratulated" on his deal with Congress for additional contra aid), and Guatemalan president Vinicio Cerezo. The discussion did not include any voices from Nicaragua, nor did it include any leaders of the anti-intervention movement in the United States. There was such a consensual atmosphere on *MacNeil/Lehrer* that one would never have known that polls indicated that a majority of the U.S. population had opposed U.S. policy toward Nicaragua for years.

The choice of Guatemalan president Cerezo to discuss human rights abuses and democratic shortcomings in Nicaragua was particularly telling, since Cerezo's U.S.-backed government stood accused by human rights monitors of involvement in the disappearances and abductions of dozens of Guatemalan civilians each month. The findings of independent monitoring groups indicated that the human rights situation in Guatemala in 1989 was significantly worse than that in Nicaragua. Although the selection of Cerezo to judge Nicaragua tended to distort human rights realities in the region, it conformed perfectly with the U.S. government's official position, contrasting Guatemala's "burgeoning democracy" with "repressive" Nicaragua. Robert MacNeil further adhered to the perspective of the U.S. government when he opened his interview with Cerezo by charging that the Sandinista government of Nicaragua made and broke promises about having free elections in the past. MacNeil did not refer to any specifics, and he neglected to mention the 1984 elections in Nicaragua, which were certified as free and fair by a range of international observers.

MacNeil/Lehrer's coverage of El Salvador focused on the March 1989 election, in which Alfredo Cristiani of the ARENA party was elected. The guests were two U.S. congressmen praising the election; there also was a "Newsmaker" interview with President-elect Cristiani. Again, no dissenting voices from the United States were heard—even at a time when there was widespread protest of Washington's support for the Salvadoran government. Furthermore, there were no voices of the armed FMLN opposition in El Salvador, nor of recently returned opposition politicians who had risked their lives to participate in the elections. In sum, *MacNeil/Lehrer*'s coverage of Central America was so narrow that it provided viewers with little substance beyond statements of U.S. government policy.

Nightline's coverage of Central America was more inclusive but displayed some of the same shortcomings. *Nightline* broadcast six programs featuring discussion of Central America: two on the Salvadoran election and four about the Panamanian election. All sixteen of the guests were men, and all of the U.S. guests were white. Three-quarters of the guests were current or former government officials.

However, *Nightline*'s few guests who were not government officials made a significant difference. Each of its two programs on the Salvadoran election—on the eve of the election and the day after the election—presented diverse views. On the eve of the election, *Nightline* hosted a debate between Elliott Abrams, former architect of the Reagan policy in Central America, and Michael Lent of CISPES (Committee in Solidarity with the People of El Salvador), a national organization that opposed U.S. policy and supported the Salvadoran opposition. This configuration of guests made for a more substantive debate than the traditional discussions limited to Democratic and Republican leadership: Abrams and Lent—both passionate partisans (although only Lent was clearly identified as such)—were able to argue fundamental issues about politics in El Salvador and in the United States.

The day after the election, *Nightline* hosted the president-elect, Cristiani, along with one of the highest-ranking members of the political opposition in El Salvador, Ruben Zamora. Unlike *MacNeil/Lehrer*, which interviewed Cristiani alone, *Nightline* had him debate a political opponent, leading to a more informative program.

Nightline's coverage of the Panamanian election also included a wider range of perspectives than did *MacNeil/Lehrer*. Although no U.S. policy critics appeared, both pro- and anti-Noriega forces from Panama were included. This coverage was markedly different from *MacNeil/Lehrer*'s, which did not include any opposing views.

Interpretation

Having reviewed the results of the comparison, we must now return to our two hypotheses. Hypothesis One—that the range of story topics would be wider on *MacNeil/Lehrer*—was partially supported by the data. In particular, *MacNeil/Lehrer* broadcast regular series that were not pegged to a daily event, including "High-Tech Frontier," "Considering the Cabinet," and "Talking Drugs."

"Talking Drugs" explored the day-to-day realities of drug use and abuse and some of the complex economic, social, and political issues involved—albeit with a focus on punishment and rehabilitation rather than the causes of drug abuse. Although the series sometimes relied on the usual government officials and academics, it included interviews with people normally excluded from the standard government/expert guest list. Charlayne Hunter-Gault, who hosted the series, talked with a former-drug-abuser-turned-drug-counselor, a former drug addict who went through a residential recovery program, and a former San Francisco drug dealer working against drug abuse in the city's African-American community. By asking these sources to evaluate the government's "war on drugs" and suggest alternatives to it, the series presented a range of new perspectives on an issue that had been saturated with redundant coverage from other news outlets. "Considering the Cabinet" provided an in-depth look at several of President Bush's cabinet nominations. Although the coverage had a decidedly deferential tone, it provided viewers with a picture of more than simply the personalities of these future cabinet officers, analyzing their careers, their qualifications, and their likely impact on policy.

Moreover, *MacNeil/Lehrer* seemed less reliant on visuals than *World News Tonight* and more willing to cover stories that were composed primarily of talking heads. As such, the *NewsHour* was less likely to spend its time on stories carried only by dramatic pictures or exciting personalities. At the same time, *MacNeil/Lehrer*, perhaps because of budgetary constraints, was more Washington-centered than ABC. It spent a good deal of time showing excerpts from congressional debates and official press conferences.

Hypothesis Two—that *MacNeil/Lehrer* would provide a more diverse guest list than *Nightline* in the aggregate and on four major issues—found little support in the data. On the whole, *Nightline* provided slightly more diversity than *MacNeil/Lehrer*, which was more focused on official voices. Although the case studies revealed only marginal difference between the two programs, *Nightline* was somewhat more likely to provide alternative perspectives. Furthermore, *Nightline* host Ted Koppel was a more active interviewer than either Robert MacNeil or Jim Lehrer, who were less likely to pose challenging questions to the government officials regularly appearing on the *NewsHour.* This type of "civil interviewing,"[8] as Robert MacNeil has characterized his method, may be one of the reasons that spokespeople from Exxon, for example, accepted invitations to appear on *MacNeil/Lehrer* but turned down several similar invitations from *Nightline*.

How can we explain these findings? One of the primary differences between the *NewsHour* and ABC's news shows is the absence of intense ratings pressure on *MacNeil/Lehrer.* Without the need to broadcast dramatic, breaking, visually oriented stories each night, *MacNeil/Lehrer* is able to focus on less "sexy" issues and take more time to explore them. The absence of ratings pressure may go a long way toward explaining why *MacNeil/Lehrer* has survived so long with its subdued look. And to the extent that *MacNeil/Lehrer* competes for an audience, it is a smaller and more select audience than that pursued by the networks. (The 1991 *NewsHour* fact sheet boasted about the high levels of income and education of its viewers.) Ultimately, the *NewsHour* does provide a small window on a different set of stories, with more depth, than *World News Tonight.*

These findings, however, do not imply that *MacNeil/Lehrer*, whether or not it is covering less orthodox stories than those carried on ABC, will provide more diverse perspectives. The data indicate that *MacNeil/Lehrer* does not provide the public with broader discussions than its network counterpart. By largely excluding a wide range of "unofficial" perspectives and alternative interpretations of issues and events, *MacNeil/Lehrer* roots itself firmly within the same narrow "consensus" presented by network news shows. Despite more in-depth coverage and occasional forays into the unconventional, the

NewsHour is little different politically from the networks, to which it ostensibly serves as an alternative.

The results of this six-month study suggest that it is problematic to argue that public television will provide more diverse news solely because it is sheltered from commercial pressures. Although these pressures, or lack thereof, may go a long way toward explaining *MacNeil/Lehrer's* ability to cover less dramatic stories, they cannot explain why *MacNeil/Lehrer's* guest list is not significantly more diverse than *Nightline's*. We should not overlook the possibility that advertiser pressure, or the threat of such pressure, is supplanted by pressure from corporate underwriters in the case of *MacNeil/Lehrer*. AT&T and PepsiCo were major underwriters, each providing $6 million of a total budget of approximately $32 million in 1991. The significance of corporate underwriting and its complex relationship to program content will be examined in Chapter 5. Although the *NewsHour* has an advertiserlike relationship with its underwriters, it does not face the whole set of commercial pressures the networks do. As such, the impact of corporate sponsorship alone cannot adequately explain why news on public television provides the same narrow range of perspectives as network news.

An adequate explanation needs to include a discussion of the norms of professional journalism and the training and socialization of MacNeil, Lehrer, and the rest of the *NewsHour* staff. Several researchers have suggested that the economic logic of the news business must be combined with an analysis of the standard methods of news gathering and reporting to gain an understanding of why news from various outlets seems so similar (Gans, 1979; Bennett, 1988; Tuchman, 1978). In a study of the effects of monopoly ownership on newspaper content, for example, McCombs found that there is no straightforward connection between ownership and diversity in content. McCombs (1988: 136) suggested that the news will be similar "due to the similarity of [journalists] professional values, beliefs, and practices. The increasing professionalization of journalism during this century has resulted in a convergence of views among journalists about what is the news of the day."

The explanation for why *MacNeil/Lehrer* is no more diverse in its guest list than *Nightline* involves more than simple pressure from underwriters or the anticipation of such pressure by reporters at *MacNeil/Lehrer*. The traditional notion held by journalists in both commercial and public broadcasting about who and what is news also serves as an important constraint. We can recognize, however, that the professional culture of journalism and the organization of news outlets are at least partially determined by the economic market within which they must operate. Journalists and producers at *MacNeil/Lehrer* are not removed from these professional and organizational forces, nor can they be completely insulated from the market forces that structure both the news industry and the U.S. economy. It is the interpretation of and response to economic market pressures—not simply the existence of these forces—that will advance our explanation of public television. Ultimately, the questions raised in this chapter cannot be answered by analysis of content alone. As such, the next three chapters will examine public television from the inside.

Notes

This chapter draws on collaborative research with David Croteau.

1. The *NewsHour* replaced the *Report* in September 1983. Traub (1985) reported that many local station managers were unhappy with the proposal to expand from thirty to sixty minutes. However, a multimillion dollar financial commitment from AT&T, coupled with the threat of losing the respected and public television–defining MacNeil and Lehrer to another broadcast outlet, convinced the local stations to support the change.

2. It is worth noting, however, that the PBS public affairs documentary series *Frontline* has been moving in the direction of more "timely" programming. One example of this was the 1991 GulfWar, in which *Frontline* produced daily updates for the first three days of the war—which served as a kind of competition for the ongoing network news coverage. It is possible that *Frontline* will continue to move in this direction in the 1990s and become more of a long-form news program than a documentary program.

3. Entman notes the existence of noneconomic reasons for the reliance on elites, including their "cultural legitimacy," the definition of news as government actions, and the "frequent dearth of non-elites with newsworthy information." However, he argues that the underlying factor is economic. "Profit seems to me to be the primary concern, however; if using other news sources were significantly more profitable, it is doubtful the media would be nearly as dependent on elites as they are" (1989: 18).

4. Data was collected starting Monday, February 6, 1989, because this was the date that a critical study of *Nightline*, which I coauthored with David Croteau, was released. The present study of *MacNeil/Lehrer* and *Nightline* was designed not only to compare the two programs, but also to examine *Nightline* before and after the release of this study. See Hoynes and Croteau (1990) for the discussion of the changes in *Nightline*'s guest list.

5. All *Nightline* stories were included in the analysis. All *MacNeil/Lehrer* stories other than those in the brief news update were included. And all *World News Tonight* stories one minute or longer were included.

6. Race was identifiable for 90 percent of guests.

7. Quoted in Hertsgaard, 1989, p. 49.

8. Quoted in Traub, 1985.

CHAPTER FIVE

■

Funding and the
Politics of Programming

One of the principal differences between public and commercial television, as I suggested in Chapter 3, is that different engines drive decisionmaking in the two structures. In public television, the process is programming-driven; in commercial television, the process is advertising-driven. At the theoretical level, there is a clear distinction between a programming-driven and an advertising-driven television system. Commercial television must sell its programs to major corporations, who literally buy shows through the purchase of advertising time. Although creative considerations are not entirely eliminated by the dictates of business, it is clear that decisionmaking ultimately must respond to the commercial nature of the industry. In the 1990s, for example, the effort by the three networks to produce programs that would attract a young audience was motivated quite clearly by the desire to attract major advertisers who wanted to reach a young market. Grant Tinker, former chairman of NBC, made the point most succinctly: Television "is an advertiser-supported medium, and to the extent that support falls out, then programming will change" (quoted in Gitlin, 1985: 253).

The ideal-typical model of public television, as we saw in Chapter 3, does not have to sell its programming to corporations, nor does it allow commercial considerations to affect its programming decisions. On the contrary, program decisions are guided by an ethos of public service, a commitment to producing and broadcasting programs that, because of commercial constraints, could not survive on network television. The principal difference between public and commercial television, then, lies in their relationships to the market. Commercial television must sell its product, and it will be constrained by buyers' preferences, identities, and goals. Public television, because it does not have to sell its product, is ostensibly insulated from the market and the accompanying constraints. It is, most fundamentally, the continuing existence of state funding that provides public television with this market insulation. By

highlighting the theoretical differences between "pure" models of commercial and public television, we have more clearly identified the questions that
we need to ask about contemporary public television. To what degree is public television actually insulated from the economic market pressures faced by
commercial television? What constraints does public television's particular
funding structure place on the system? In this chapter I examine the funding
picture at public television and explore its impact on programming.

Since the Carnegie Commission report in 1967, the funding of public television has been one of the central issues in both popular and industrywide discussions of the future of public broadcasting. As we saw in Chapter 1, public
television was never funded like European television—with an annual user fee.
And the original proposal to fund public television through a tax on the sale of
television sets was not included in the Public Broadcasting Act of 1967. What
public television has had over the past twenty-five years is a complex hodge-
podge of funders, some more stable than others. The principal sources of
funding for public television have been the federal government, through both
CPB and federal grants; state and local governments, including state colleges
and universities that operate stations; private foundations; viewers, through
both subscriptions and local auctions; and private businesses. Also, some programming is coproduced, with the partner (the BBC, for example) assuming
part of the cost of production.[1]

For most national programming, producers put together funding from a
mélange of the above sources. Such a process, as is well known within the industry, takes both perseverance and patience. The fast track on raising funds
for a major documentary project may still be about two years. Member support—the money viewers contribute for subscriptions each year—goes to the
local stations and is only marginally related to national production. In fact,
since there are no restrictions on it, member support is principally used to pay
for the day-to-day costs of operating a local public television station. At a national production house such as WGBH in Boston, member support may spill
into a discretionary fund that can be used to cover cost overruns on national
production or to help with the development of new ideas. But there is a clear
difference between member support, which is unrestricted, and corporate and
foundation money, which is restricted to the purpose of producing a particular show. That is, corporations and foundations do not provide resources for
the operation of a station; they provide funds for a specific program.

In Chapter 1, we saw how public television's funding increased in total dollars and changed in character between 1973 and 1990. For our purposes, the
most important change was the decrease in the relative importance of public
funds and the dramatic increase in the importance of private funds. As Table
5.1 shows, government funding (federal, state, and local) accounted for more
than 70 percent of public television's income in 1973; by 1990, public funding accounted for 46.6 percent. What explains the rising importance of pri-

TABLE 5.1 Federal vs. Nonfederal and Public vs. Private Support for Public Television, 1973–1990 (as a percentage of total income)

	1973	1974	1975	1976	1977	1978	1979	1980	1981	1982	1983	1984	1985	1986	1987	1988	1989	1990
Federal	21.4	22.5	24.7	28.9	26.6	28.4	25.8	26.2	23.7	22.1	17.1	16.1	15.3	15.6	18.1	17.1	16.3	16.2
Nonfederal	78.4	77.5	75.3	71.1	72.8	71.5	74.1	73.9	76.4	77.8	82.8	83.8	84.6	84.6	82.1	82.6	83.7	83.8
Public	70.7	69.6	66.8	69.0	65.4	67.4	66.4	64.6	59.7	57.5	52.2	50.2	47.5	48.9	48.0	47.5	45.5	46.6
Private	29.1	30.4	33.2	31.0	34.0	32.5	33.5	35.5	40.4	42.4	47.7	49.7	52.4	51.3	52.2	52.2	54.5	53.4

Source: Corporation for Public Broadcasting.

TABLE 5.2   Ratio of Federal Government to Business and Subscriber Funding of Public
Television

	1973	1979	1985	1990
Federal government/business	5.35	2.46	0.94	0.96
Federal government/subscriber	2.97	2.13	0.74	0.74
Federal government/combined Business and Subscriber	1.91	1.14	0.41	0.42

Source: Corporation for Public Broadcasting.

vate funding, from less than 30 percent of the total to more than 53 percent, over a seventeen-year period? Two sources in particular are responsible for the bulk of this change: businesses and subscribers. As Figure 1.4 illustrated, between 1973 and 1990 business contributions as a percentage of public television's total income increased more than 300 percent, from 4.0 percent of total income in 1973 to 16.8 percent in 1990. At the same time, subscriber contributions, again as a percentage of public television's total income, increased 200 percent, from 7.2 percent to 21.9 percent of total income. These figures are even more stark when they are compared to federal government support, which decreased from 21.4 percent to 16.2 percent of total income over the same period.

When we look at the data from another perspective in Table 5.2, the full measure of the change becomes clear. Federal government support, almost two times (1.91) that of the combined contributions of business and subscribers in 1973, was less than half (0.42) that of these two private sources by 1990. In essence, there has been a total reversal, as private sources of money have become increasingly more important than federal money.

What are the consequences of the shift away from the public sector and toward private funding? As I detailed in Chapter 3, critics have long suggested that public television's reliance for funding on major corporate dollars affects the content of PBS programming. The old joke in public television circles is that PBS stands for "Petroleum Broadcasting Service" because of the money it has traditionally received from large oil companies. In its simplest version, this critique suggests that those who pay the bills—increasingly corporate America—influence the content of programs. Although such a critique provides important food for thought and cannot be dismissed out of hand, as it is by many public television supporters, the equation of private *support* with private *influence* needs to be examined, rather than simply asserted. In fact, it is not at all clear that PBS's corporate funders have any direct influence over the content of programming. My interviews suggest that the effect of corporate sponsorship, though important, is much more subtle and hard to identify. Moreover, in order to fully understand the role of corporate underwriters, it is necessary to first examine the larger constraints imposed by the overall funding situation.

Funding and Risk Taking

In public television, uncertain and unstable funding is a major obstacle to producing creative or "risky" programming. The importance of and structural obstacles to risk taking were a regular theme in my interviews. Although there were other obstacles named (e.g., fear of terrible ratings even by PBS standards, to maintain one's personal reputation), the need to attract funding, largely on a project-by-project basis, was cited as one of the primary mechanisms keeping programming "safe."

Gitlin's study of network television provides a useful context for the discussion of risk. Gitlin reports that "safety first is the network rule" (1985: 63). The logic of safety, for the networks, revolves around economic success. Risky programs are those that seem unlikely to attract a mass audience or that create controversy and might offend a portion of the audience or, even worse, major advertisers. This formula might sound simple: If safety is the cardinal rule, those programs that are either controversial or obvious ratings losers will be avoided at all costs. However, as Gitlin points out, ratings "hits" are few and far between, and most network television programs are not successful in economic terms. What, then, are the consequences of the logic of safety in network television?

One consequence is the general tendency to avoid controversy, even if it might bring high ratings. Controversial programs do occasionally appear on network television. But Gitlin argues that in the 1980s the networks found that "it was safest to err on the side of puffery. Whatever projects smacked of controversy got scrubbed" (1985: 195). The logic of safety, however, has much broader consequences than the avoidance of controversial programs. Since network executives and producers are never sure what audiences will watch or why some programs succeed and others fail, Gitlin points out, the corollary to "safety first" is the notion that "nothing succeeds like success." As a result, network television constantly imitates itself, creating what Gitlin has called a "recombinant culture." The prime time network lineups are filled with copies, spinoffs, and repackagings of previously successful programs. However, as Gitlin suggests, recombinant cultural products are hardly satisfying for audiences and are rarely commercial successes.

> The pursuit of safety above all else makes economic sense to the networks, at least in the short run, but success anxiety reduces many a fertile idea to an inert object, which usually also turns out to be a commercial dud. For all the testing and ratings research and all the self-imitative market calculation in the world does not produce that originality or energy that makes for much commercial success, let alone truth, provocation, or beauty (1985: 85).

The logic of safety is also prevalent in public television. However, safety and risk have different meanings within public television, reflecting its different

relationship to the market forces that define these terms. In order to understand the consequences of the quest for safety within public television, we
need to examine what risk is and how safety is pursued.

Unlike network television, public television does not define risk in terms of
ratings, nor does it define success solely within the framework of audience
size. Since ratings are comparatively small and revenues are not pegged directly to audience size, risk is not so clearly associated with the mass of viewers. The question of risk within public television is more complex. Risky programs are, most fundamentally, programs that might offend a segment of the
public television community: major funders, including corporate underwriters; local public television station managers; subscribers, particularly if they
are organized; and increasingly, as conservative U.S. senators admonish public television, Congress. The logic of safety is not connected to the pursuit of
profits, as it is for the networks. It is, however, a result of public television's
peculiar funding structure, which breeds a mentality of both scarcity and dependence. By examining the relationship between economic considerations
and the logic of safety, we can better understand why public television seeks to
minimize risks and discern the ultimate consequences.

At the most general level, public television does not have the resources to
take risks. Funding is tight enough that there is no expendable money with
which to try something new that may not work. One veteran WGBH staffer
indicated that "we do not ever have funding to take a risk; we don't have failure money." Even those who are consciously trying to make the kinds of programs that are considered risky—offbeat, visually different, or controversial—
find funding scarcity an obstacle. One producer, a self-defined innovator, suggested that an important constraint is that "you've got to find somebody to
finance whatever these ventures are. ... You would have to raise a huge
amount of money for a program that might be a couple of years finding its
voice and style. So it is really just beyond our means. I think everybody recog-
nizes that this is desirable but we just don't have the wherewithal to make it
happen." Public television simply does not have the resources to regularly invest in a risky project, whether it be a new idea, a different style, or even an un-
tested producer.

This constraint affects not only the development of new programming but
also the regular series on public television. One producer indicated that the
bottom line is money: "It's a problem that we have a documentary series and
we don't kill two or three programs a year. I think we sort of should figure
that you should have a budget that would allow you to say, oh well, that project didn't pan out, let's kill it, let's absorb a $200,000 loss on it or a $100,000
loss. ... *Risk means money.*" Another producer noted that scarce resources
make it difficult to experiment for even one day. With such high costs,
"$1,300 a day for a crew plus 21 percent overhead, we simply don't have the
option to burn a day on some wild idea." As such, each program and each

project has to succeed. And the easiest way to ensure success, as Gitlin found at the networks, is to repeat a successful formula. That is one of the principal reasons that public television programming has maintained such a traditional style over the years. There may be various definitions of success, a point I will address further in Chapter 6, but there is no room for outright failure. And, as several producers pointed out, television is a difficult medium, one in which it is only too easy to create something that simply does not work.

The pressure on individual producers, then, is to produce what they have produced in the past and not to try anything new. One industry veteran noted that

> sometimes you do something very original and different, but often it's a struggle, because people tend to want the thing that you did before that they liked. It's hard to do things a new way. It's always hard to sell something that's new, and that's why often the people who break through and do something are working on the outside and are independent. And there is an enormous struggle ... and when they finally succeed, they're so exhausted by it that they'll never do a new thing again. ... And people who do like taking risks are not rewarded and are discouraged and are seen as basically loose cannons. ... It is totally the wrong environment for taking risks. ... So people tend to do exactly what they have done for years and years. ... You *better* do what you've done before, what you have a reputation for.

Another producer wondered whether there were benefits to taking chances. "In terms of risk taking, I think the general answer is why take risks? Why make waves? What is to be gained?" The formula, then, for continued employment as a producer for public television is to play it safe.

Other observers noted that the Station Program Cooperative (SPC), until 1990 the body that decided which programming local station money would support, imposed similar constraints. One producer suggested that "the SPC has always had the reputation for being a very good vehicle to kill a program, but not to introduce a new one, because they want to see something that's sort of [been] tried. And if you get money, get it on the air, and they like it, then they're likely to help bankroll it in upcoming years." Another staffer suggested that more conservative local stations helped make the SPC risk-averse.

> We have all these other stations voting on what they think programming should be like, and that's as far as who should receive funding. And that creates a problem because what New York likes, someone out in the Midwest isn't going to like. ... And I think that is what's keeping a lot of independent producers out of the ball game. ... Because a station in Idaho doesn't want [a program], we can't give you the money. They don't take enough risks in that sense.

The 1990 centralization of PBS funds under the control of new programming chief Jennifer Lawson may create some additional room for risk taking. One producer, thinking aloud about the change, wondered "whether or not a centralized outfit like Jennifer Lawson's is going to be able to take risks in putting money into an idea that only exists on paper, because they like the idea and they have faith in the producer, I don't know. I don't know if they have that kind of money." Another, less sanguine producer indicated that the pressures will be the same even under a more centralized system. Limited funding will make it difficult to take programming risks.

> All of this is easy to talk about from a distance. If you get closer to the point where you really have to be willing to commit millions of scarce dollars to ventures that may fail, the more difficult it is actually to take that kind of risk. And the pressure on her is going to be ferocious to deliver results. ... Everybody pays lip service to the notion of innovation and risk-taking and so on; the fact of the matter is, she makes two or three big mistakes to the tune of a few million dollars each, and they're going to be on her like a pack of wolves. This is not going to be an easy set of choices to make. Everything will drive her in the direction of safer choices; the closer she gets, the harder it's going to be really to take a chance on something that by its very nature is uncertain to succeed.

The dilemma for public television was posed clearly by a longtime freelancer. "They think that doing innovative programming will deter viewers, but if they don't do innovative programming, they'll lose viewers. So they don't really know what to do." Even the centralization of resources, which was intended to provide room for risky and innovative programming, cannot solve the pressures associated with scarcity of funding and the fear of losing viewers.

Other producers noted the personal risk involved in trying out new ideas in a system in which there are limited resources. One producer suggested that "you often go in with all these expectations about what you are going to do differently, but when you get down to it, you don't have the time. It is easy to fall back on what you know. And why should you take risks? You're not just taking risks with your program, you're taking risks with your own career." Another producer indicated that in order to raise funds for a program "you've got to raise expectations too frequently to an unreasonable level, right from the beginning, in order to raise the money to make a show happen, and then you're stuck with this inflated expectation of what you're going to be able to deliver. And it frequently dooms you either to fail or else to be very safe in what you do." Economic considerations make both producers and executives wary of projects that are either too experimental or too politically sensitive, whether the risk be personal or organizational. This caution is not the result of individual commitments to tradition or personal political preferences. Risk aversion is a consequence of resource scarcity and the need to satisfy, or at least not offend, current and potential providers of funding. Although the structural roots of the logic of safety are different in public television than at the networks, the end product is the reproduction of the same formula that has "worked" in the past. At the organizational level, it is easier and, of course, safer to invest in the kinds of programs that carry less potential to either fail or offend than it is to support innovation and risk taking. For individual producers, even those who want to be risk takers, it is difficult to negotiate the obstacles associated with the funding process all the way to the production of an innovative program.

Funding-Driven Programming

These obstacles to risk taking raise important questions about the relationship between programming and funding. Is programming on public television, supposedly the programming-driven system, driven—at least in part—by funding considerations? My interviews suggest that in a subtle way, the answer is yes. First, producers and administrators have assumptions about what is fundable and what is not. These assumptions pervade the decision-making process from the earliest stages. There was no consensus among my informants about the specific nature of these preconceptions, but there was, of course, a clear understanding that programs cannot be made without adequate funding. And a great program idea without possible sources of funds to produce it is no longer a great idea. One staffer noted that one of the main factors in the process of developing new programming ideas is "whether it's fundable or not."

Another producer noted that there is little connection between funder and program once production is underway, a sentiment that was echoed frequently. At the same time, s/he suggested that

> it would be naive to not realize that most of the kind of crucial decisions about the film are going to have already been made before the film is shot. And I think that's where those kinds of questions come into play. When proposals are written for films, proposals are written with funders in mind. There's absolutely no doubt about that. A recent series, a series that is going into production as we speak ... was written because it was perceived that it was a fundable topic.

Producers have a good sense of what ideas are most likely to be funded. In fact, one producer bluntly stated that

> we know what's going to sell. I got to the point where I knew exactly what the proposal had to say and what kind of proposal these people were looking for. ... You should see some of the proposals; they're almost a parody of themselves, their seriousness, the high-mindedness, the educational content ... because a lot of funders want that sense of high-mindedness and seriousness.

Other producers noted that they have worked on several projects that did not come together. These experiences prepared them for the future, when they would have a clearer sense of the financial feasibility of each project. One producer indicated that funding is something that "one is always aware of. And projects don't get made because we say, 'No one's going to fund that.'" Another suggested that funder interference is not a problem but that "there are certain things you don't do because you can't get funding for it, that's all. People would love to do it, but no one will give them the money for it." A third producer pointed out that the entire process can be very demoralizing.

> There is a certain feeling of whoring that goes on, and that pervades everything we do. The shows are designed around who will fund them. So there's a constant compromise around doing shows, and shows that will be funded. ... There is a continual kind of cynical, jaded acceptance of the kind of lack of substance of the show that we're given to work on because we know that this is what the funders will support.

This theme ran through the interviews: Often the primary obstacle to making interesting, innovative programming is the lack of a suitable funder. Since the process of funding a program in public television can take years—witness the multiyear effort required to fund two of public television's most well-known series, Henry Hampton's *Eyes on the Prize* and Stanley Karnow's *Vietnam: A Television History*—program ideas can have a long shelf life, to be resurrected when a potential funder's interest is piqued. It would not be surprising to hear that a long-forgotten program proposal could have new life breathed into it if a potential funder inadvertently expressed interest in the subject. One staffer noted that with some program proposals,

> when you think they're dead, something revives them. ... There was one, a weekly science magazine show that had been kicking around for three years, and then it had this brief renaissance when one of the people in underwriting was talking to somebody at some company and they were interested in a weekly science show. And they said, "We have this proposal from a couple of years ago," and we pitched it to them and they almost bought it. ... And in the end it didn't happen, but that can happen.

Still, s/he indicated that few proposals stick around for very long: "Now the tendency is to abandon them before that long, if nothing has happened."

The pressure, then, is to make an accurate assessment of the fundability of a project before moving forward with it. If it is perceived to have little chance of finding support, a producer may not even pursue it; even if the producer pursues it, management may not give it a green light. There are no rules to this calculation process, and several producers expressed anxiety about the uncertainty. Veterans of the process, however, seemed to have developed a clear understanding of which ideas will be rewarded. One producer noted that s/he knows exactly what her/his boss is "going to say in a screening. I mean, I know exactly what he's going to like and what he doesn't." As such, it is clear to producers which ideas will be useful to bring forward and which to forget.

Ultimately, then, funding serves as a subtle, but important, drive on programming. Producers and managers know the sources of potential funding, and they know the priorities and interests of these sources. As one staffer put it, "It's not a matter of them telling you, 'this is what we want,' but it's a matter of, if you want the money, then you have to sort of just fit their expectations." There is little sense that funders intrude on the production process in any direct way. They do not have to intervene. The various agendas of potential funders (who, given the amount of money it takes to make a program, are very limited) are well-known, and producers either have to meet them or look elsewhere for funding.

All of this adds up to a system with real constraints on the range of programming. This is not to say that funders serve the same role for public television that advertisers do for commercial television. Rather, the need to attract funding and the inability to "waste" money on projects that don't pan out means that from the development of a program through the actual production, a set of assumptions—assumptions that largely reinforce what has been successful in the past—pervade the decisionmaking process. As one staffer put it, there is a

> certain complacency about the type of programming that has been successful ... before and that people assume will be successful forever more. It's also the way that funding issues are a problem. ... WGBH is in a position to ask people to give them money. I mean there's really no other way of saying that. So whatever we put on the air has to be something that will not fly in the face of funders. I don't know if WGBH errs on the side of being too conservative about what they assume funders will like or not like. I don't know how willing they are to push those limits. When you're that dependent on those funders, it's a problem! And I'm not saying that there's an easy solution to it at all.

This situation does not mean that public television faces the same pressures as the networks. One producer noted that the pressures at public television are much more subtle. "Commercial television just reacts to the numbers immediately, and it's clear cut. You know if the numbers are low, the program goes off the air. But here it's much more subtle. But there still exist pressures." S/he went on to suggest that the underlying assumptions about how things should be done—and what is ultimately possible—are well ingrained in the minds of producers. It is a "feeling that everybody shares; it's not really brought out into the open and analyzed that much."

Ultimately, although no one seemed particularly comfortable with this conclusion, there was a general consensus that the funding process does make a difference. The lack of stable, independent funding means that the entire programming process is connected to the fundraising process. As one producer put it, "you have to be quite agile in this little dance in which you court the funding ... without, in the process, compromising the integrity of ... the pro-

gramming vision that you started out with." It is clear that not all programming is compromised by the funding process. Still, funding puts constraints
on the entire enterprise—constraints that are felt at all phases in the programming sequence. One longtime staffer who was critical of those who simply
dismiss public television as funder-driven nevertheless admitted that "there is
no question that the sources of money make a difference in program forecast-
ing." They make a difference primarily because they limit what is considered
possible.

Corporate Funding

The influence of corporate funding on public television continues to serve as a
major area of concern for proponents of noncommercial broadcasting. The
focus of this concern revolves around the fact that major corporate funders are
also large advertisers on commercial television. Has public television, in looking for funding, become privatized by its reliance on corporate contributions?
If so, how does this process work?

Earlier in this chapter, I discussed the dramatic growth in corporate support
for public television in the 1970s and 1980s. Whereas corporate support
made up a tiny percentage of total income in earliest years of public television,
it accounted for approximately 16 percent in the late 1980s and early 1990s.
Other providers of income—including CPB, subscribers, and state governments—contribute a similar amount of money, but they have a different relationship to programming than corporate underwriters do. Corporate underwriting does not simply support public television stations, as do subscriber
dollars, most state government dollars, and most CPB money in the form of
community service grants to local stations. Rather, corporations support particular programs. Not only has public television's reliance on corporate underwriting increased, but regulations differentiating underwriting announcements from traditional advertisements have been relaxed.

Corporate underwriting clearly provides benefits to the sponsors. Between
1982 and 1991, seventeen major corporations provided at least $5 million
each to support public television programming. The list includes some of the
largest concerns in the United States: Aetna Life and Casualty, AT&T, Chev-
ron Corporation and Foundation, Digital Equipment Corporation, Exxon
Corporation, Ford Motor Company, General Electric Company, General
Motors Corporation, GTE Corporation and Foundation, IBM, Johnson &
Johnson, Martin-Marietta Corporation, Metropolitan Life Insurance Company, Mobil Corporation, Nutrasweet Company, Pepsi-Cola Company, and
Texaco Inc. and Foundation.[2]

Although corporate sponsorship increased steadily through the 1970s and
1980s, there was a firm consensus among my informants that corporations
have no direct influence on the content of programming. Once the contracts

are signed, underwriters do not see rough cuts or fine cuts, nor are they consulted about such issues as choice of narrator or specific points in the story line; they do not see the program until it is aired. Furthermore, those who work closely with the funding process indicated that corporate funders are in many ways less trouble than other funders. Private foundations, the NEA and NEH, and the Corporation for Public Broadcasting all have elaborate reporting procedures, whereas corporations generally make their contribution with little or no reporting required. So on one level, production staff find it easier to work on a day-to-day basis with corporate underwriters.

The possibility of corporate underwriter intrusion, however, is not so remote that producers are not concerned about it. When the notion of interference does surface, it is in the context of discussions of "conflict of interest," where a funder has a clear political or economic stake in the content of a particular program. Many indicated that they were particularly vigilant about avoiding such situations. One staffer indicated that "we have generally tried to avoid conflicts and in fact I know of cases where shows have not been aired because of perceived conflict. That is, they have not been funded in ways that we originally had thought." And a producer noted that

> there are all kinds of tricky questions that come up, in terms of conflict of interest and things like that. I think systemwide, the rules are not strictly enforced. I mean, I think [we] tend to be much more strict about it. You can get yourself into trouble very quickly. Or you could find money pretty easily in some cases. And we have had to turn money down because we feel it's tainted, not in reality, but there's a perception that money has been tainted. And that counts. We don't want to have anything to do with it.

Others were more pessimistic about their ability to avoid such conflicts. One producer, for example, suggested that "you make these deals with the devil. ... Everybody's working right along the border here, and the question is: How do you secure the perimeter? I don't know what the answer is, except have vigilance. And I think we've done a pretty good job of it, but I think it's going to get harder rather than easier. I'm not sanguine about what the future holds for this kind of conflict of interest."

In either case, producers are not immune to the opposing pressures of, on the one hand, raising money to make programs and, on the other hand, avoiding any perceived conflicts of interest. One staffer noted the high stakes involved in negotiating this line. "We don't want to be perceived to have made a devil's bargain, that we basically have sold ourselves out. We don't want to have a conflict of interest because there is, in fact, I think, a moment in every broadcaster's life that the minute you do sell yourself out you can't come back. Once you [have] dirtied yourself, you can't get clean again." There is no universal response to the dilemmas posed by interested funders, but several producers indicated that it is not smart to be overcautious. One producer who

was particularly concerned about avoiding conflicts wondered about the corporate funding of one of his/her own recent programs.

> Is there a point at which we somehow crossed some uncrossable line? I don't
> think so, but again, if the choice is between accepting the money and not doing
> the show, then my choice is to accept the money. So you could argue that the pur-
> ist answer is, "You've been bought, and you shouldn't do it." And you have to
> draw the line somewhere. I don't have a simple answer to that, except that you try
> to be constantly sensitive to what the perception will be.

But the experience of sifting through such quandries can be discouraging.
One staffer perceived a clear conflict of interest in a particular case, but no action was taken.

> Everyone complained, but I think maybe the people in public television are too
> timid to say, "we're going to do what we want." ... They're so worried about
> money that they're really careful not to buck the system, I think. And money for
> public television is so hard to get that they aren't going to buck people, and that
> includes government, too. So, I feel it is sort of compromising.

Another producer indicated that, ultimately, each producer has to draw his or
her own line. "And there is the argument that you take the money and do
something good with it. ... You can always justify taking the money some way
or another. Each person has his own different point at which they say no."

Discussions of conflicts of interest, then, become the forum in which the issue of funder intervention is seriously addressed. Although avoiding the perception of a conflict is a high priority, finding the money to make a program is
equally important. Since there is no fixed line that cannot be crossed, the concerns about conflicts of interest are not likely to be resolved anytime soon.
Despite, or perhaps because of, the ongoing nature of the discussion, the focus on this kind of funder interference serves an important function both for
those inside public television and for its outside critics. It narrows the discourse about corporate influence to the terrain of "selling out" and effectively
obscures the broader and more subtle ways in which the funding process can
influence programming.

Regardless of their particular experience with corporate funders, none of
my informants was naive about why corporations underwrite public television
programming: It is clear that they fund PBS programs for self-interested reasons. As one staffer put it, "The private sector is not going to fund a show out
of some sense of noblesse oblige. They are doing it for business; they want to
get something out of it." One line of argument suggests that it is good public
relations for major corporations to be associated with public television. This
kind of association can give underwriters a positive image in the community
or help to polish up a tainted one. It is interesting, for example, that large corporate polluters are major sponsors of PBS nature and animal programs. Cor-

porations such as BASF, Du Pont, W. R. Grace, and Waste Management, Inc. sponsor such programs as *Adventure, Discoveries Underwater, Victory Garden,* and *Conserving America.*[3] Such corporate image polishing is not lost on public television professionals. In fact, one staffer involved in fundraising indicated that it is something of which public television tries to take advantage. S/he noted that WGBH has been "pretty successful in corporate underwriting in the past few years, more than a lot of other stations have been, and I think it's largely because the salespeople focused on identifying a company that needed good PR, basically. And they would go after them with a series they thought would help them."

Others argued that corporate underwriters were looking for a much more specific payoff than simple image enhancement. In fact, it was clear to many of the producers that corporate underwriters are essentially "advertisers" who want to reach a certain audience. The staffer who works in fundraising noted that corporations are sold on this notion. "It's pitched to corporations as, 'why is this going to benefit you?—because people that you want to reach are going to watch it.'" Another staffer noted that corporations are "looking for a very much more specific payoff ... and if you can't always provide it, that's a problem." And in a 1991 *Fortune* magazine interview, Steven Blass, the director of PBS's corporate support department, put it most bluntly: "PBS is a different way for companies to get into the mind of the consumer."[4]

Overall, there was no question in the minds of these public television workers that corporations' reasons for underwriting programs are similar to their reasons for advertising on commercial television. On PBS, they can reach a different, often more upscale audience. One producer suggested that public television should be more up front about what corporate funding really is; rather than the term "underwriter," s/he indicated, "'sponsor' is a perfectly adequate word. We ought to use it, but that's just that we're sanitizing all of those words." A staffer pointed out that "we approach corporate contributions ... as sponsorship. They, and we, do; we sell it—look, there's no secret to that. We sell time on TV. We're not mercenaries but simultaneously not fools. We recognize that this is a business. That may be a little harsher than somebody else might say, but that's basically how I look at it." Others simply referred to underwriting as "advertising" or "sponsorship" and suggested that it needs to be understood as such. Given that the PBS pitch to potential corporate underwriters stresses advertisement-oriented benefits, it should not be surprising that many of my informants saw little difference between underwriting and advertising.

Funding Controversial Programs

Public television workers have a clear understanding of why corporations fund public television, as well as what they will and will not fund. As such, I heard repeatedly that corporations will not support "controversial" programming. Several producers noted that they had worked on programs for which corporate dollars were impossible to raise because the programs were "too controversial." One producer suggested that "it is a question of corporate willingness to take risks. ... The problem is that whatever program we do, there's probably somebody who's unhappy. ... It isn't quite the subject or editorial control or anything like that. I think it has to do with their name associated with something that made somebody unhappy." Another producer explained why some programs are too controversial for corporations, arguing that the reasons are content-specific. "It means, practically speaking, that no corporation wants to be identified with that subject. And it means that the corporate funders who are close to the issue worry that you are going to be fair to the controversy and therefore deleterious to their interest." As a result, any program with potential for controversy is perceived by producers as an unlikely candidate for corporate funding. One staffer suggested that it is not simply programs that are obviously controversial, but public affairs programming in general, for which it is difficult (perhaps even impossible) to bring in corporate underwriters.

This perspective suggests that there are a whole range of programs that do not have access to corporate dollars. This is not to say that only procorporate programming can be produced; clearly, corporate underwriting is only one source of funding for public television. However, it is an important source of funding, one that can be the difference between a program proposal's ending up in production or in a file cabinet.

Nor does this mean that programs that accept corporate dollars become slaves to corporate interests. In fact, my interviews indicate that there is a very strong sense that underwriters must keep their noses out of the production process. As one producer put it, "more sophisticated funders understand that they can't call the shots." If an underwriter did try to interfere directly, the attempt would likely backfire, because producers are sensitive to the importance of remaining independent.

The impact of corporate underwriting is much more subtle than direct intervention. The most significant impact of underwriting is that corporate dollars can often be the key variable that determines whether a program will make it on the air. That is, when all other things are equal, the program proposal with access to corporate dollars is more likely to get produced and broadcast. And because controversial programs rarely, if ever, have access to major corporate underwriting dollars, the inevitable result is a narrowing of the range of discourse on public television.

This narrowing operates on two distinct levels. First, major production houses inside the system, in particular WGBH in Boston or WNET in New York, have a limited capacity to raise funds for national programs. They have access to system money (CPB, PBS), foundation grants, corporate underwriting, and some of their own discretionary funds. But there are a limited number of projects that such funding can cover. When producers and managers make calculations about how best to use their time, the funding limits are clearly a factor. Because of the narrow range of programs that corporate funders will support—and according to one of my informants, the NEH in the late 1980s was similarly narrow in the projects it would fund—potentially controversial programs face an extra obstacle in their pursuit of financial backing. Ultimately, the general understanding of the types of programming corporate underwriters will and will not support influences whether a program proposal will move forward, languish until it disappears, or simply be discarded.

The long-term effects of such a situation may be that the limitations posed by corporate considerations move beyond the realm of rational calculation. As one producer put it, "people who decide they want to work within the public television structure, they want to make films within this highly bureaucratized organization that really in a way mirrors a corporation. Those people decide to a certain extent they're going to play the game. And so it's a kind of internalized set of understandings about what is and is not acceptable." Producers have not fully internalized the corporate worldview, and public television is no slave to the corporate agenda. There is no question, however, that the promise of financial support—or the fear of finding no support—not only limits what programs are produced but also limits what programs are even proposed in the first place.

Equally important are those programs made outside of the major public television production centers and then broadcast by local public television stations. In the 1980s and early 1990s, major corporations sponsored an inordinate number of public affairs and business programs that were carried widely by local stations. Talk shows with a decidedly conservative bent, such as *The McLaughlin Group* (funded by General Electric) and *One on One* (Pepsi-Cola, Metropolitan Life), are funded by major corporations and are available to local stations at little or no cost. Business programs such as *Wall $treet Week* (Prudential-Bache, FGIC, The Travelers), *Nightly Business Report* (Digital Equipment Corporation, A. G. Edwards, The Franklin Group), and *Adam Smith's Money World* (Metropolitan Life, Panasonic) were regular components of the public television schedule in the 1990s. Although some of these may in fact be the kinds of shows that a programming-driven public television system would support, it is unlikely that all would be supported. In fact, it should be clear that these programs exist in such abundance because of a convergence of two factors: local public television stations' need to obtain inexpensive programs, and the desire of corporate funders to have such perspectives aired on a regular basis.

However, attempts to put alternative public affairs programs on PBS have run into one major obstacle: inadequate funding. *The Kwitny Report,* a weekly public affairs program from a liberal-left perspective, ran for one season in 1988–1989. *Kwitny,* hosted by investigative journalist Jonathan Kwitny, was broadcast twenty times in its first and only season. The programs covered a wide range of current issues and mixed documentary reporting and in-studio discussions. *Kwitny* was, in many ways, the flip side of a program such as *McLaughlin Group* or *Firing Line,* and it regularly presented perspectives that did not frequently make it onto national network television. During its only season, government officials (35 percent) and representatives of public interest organizations (33 percent) accounted for roughly equal percentages of the forty guests. As a general rule, *Kwitny* provided more inclusive discussions than other programming on PBS, including the *MacNeil/Lehrer NewsHour.* For example, a program about nuclear weapons included defense establishment figures McGeorge Bundy and Gen. Daniel Graham, along with policy critic Daniel Ellsberg; a program on energy policy included a U.S. senator, a corporate representative, and an environmentalist; and a program on the U.S. presence in the Philippines included the former U.S. ambassador to the Philippines, a Filipino policy analyst, and Admiral Gene La Rocque, a policy critic from the Center for Defense Information.

The contrast between *Kwitny* and the *MacNeil/Lehrer NewsHour* was demonstrated starkly in February 1989, when the *NewsHour* presented U.S.-backed Guatemalan president Vinicio Cerezo as an expert on human rights in Nicaragua without discussing the dismal human rights situation in Guatemala. During the same month, *Kwitny* presented a two-part program examining widespread human rights abuses being committed by the Guatemalan government, with panels that included a representative of the human rights group Americas Watch, a Guatemalan labor leader, and former U.S. ambassador to El Salvador and current policy critic Robert White. On both programs, Guatemalan and U.S. officials declined to send spokespeople.

Ultimately, *Kwitny* was unable to secure funding for a second year, and it ceased production. One of the major reasons was that it was unable to attract the support of a corporate funder, the kind of underwriter that *McLaughlin* and *MacNeil/Lehrer* rely on to such a great extent. No alternative public affairs program has yet filled the gap left by *Kwitny's* cancellation. Given the virtual necessity of finding a corporate sponsor, this failure is not surprising.

South Africa Now, a weekly news magazine produced by Globalvision, was another victim of the inability to attract a major funder. After a three-year run of 156 programs, *South Africa Now* folded at the end of April 1991. *South Africa Now* was a unique television program, one that clearly could not have existed on commercial television. It never attracted a mass audience, and its subject matter was highly specialized. But it offered information and imagery that was not available elsewhere on either commercial or public television. In particular, *South Africa Now* served as a vital source of news about unfolding events in South Africa, Angola, and Namibia at crucial moments in history for each country. With severe media restrictions in place in South Africa, *South Africa Now* was often the only U.S. news outlet to broadcast images of the repression and resistance. As such, it served as an important supplement to the evening news and was often recognized in this capacity by members of the national media. *South Africa Now* was also an important player in the U.S. antiapartheid movement, providing activists with regular updates on the situation and Randall Robinson, of the advocacy group TransAfrica, with a frequent commentary spot. *South Africa Now* also presented a regular "culture" segment at the end of each program, with music, art, film, literature, and dance from southern Africa. Although the program was perhaps best known for providing information and analysis, one of its most important contributions was in blending culture and politics to give viewers a sense not only of the conflict in the region but also of the life of southern Africa.

Finally, the program was a rare breed for television as it was developed and produced by a diverse group of people. Much of the on-camera talent was African-American, and the show developed a strong connection to various segments of the African-American community. It was the kind of programming, alternative in its orientation and diverse in its staff and audience, that one would think a public television system committed to diversity would enthusiastically support.

However, *South Africa Now* was never fully embraced by either PBS or the local stations. Although it did air in most major markets in its second and third years, it was rarely allotted a favorable time slot. It seemed always to be on the brink of extinction. In December 1990, for example, PBS stations in several major markets, including Boston and Los Angeles, abruptly announced that *South Africa Now* was to be removed from the schedule. After letter-writing campaigns and pressure from local elected officials, the program was restored in both cities.

Despite the fact that *South Africa Now* won Long Island University's prestigious George Polk Award for "courage and resourcefulness in gathering information" in 1990, it folded only a few months later because of a lack of funds. Globalvision was unable to secure funds from PBS or CPB to support *South Africa Now*, nor was it able to obtain substantial foundation money. And the program was not able to find a corporate underwriter, which, as in the case of *Kwitny*, seemed to be the only hope for staying on the air. With lucrative investment opportunities in South Africa blocked because of U.S. sanctions that *South Africa Now* supported editorially, it is not surprising that no major corporations believed it was in their interest to support such a program.

What is perhaps most interesting is that the producers of *South Africa Now* were former network producers who left to make more meaningful, less commercially constrained television. Public television, which seemed to be the site for making such programming, turned out in this case to provide similar constraints: Without a major corporate sponsor, existence was not impossible, but it was certainly short-lived. The current state of public television funding may mean that independently produced programs offering an alternative perspective will not be regulars on PBS stations.

This situation suggests the major role that corporations play in influencing PBS programming. Corporate dollars can give programs life and get them on the air; they do not necessarily influence the specific content of particular programs, but they are an important determinant of what viewers ultimately have access to. Potential underwriters make their priorities and interests well known, and PBS and member stations factor this information into their decisionmaking process. Critics who argue that PBS is simply controlled by corporations are missing the more subtle corporate influence that occurs during the idea formation, proposal preparation, and fundraising stages. The fact is that corporate underwriters provide resources for the production and distribution of only a narrow range of programs.

Frontline

One program with no corporate underwriting dollars is *Frontline,* the PBS public affairs documentary program. Over the past ten years *Frontline* has produced scores of documentaries on a wide range of issues, often not shying away from controversy. It is funded entirely by public television and has the strong support of local stations. What makes *Frontline* so interesting is the role it played in my interviews—as a sort of "pure" cousin that is regularly singled out for its unique virtue. In other words, the fact that *Frontline* exists without corporate dollars provides solace to those who are not entirely comfortable with the existence of corporate funding. Most fundamentally, this attitude suggests that it is clear to public television workers that large infusions of corporate money can taint a program. Even if they believe that there is no direct influence in the production, many are still concerned about what has to be done in order to actually get the money. They are also concerned about the *perception* that their programming is tainted, even when they are confident that it is not.

Frontline, then, takes on a kind of mythical character as the controversial program that cannot be perceived as corrupt. One producer noted, "It's so important that *Frontline* survive because that becomes the outlet for programming that nobody else would ever pay for." As such, *Frontline* proves that PBS can produce whatever it wants to produce, that there are no constraints, either political or economic, affecting the content of its programming. It is a tall order for *Frontline* to fill, one it does indeed often live up to. But the legendary nature of *Frontline* both highlights and obscures the importance of corporate underwriting.

First, it suggests that, indeed, there is some reason for concern about the impact of corporate money. If not, there would be no reason to identify *Frontline* as such a significant program. But it is important precisely because people *are* concerned about the subtle ways in which corporate money impacts programming: As long as there is a *Frontline* around to provide an example of programming that is not tainted by private interests, the overall integrity of the system cannot be questioned. Second, *Frontline*'s status points to the inconsistency with which people view corporate underwriting. Although *Frontline* was singled out because it tackles controversial and sensitive issues, there was little concern about the fact that an evening news program such as the *MacNeil/Lehrer NewsHour* receives significant corporate support. In fact, the very argument that a program such as *Frontline* should not have corporate dollars so that it can tackle politically sensitive areas seems equally appropriate for *MacNeil/Lehrer.* Nevertheless, I did not find evidence that producers were concerned about corporate sponsorship of news. Third, the "purity" myth implies that the absence of corporate funds for *Frontline* is the result of some kind of firm ethical stand taken by the show's decisionmakers to avoid the pressure to satisfy potential funders. However, my research indicates that, in fact, there is not any kind of firm position at *Frontline* against accepting corporate money. *Frontline*'s efforts to obtain corporate money after its first season have proved unsuccessful. The program does not shy away from corporate dollars, as several of my informants assumed; rather, corporations avoid *Frontline.*

Still, *Frontline* remains an important program. It does tackle issues that other PBS programs and the networks seem reluctant to examine. And the perception that its ability to engage controversial issues is related to the fact that it does not have corporate funding may be one of the keys to understanding how corporate money affects public television—and why producers and executives are so sensitive about this topic. One staffer who pointed out *Frontline*'s freedom from corporate pressures summed up the contradictions well: "If everybody had their way we would not have to go to corporations, I bet. Nobody at PBS likes the tag that we are becoming more and more commercial, even though we clearly are."

Self-Censorship

Does the constant need to find funding for the next project lead to a subtle form of self-censorship, of which producers themselves are only barely aware? This question is difficult to answer definitively, but there are indications that this kind of self-censorship exists. I have argued that in the early stage of conceptualizing projects, the demands of fundraising and the assumptions about what is fundable limit what gets produced. However, there is also a sense that producers of programs that have already received corporate funding may feel pressure, albeit unconsciously, to please their funder. One producer indicated that "if you are a big enough funder, we want your return business. And so what happens is not a formal kind of intervention, but a subtle and often unconscious kind of self-censorship. But I don't think that we're any more susceptible to that than the networks are." Another staffer expressed concern about "sins of omission" and suggested that "it would be a foolish producer who didn't think twice about what they were doing if it affected their source of funding." Still, s/he noted that "it's not any different at the networks."

There are two points worth highlighting here. First, individual producers are an important piece of the fundraising puzzle. In fact, they are often the key selling point to a potential funder, who is buying not simply the idea but also the people who will turn the idea into a program. It is not unreasonable to suggest, as do the two individuals quoted above, that future funding, both in terms of return business from a current funder or new business from a prospective funder, is an important consideration. It may not be an overt process, whereby producers weigh in their mind the costs and benefits of certain editorial decisions. At the same time, the pressure to avoid anything that will jeopardize one's next production should not be underestimated.

Second, producers regularly asserted that even if there are funder pressures, they are similar to or less severe than those faced at network television. Many of the producers in public television have worked at the networks and have come to public television to avoid these very pressures. But when they feel similar pressures in their new environment, there is not the sense of outrage and resistance that one might expect. These pressures come along less frequently and are probably more subtle than at network television. With network pressures as a reference point, funder-related pressures in public television do not seem so problematic.

Several other staffers told stories—often ones they did not want repeated—in which questions about pleasing (or not offending) a funder came out into the open. The issues were apparently small: using a particular host, altering a few spots of narration, mentioning products (either favorably or unfavorably) manufactured by the underwriter on the air. The implications were that this kind of funder-oriented self-censorship—or, as Gans (1979) has called it, "anticipatory avoidance"—is not uncommon in public television. What appears to be uncommon, however, is for people, even those who are uncomfortable with self-censorship, to name it as such. In fact, what emerged most clearly from my interviews was the sense that "you want to keep a funder happy; you don't want to lose a funder."

Beyond the tendency to avoid, whether consciously or not, situations that will pose funder problems, the overall scarcity of resources imposes an even subtler form of self-censorship. Each program or series is likely to be the only one on that topic, and producers understand that they are expected to make the definitive program. That is, when PBS puts resources into a series on Central America or the criminal justice system, producers are expected to make an authoritative statement, which leaves little room for trying a new approach or introducing unorthodox ideas. The system is not structured to accommodate several programs with a variety of perspectives on the same issue. Producers internalize these pressures and, by accepting the limits set by the need to say the final word, effectively engage in a form of self-censorship. One producer noted that

> there are all kinds of stories that we choose not to do for good reasons in and of themselves. But the net result is self-imposed. ... I mean, we regard ourselves as the high church of public broadcasting and the high church of television. ... In a sense, that is the same kind of values as they would write in the *New York Times*— all the news that's fit to print—which is itself a self-censoring kind of approach. And we have that. And we have it for the same reason. We think of ourselves as the ultimate authority. We are establishing a record. You get so much within the institutions and the establishment.

Another producer suggested that adherence to such values is key to individual success within public television, that those who succeed are those

> who show that they have "judgment." And judgment means not only the ability to do the work, but it means the ability to present ideas in the appropriate way. And to present the appropriate approach. And the values that are contained in appropriateness seem to be a certain kind of mainstream worldview, a certain kind of balance, a certain kind of academic distance. ... and a kind of noncontroversial approach. There's a great concern for minimizing exposure to controversy.

Still another producer provided some historical perspective on the values associated with public television programming.

> Television doesn't take place in a vacuum, and the kind of *World at War*–paradigm public affairs documentary comes out of a particular view of the world, and that view is not really holding any more today, and there's a little bit of—I wouldn't say crisis—but a difficulty for WGBH, which is the inheritor of that. The line from *World at War* to *Vietnam: A Television History* to *Central America* to *War and Peace in the Nuclear Age* is a pretty direct line. The problem is that it's a bunch of white guys in suits, at a time when a bunch of women and a bunch of blacks and all other kinds of people look at that stuff and say, "I don't believe that. That's just a bunch of white guys in suits." So the idea of there being a sort of predigested history that stands up is called into question now.

The need to make the definitive program and the values associated with such a program have important consequences. The same producer argued that politically charged or controversial programs do not arise from this formula.

> The classic public television method ... is the "canoe theory," that generally we're going to do a stroke to the left, a stroke to the right, and the canoe goes in

the middle. But the strokes are actually pretty close to the boat, too. I mean the
spectrum of opinion that is seen as responsible by the sort of mainstream academic community, which is where we make our living, is sort of five degrees to
the left of center, five degrees to the right of center. ... If you get a chance to do a
documentary on Nicaragua it has to be the authoritative thing on Nicaragua, and
so you have to make it five degrees to the left, five degrees to the right. It's much
less engaging television.

When such values are internalized and such techniques become the appropriate method, the very possibility of making a different kind of product becomes more remote. Ultimately, definitive statements are, even in their de-
nial, highly politicized. Cumings (1992), a noted historian, argues that the
desire to stand in the center, to create consensus, is fundamentally disingenu-
ous. He believes WGBH's changes in the British documentary *Korea: The
Unknown War,* to which Cumings served as a consultant, were driven by the
need to broadcast what would be perceived as an authoritative, "unbiased"
view. Cumings argues:

> For WGBH, it was a matter of appearances, of simulation, of getting the sign
> straight, 'control of the code'—not getting 'the facts' straight, and certainly not a
> consistent logic of interpretation. Seeking the truth was as much a pose as
> [WGBH's Director of National Programming] Peter McGhee pretending to be
> the historian lecturing me about proper standards of inquiry. What was critical
> was that the documentary should *seem* to heed these principles. In the end
> WGBH wanted an appearance of probity, a semblance of objectivity, a package
> that would not offend, and a position in the 'middle' of television's fictive consen-
> sus (Cumings, 1992: 266; emphasis in original).

Cumings was not describing a unique happening; his account characterizes
the underlying sensibility of creating programming that is definitive. The political implications of "definitiveness" may lie below the surface, obscured by
the certainty with which the programs define themselves as authoritative, but
they provide powerful incentives for a kind of self-censorship that is rarely recognized.

Member Considerations

The need to raise money from the public, which provides increasingly important revenue to local stations during pledge drives—totaling over 20 percent
of public television's annual income—imposes yet another constraint on public television programming. Although public television has been committed,
at least in rhetoric, to diverse programming, it is not clear that serving a diversity of audiences is an effective strategy for maximizing member support. Staff
concerned about the lack of variety in PBS programming suggested that public television caters to the segment of the public having the resources to contribute to public television: the affluent. One producer noted that

you have to do programming for people that are going to fund public television
… and the viewers that are going to support public television are not single black
mothers in a housing project. I mean, you can't expect that. Or, I mean, very low-
income people. But I think that a lot of programming is geared more toward the
people that contribute. And I don't know if that's conscious or not.

Another agreed that there was a problem, noting that public television has
to "appeal to its viewers to support public programming by becoming a member. People who can't afford that membership, then they're lost, or they are
not as clearly targeted as people who can afford and will be able to devote part
of their income to that." Programs geared toward those with little purchasing
power are not likely to attract advertising dollars on commercial television.
But they may also be of little help in attracting support for public television either from corporations or from those members of the public who have the
money to spare. One producer suggested that this point has been largely overlooked.

One of the things that people fail to note is that in this age of a thousand points of
light, we need to raise money. … And minorities are minorities. There aren't
many of them, and they often aren't very rich. … A preponderance of dollars cre-
ates an overwhelming preponderance of coverage. And that's a real problem that
people really haven't begun to address.

The need to raise money from members can have the same impact that advertising has on network television: Programming is geared toward the tastes
and interests of high-income people. This is the source of the often-repeated
argument that public television broadcasts programs for elites. Although the
system may be committed to producing and broadcasting a more diverse selection, its financial structure and its growing reliance on member contributions in the 1970s and 1980s provide not-so-subtle incentives to focus programming on the interests of one specific constituency—those who have the
disposable income to contribute to public television.

As long as local stations rely for their operating budget to a great degree on
member support, there will be little pressure from the stations for more diverse national programming. If more diverse programming comes from the
top, as the new PBS programming chief has suggested, there may be resistance from the local stations, who do not want to alienate an important source
of revenue: local elites. Ultimately, the growing reliance on private revenue,
whether from well-off individuals or major corporations, is another pressure
to create programming that is careful not to offend.

The Funding Market

The funding structure in public television, although vastly different from that
of commercial television, exerts powerful market pressures. Public television
programs are fundamentally products that have to be sold in a highly competi-

tive market. Program proposals must be sold to potential funders—increasingly, private corporations. Programs must also be sold to the public, particularly those members of the public who will actually "buy" public television by making a contribution. And programs have to be sold to local station managers, who are often wary of broadcasting anything with the potential to displease their constituencies. Although the constraints imposed by the funding market do not yet rival those faced by network television, which relies much more on corporate support (in the form of advertising) and requires a mass audience, the lack of market insulation at public television plays a significant, though subtle, role in the process by which ideas are turned into programs.

Increasingly, public television competes directly with commercial television for the patronage of large corporations. These corporate funders are not likely to see support for public television as any different from advertising on the networks; they simply believe they can reach a more upscale audience on public television. In the 1980s, particularly when the Reagan administration imposed federal funding cuts, public television acted more aggressively to sell television time to corporate buyers, thereby further integrating itself into the commercial television market. As major corporations increasingly provide resources for PBS programming, public television will increasingly reflect the narrow interests of these winners in the larger market system.

Because the search for funding under the current structure is a continuous, uphill battle for public television, the choice to move toward a more market-based funding model may have been virtually inevitable. As the system continues to grow, the market pressures that I have discussed in this chapter are likely to become stronger. Public broadcasters will feel more pressure to deliver the "appropriate" audience to their underwriters—which is, not coincidentally, the same audience that will give money directly to public television. And the need to attract funders, as well as the appropriate viewership, will lead public television further in the direction of safe programming choices. Without a funding structure that will provide more insulation from market forces, public television will continue to face constraints on its ability to produce and broadcast innovative and challenging television.

Notes

1. Public television may be moving in the direction of co-producing programs with the networks. Public television's coverage of the 1992 Democratic and Republican national conventions was co-produced with NBC.

2. Data is from CPB's 1991 Annual Report, p. 45.

3. Peter Dykstra, Media Director of Greenpeace, calls these contributions "Polluters' PBS penance." *Extra!* May/June 1990, p. 4.

4. Quoted in *Fortune,* April 22, 1991, p. 17.

CHAPTER SIX

■

Audiences, Markets, and the Public

In its ideal-typical form, a public television system must provide a role in which citizens can be involved as more than simply passive audiences; public participation must be structured into the system. The specific contours of such participation will be explored further in Chapter 8. In this chapter, I will examine how public television workers perceive the role of the public and compare it with the traditional role reserved for commercial television audiences. Ultimately, I want to assess whether members of the public do indeed have a distinct relationship—at the structural, but perhaps more important at the ideological, level—with public television, a broadcast system explicitly designed to "serve" the public's needs.

By focusing on the relationship between broadcasters and the public, we have stepped into the middle of one of the principal theoretical debates in contemporary media studies: What is the definition of a television audience? And what does the term "audience" suggest about the nature of those included in the collective defined by that term? Before moving on, we need to clarify the parameters of this debate and suggest its implications for our exploration of public television.

Fiske (1987: 16–17), in a widely cited work, argues that the term "audience" is fundamentally problematic: "It implies that television reaches a homogeneous mass of people who are all essentially identical, who receive the same messages, meanings, and ideologies from the same programs and who are essentially passive." Fiske suggests the use of either "reader" or "viewer" rather than "audience" to indicate that television viewing is a less passive, more active process. At the theoretical level, Fiske's argument is compelling: The very term "audience" seems inadequate to describe those groups and individuals who watch and interpret television. At the practical level, however, "audience" is in such wide currency that it is difficult to envision its abandonment. Despite Fiske's advice, most discussions of television viewing, in both industry and scholarly circles, use the term "audience," with all of its ideological baggage, to describe those people who turn on the television set—and who are so highly coveted by both the producers and sponsors of television programs.

However, we can make distinctions between the various uses of the term. Ang's (1991) analysis is the most theoretically sophisticated exploration of the television audience that I have seen. Drawing on McQuail (1987), Ang describes how the positioning of the audience differs between commercial and public service broadcasting. On the one hand, the political economy of commercial television means that audience maximization is the ultimate goal: "In the commercial system, the imperative of conquering the audience ensues from the positioning of the audience as market in which audience members are defined as potential consumers in a dual sense: not only of TV programmes, but also of the products being advertised" (Ang, 1991: 27–28; cf. McQuail, 1987). On the other hand, the audience for public service television is not conceived as a market, nor are the individual members of the audience seen simply as consumers; this audience is perceived as a public. In Ang's words, "The audience-as-public consists not of consumers, but of citizens who must be reformed, educated, informed as well as entertained—in short, 'served'—presumably to enable them to better perform their democratic rights and duties" (Ang, 1991: 28–29). The differences between these theoretical positions are indeed vast. The audience for commercial television is a passive market to be "conquered," to use Ang's term. Audience members are, most fundamentally, potential consumers in a commercial transaction. Conversely, the audience for public service television is not a market to be conquered but a public to be served. Rather than consumers, members of the public television audience are citizens, active members of a democratic society.

Is there a fundamental difference between "serving" a public and "conquering" a market? This is the central question raised by Ang's distinction between public service and commercial television. For Ang, the ultimate answer is that "in both systems the audience is inevitably viewed either from 'above' or from 'outside': from an institutional point of view which sees 'television audience' as an objectified category of others to be controlled" (1991: 32). The fundamental reason for this, according to Ang, is that in both cases the members of the audience are depersonalized: "They are not seen as individual persons or social subjects with their own particularities, but are given the status of serialized parts of an objectified whole (market or public)" (1991: 36). It is premature, however, to accept Ang's argument that there is ultimately little difference between the audience-as-market and the audience-as-public. At least at the rhetorical level, as we saw in Chapter 3, public television has a commitment not only to serving citizens, as a broadly defined group, but also to including them in the functioning of the system itself. At least temporarily, then, we must set aside Ang's conclusion and concentrate on the questions that the market/public distinction suggests: How do public television workers understand their audience? Is the audience perceived as a market or a public? As we move forward, we will want to examine which set of ideological assumptions underlies the perspectives of our public television workers.

We begin by focusing on the role of audience ratings, one of the principal ways that commercial television audiences are turned into markets. Ang points out that "the hard, economic need for ratings data is missing in television systems that are not dependent on competition for advertiser investments. Still, audience measurement has become a large-scale enterprise in many public broadcasting institutions" (1991: 140). This is clearly the case in public television in the United States. In the 1980s and 1990s, PBS has exhibited a growing interest in the nature of its audience. As a result, audience research has become increasingly important; demographic analysis is taken seriously as a means of "knowing" the audience. In the spring of 1990, for example, PBS hosted a conference for producers and station managers in Hilton Head, South Carolina, called "Exploring Prime Time." The meeting was designed to examine public television's viewership—who PBS is losing, who it is holding—as a means for planning future programming. Central to this task were a series of presentations based on audience research. Unlike commercial television, public television does not use audience research primarily for the purpose of selling advertising time, although potential funders (particularly corporations) certainly are interested in such research. Audience research is understood as a means of determining who public television is reaching and who it is not, with an eye toward "broadening" the audience. Nevertheless, traditional ratings continue to provide the easiest and most straightforward way for public television to learn about the public it is intended to serve.

Ratings in Public Television

Ratings are the principal means by which network television "knows" what the public "wants." They are also the primary means of measuring success at the networks. The situation in public television is much more complex. Ratings are not insignificant, but they do not have the same power as they do in commercial television. As one producer explained, public television programs "don't have to appeal to the greatest number of people, which in commercial television they do. So there's a lowest-common-denominator element in regular TV, just to get the numbers, because that's how everything works. And public television doesn't have to be a slave to that system in such a direct way."

There may have been a time in the early years of public television when ratings were of little or no concern; however, few people in the system would make a similar argument in the 1990s. Many of my informants referred to the days (which may be more mythical than real) when "purists" existed in public television—people who wanted to make innovative programming, with no interest in the size of the audience. One producer indicated that "there are some purists—actually I heard somebody say, 'I don't care if anybody looks at it. All I know is it's my show, and I did it right. Why would you want anybody to look at it?' I mean, to me, that seems crazy, and sort of shortsighted." A longtime staffer made a similar point: "There was a school of thought in public television that ratings should never be a concern, and there are still people who represent that school of thought. I think that's a little bit elitist and behind the times now." There may be some remaining "purists," but if so they are not easy to find. Only one of the twenty-five people I interviewed suggested that ratings should be of no importance—both to the producer personally and to the system more generally.

Although audience measurement has grown in importance in public television, ratings considerations here are substantially more subtle than they are at the networks (which may not provide a very rigorous yardstick in this regard). In fact, as public television workers respond to ratings considerations, they are pushed in contradictory directions. On the one hand, they see ratings as some relative measure of public interest and public need. As public servants, they want to adequately respond to these apparent needs. On the other hand, they do not want to duplicate the networks with least-common-denominator programming designed for a mass audience. As a result, they are suspicious of audience ratings and do not want to respond too directly to them. One producer indicated that public television institutions are unsure of just how to respond to ratings.

> I think you need a couple of ratings blockbusters, but the show that has consistently been the highest-rated for WGBH is one that we don't even much like to talk about around here, which is this ballroom dancing program. And it's never been really a public television program and it is kind of the bastard stepchild here in a way. I don't think anybody would say this publicly, but it's almost as if we're a little embarrassed about having it in our portfolio here. And it's the program that year after year pulls in staggering numbers for us. And you don't see it listed anyplace. I mean, it is not a program that WGBH mentions in its magazine; it doesn't get listed up there with the Vietnam series. Probably, it shouldn't; I am not disputing the decision, but I'm just saying there is some confusion about how we respond to ratings considerations.

Even when ratings are considered, public television does not measure ratings at the same levels as the networks. It is clear to PBS producers that they are working on programs that would never make it on network television because they would not, to use the jargon, "pull the numbers." The fact that they do not have to attract such a large audience is appealing to these producers, who are often trying to make programs that they see as more than simple entertainment. Low ratings are, on one level, worn as a badge of honor by producers, as evidence of the "quality" of their programs. There is even a sense that public television should *not* pull such huge numbers. As one producer argued, "if our audiences are the same size as the network audiences, ... we're doing something wrong. I mean, that sounds like a kind of a snobbish way of looking at it, but I think by and large, that's accurate. We are simply not trying to compete for volume business. And we shouldn't.''

Another producer pointed to the growing importance of ratings but noted that there is an important quantitative difference between public and network television ratings. "We should not be measuring ourselves against the commercial networks. You have an explosion like Ken Burns' *Civil War* and you have to be very careful not to get carried away and think that all public television series are going to do that well, or that we should begin to aim all our programming to do that well. Because I think that would be a big mistake.'' The basis of comparison, then, is other PBS programs, which draw small numbers relative to those of network shows, although such ratings bonanzas as *The Civil War* may begin to change this pattern. Previous public television programs of a similar nature set the parameters within which future audience size is compared.

Given that the numbers are so small, stability is a key factor. Regular series are watched over the long run—a single ratings smash or bomb on a *Frontline* or *Nova*, for example, will not make people rethink the strengths and weaknesses of the series. One staffer explained how long-term ratings stability is watched.

> Are the ratings steady or are they declining? That is one thing that you can look at from season to season. Because one season may not be enough. If the trend over two seasons looks down, then you wonder what's going on. So I think you keep vigilant with that eye peeled to whether things are holding their own or getting worse. I think in the environment of cable, holding their own is probably very good.

To the degree that ratings are a consideration, then, they are responded to much more slowly in public television than at the networks.

At the same time, the ratings are examined very closely, especially with documentaries, as a means of assessing the merits of a particular program. One producer indicated that there are various ways of making sense of the ratings. For example, one question is whether "the audience increased over the quarter-hours. If it decreased, if you do a show that decreased over the quarter-hours, then you have to think of whether you told the story right.'' The same kinds of calculations are made for limited, multiple-part documentaries such as *The Civil War, Columbus and the Age of Discovery,* and *Vietnam: A Television History.* Managers and producers look to see if ratings are increasing or decreasing from one episode to the next. If they are increasing, or at least holding stable, the interpretation is that the story was told in a compelling enough fashion to keep people's interest. If not, there is perceived to be a flaw in the filmmaking. In this context ratings do matter, because they suggest something about the relative strengths and weaknesses of a particular program. This type of analysis is substantially different and more complex from the way ratings are used at the networks.

When producers focus on ratings, either for their own personal desire to produce a hit or because of pressure from above to maintain consistent numbers, it is not always obvious to people in public television what to do in order to increase the size of the audience. Since it is clear that public television, even when it does feel ratings pressure, is not simply trying to attract the largest possible audience, producers have a difficult time reading the lessons of programs with particularly high or low ratings. One producer noted that "the question is what to do about the ratings, and how you respond to it. It's much harder to come up with a really good answer because we never really know why some programs do well and others do poorly. Particularly in nonfiction television with certain exceptions, ... it's very hard to say what it is that will make a sure-fire winner and what won't." Even when people do have a good sense of how to increase the ratings—which often means making programming that looks and feels more like network programming—there is discomfort with the notion that ratings should be the principal basis for decisions about future projects. One producer indicated that

> it helps me if a program that I've done ends up with a good rating. On the other hand, if you try to start with that as your objective, I think you're not going to get anywhere. At least, the kinds of programs I want to make aren't going to emerge from that kind of thinking. And I don't see any value in trying to concoct some sense of who the viewership is, and then figure out what they want. That seems to me a foolhardy and misbegotten strategy for designing programs. ... It seems to me to be pandering, and also to be mistaken—I don't think you can do it, never mind the ethics of it.

Since public television does not have to attract a network-size mass audience, producers do not feel the constant pressure to make programs that are as slick or "sexy" as those on network television. In particular, public television is not nearly as visually oriented as the networks, nor is it as image conscious. This fact has led some critics, and perhaps many viewers, to charge that public television programming is dull. Several producers addressed the issue that public television can be boring, a charge they generally did not deny but to which there is no simple answer. One producer indicated that PBS

> wants to pull up our ratings. But it's not like they are going to do that. You have to look at the whole picture. You have to look at what is impacting on the ratings—I mean, what's causing the slippage, or where's the industry at? What's happening with cable? So, if I talk to my parents and my dad says, "Well, I fell

asleep during that program" and my mom says that, that doesn't make me feel good, because I think [the program] can be boring sometimes. I think that we can really pick up the format a little, in different ways. I want to feel that the show's interesting. That's really the main thing for me.

Another producer noted that the relative weakness of ratings concerns has led to a more toned-down kind of programming but suggested that new ratings pressures are beginning to foster change.

> And so I've heard the talk that now we need to get "slutty," we need to get sexy shows to boost the ratings. In a sense, you can make the case that we've been somewhat sheltered. I mean, we're allowed to do boring shows. And in fact, we're sort of encouraged to do boring shows. Not to make them boring intentionally, but we've been sheltered from those kinds of commercial concerns. We do shows that had academic or intellectual content that wouldn't attract a large audience. And now we're being told we need to make the shows lighter. We need to make the shows fluffier, more accessible. This last show that I worked on ... has a new format ... with the hope that it's a more palatable format, and also the content is much thinner. ... We're not trying to teach a course, we're just entertaining, give the impression of having some content. But with the hope that this would [bring] a high rating. ... If this show that I'm working on now has high ratings, there are going to be many more shows like it in the future.

However, "boring" has its defenders. Postman suggests that one of the strengths of the *MacNeil/Lehrer NewsHour* is that it brings to television "some of the elements of typographic discourse" (1985: 106). He argues that the more public television takes on the "show business" flavor of the networks, the less it will be providing the public with a unique service; if the price of a more typographic sensibility is low ratings or a "boring" program, so be it. It is not clear that public television producers share Postman's sentiments. They see themselves as working with a visual medium, and the challenge, as they see it, is to make good television. Although producers neither desire nor intend to make programs that are boring, they also do not want to make programs whose only goal is diversion. Ultimately, the question of boredom is linked to the issue of ratings: Programs cannot be so boring that nobody watches them; but the toned-down style of PBS programs both attracts a certain audience and differentiates public television from commercial television. Producers constantly have to straddle the fence on both of these issues: trying to make the programs they want, without fear of a small rating or the charge of boring the audience and the critics, while satisfying their own, and their superiors', desires to make a program that is watched and highly regarded.

Increasingly in the 1990s, the size of the audience is not something that people in public television believe they can ignore. There is a growing sense that PBS management has become more interested in high ratings, putting more pressure on producers to keep closely in touch with their numbers. One producer noted that "there's more pressure now to pay attention to ratings. ... They [PBS] weren't excited about *The Civil War* because it was just good programming, right. It was a huge ratings success."

Others indicated that their own attitudes about ratings have changed. One longtime staffer noted that since ratings have become more of a concern in recent years, s/he has taken to paying closer attention as well: "I look at the overnights for Boston. I think that they are becoming more important to various people, like programming people. Broadcast people at public television stations ... everybody looks at them. The funders want to know, 'How many people did we reach?'" Another producer noted that her/his boss is very concerned about ratings and that as a result, "I'm getting more concerned because I realize now the importance of it and I care enough about each particular series to want our ratings to be good."

Concern about ratings is not simply imposed on public television workers by management. It is a concern most producers and staffers have internalized and do not hesitate to articulate. In particular, producers do not want to make programs that nobody watches. Even though public television professionals know that they will never have audiences comparable to those of the networks (nor do they necessarily want them), they still want to know that there is some substantial audience for their programs.

One producer stated, "I feel like people should be watching our show. So if they're really not watching it, that's a problem. ... I mean, I don't think a series should exist if no one's watching it. You know, you have to have people watching it, and have to have some impact." Another producer argued that "it's no good to make the best television in the world if nobody watches it. The whole point of doing this at all is for people to see what you had to say." For their own sense of efficacy, producers want to know that their programs are being watched. For many, in fact, the ability to reach a large audience—even programs with very low ratings generally are viewed by more than a million households—is one of the principal attractions of working in a mass medium such as television, whether it be commercial or public. In addition, connection to a highly rated program may also help people find work on future projects.

Others believe that it is their responsibility to make programs that at least some sector of the public finds useful. This perspective stresses a kind of public service ethos: Programs should fulfill a public need. Such needs are measured, ironically, in the same way that commercial broadcasters measure public "wants"—through audience ratings. One staffer commented, "I don't think you can say that if very few people, not literally no one, but below measurable standards of numbers, are watching the program then you're necessarily spending, especially the public's money—it's public funded—as wisely as it might otherwise be spent." A producer offered a similar sentiment, indicating that "ratings are some reflection of what people are interested in, and I believe in some measure of democracy in all this—that we should provide programming that people are interested in watching." In an age of scarce public resources, there is a sense that low ratings by network standings are fine, but minuscule ratings even by PBS standards are not something public television should tolerate.

The institutionalization of cable television is an increasingly significant factor. The rise of cable has meant ratings losses for both the networks and public television. As such, cable has put new pressure on public television to maintain its audience. The term that has emerged in public television circles to explain the growing focus on ratings is "competition." It is clear that people believe that cable stations are competing directly with public television for the same, relatively small audience. In fact, several cable channels now broadcast the same kinds of programming that PBS does. As such, PBS is not as obviously unique as it once was. One producer noted that

> the proliferation of cable made public television much less special. You can flip through the dial and you'll land on A & E, and Bravo, and you can't see a huge difference—viewers don't see a big difference. So it's no longer that Channel 2 [in Boston] or Channel 13 in New York stand out when you flip through the dial. Because there's such a variety of programs. So I think that puts more pressure, and I think that that's diluted ... everybody's ratings.

In fact, some of the programming that appears on cable television was originally broadcast on PBS. It is not surprising, then, that viewers might see little difference between public television and, for example, the Discovery Channel.

In the short run, the rise of cable television has coincided with a decline in the audience for public television, along with a much larger decline in network television's audience. However, the growth of cable television has also provided some benefits for public television: Cable wiring has made public television more accessible in a variety of rural areas and resulted in a better reception in those communities where public television is only available on a UHF station. The data on cable television's impact on public television ratings do not present an unambiguously dim picture. Agostino's (1980: 359) study of public television viewing in twelve markets found that "circulation of public television increased because of cable's extension, [but] the amount of public television viewing as a proportion of total TV use fell."

By the 1990s, the impact of cable on public television continued to be less than clear. Based on data from the winter quarter of 1992, there is no unequivocal pattern of declining public television viewership within those households with basic cable (32 percent of U.S. TV households).[1] If basic cable had seriously eroded the size of public television's audience, the percentage of PBS viewers who had basic cable would be less than 32 percent. However, this was the case for only fifteen of thirty-one programs for which data was available. For fourteen programs, basic cable viewers made up more than 32 percent of the audience, and for two programs, basic cable households constituted exactly 32 percent of the viewers. Moreover, over a four-week period in March 1992, households with cable television, both basic and pay, watched public television, over a full day, in higher proportions than those without cable. The data are different for prime time television, but households with basic cable still watched public television in higher proportions than those with no cable at all. Although public television workers and administrators are concerned, even alarmed, about the impact of cable television on their audience, the data suggest that the correlation between cable and public television viewing is weak.

Despite this weak correlation, it is clear, as I indicated in Chapter 1 (see Figure 1.5), that the size of the public television audience has decreased in the 1980s. The new choices offered by cable, satellite, and the VCR are undoubtedly related to this decline. Still, we should not forget the fundamental political economic differences between cable channels and public television. It is likely that as cable companies become more successful and raise the expectations of their advertisers, they will feel the pressure of ratings as other commercial networks do. Ultimately, many cable stations may move away from showing traditional PBS-style programming and toward the production of slicker, network-style programming. In this case, public television could once again look very different from the competition provided by both the networks and cable. One producer indicated that this school of thought does exist within public television circles. Describing a colleague's perspective, s/he noted that some people believe

> that the more they start to wire the country [with cable television], the more money they expect to make, the more their investors are going to insist on an increasing rate of return every year, just as investors do everywhere else, and that because they are commercial and profit-driven, the pressures are going to mount on them to deliver audiences, and that is going to start to push them away from the kinds of programming that public television has traditionally done. And that will leave us once again as really the only place that is insulated, and we're not even completely insulated from it, but more so than anybody else by a considerable degree, from the kinds of pressures that turn you away from doing useful, valuable programming of the sort that doesn't pay off in any tangible way.

From this perspective, it is specifically public television's noncommercial nature that will save it from the threat posed by cable television. This attitude, however, is the exception, rather than the rule, in public television.

The fear that cable television will diminish the size of the audience has people at public television (and the networks) on the defensive, looking for new ways to maintain their audience. At least one response is to focus less on content and more on making a program visually exciting. One staffer indicated that with the growth of cable television, more and more pressure is on documentary filmmakers and producers at PBS to get better ratings, to make their shows have more mass appeal. And I don't want to cite any specific examples, but there are recently some documentaries that I think are a little lighter, more. ... I don't want to say entertainment, but 'infotainment' perhaps, is a word I've heard passed around a bit.

And one producer indicated that "in the current climate ... there's this need now to compete. ... It used to just be, 'Okay, we're PBS and we're different, we're not like the networks, and there's a reason why we're like this.' But now I personally do feel there's a pressure to impress, or make it flashy." The signals coming down from PBS are not that poor ratings will lead to immediate cancellation or that ratings need to increase dramatically. Still, there is a clear sense among public television workers that in the new "competitive" climate, a new attitude has emerged in which steps have to be taken to maintain ratings and that programs that continue to lose their audience will be in jeopardy.

One of the first steps in the privatization of public institutions is their colonization by the ideology of commercialism. As ratings become more important in public television, market-based assumptions also become more prevalent. The distinction between citizens and consumers becomes less significant, as both appear to make choices, at least in what to watch on television. Ultimately, the difference between serving the public and conquering an audience—when public service increasingly depends on the same measurements as commercial marketing—can become very fuzzy.

Ratings and Success

In commercial television, high ratings are the principal indicator of success. Industry awards and positive reviews also play a role, but fundamentally a successful program is defined as a program that attracts an acceptable-size mass audience. For public television, the calculation is much less straightforward. High ratings do bring some degree of personal satisfaction to the people who produce PBS programming. And it is clear that "the numbers" are well known within public television circles. As competition from other sources grows, the pressure to maintain audience share will continue to increase. Still, there is some discomfort with the notion that ratings provide an unambiguous measure of success. In fact, even those people who pay close attention to ratings and are concerned about audience slippage indicate that ratings are, at best, only a partial indicator of success in public television.

Ang makes a similar point for public service broadcasting more generally: "Knowing the size of the audience alone is not sufficient to gauge the degree of success or failure of public service television's communicative efforts, not least because success and failure are a normative rather than a material issue here" (1991: 30). If success is defined at least partially on normative grounds, then what are the specific norms upon which success is measured? One producer remarked, "That's the perennial question, isn't it?" and indicated that "without ratings, it's a hard question to answer." Another producer was more direct: "I do care about ratings. I mean, it's not the same as in commercial television, but it's important, it has become more important, too. Ratings are a criterion by which films are judged, by which the success of the film is judged. ... So when ratings slip, people get nervous and when ratings go up, people are happy." At the most fundamental level, the degree to which ratings are considered an important measure of success coincides with the lack of any other yardstick for measuring success. Ratings are particularly attractive because they provide an ostensibly objective, precise, and unambiguous measure. Ultimately, ratings serve in this capacity by default, because there is no suitable alternative measure available to fill the role.

Although ratings clearly contribute to the definition of success in public television, other measures of success are widely acknowledged, although they are perceived to be less precise and more ambiguous than ratings points. Many public television programs are distributed on videocassette to schools and other educational institutions. Some of the more popular programs, such as *The Civil War*, even appear in neighborhood video rental stores. This means that there is a kind of ongoing number-counting—and with success in the videocassette realm, a program can have a real presence well after it has been broadcast. One producer indicated that "when orders came in from dozens and dozens of universities so that people could show it in their classroom, then that, to me, that is a success." A farsighted view, particularly for those interested in reaching a large audience, might value videocassette distribution over broadcast ratings and see that the long-term impact of a program is ultimately more important than the size of the original broadcast audience.

Others suggested that purely quantitative measures, whether in ratings or videocassette sales, do not do justice to the ways in which programs can be successful. One staffer argued that

> what public television really needs is some qualitative measurements, because to the extent that some of the things that we air actually impact on someone's life, cause them to think about something, make a difference to them—that's a really wonderful thing to have done. ... And I think that's one of our goals, and I don't know that it's a goal of the networks. That just the raw numbers, showing not that many people saw our program, but how affected were they by that watching; I don't mean that all of what we do is profound and incredible and earth-shattering, but there are those moments, when you reach—*Vietnam* had a tsunami of mail, from people who just were unbelievably touched by it. Those moments are very interesting. The *AIDS Quarterly* has had that same thing, causing people to have an intimacy with their own families, and to talk about the disease that they have and they hadn't even had the nerve to tell them about. I mean, that's just, that's a huge thing to have done, even to one person.

Similar qualitative measures of audience "appreciation" have been used by European public service broadcasters. On one hand, the interest in such measures indicates that success is defined by a program's impact, not simply its audience size. It suggests that producers want the public to engage with their programs and to find them to be more than simple diversionary activity. On the other hand, as Ang points out, "measurement of appreciation does nothing other than register the volume of applause, and as a form of information applause generally tends to be particularly meaningful from the narcissistic perspective of the institutions themselves" (1991: 145). Such "applause" is highly valued and a good sign of a successful program. The absence of such applause, however, is not taken to mean the absence of success. Qualitative measures of this type may provide a useful morale boost, but without a comparative framework and a clearer definition of what, besides applause, is being measured, they will do little more than register varying degrees of support.

Direct audience response, in the form of letters to stations and calls to response lines, is also taken seriously as a measure of the success of public television programming. In contrast, Gans (1979: 230) found that network television journalists "had little knowledge about the actual audience and rejected feedback from it." In public television, my informants expressed a real interest in how viewers respond, and even though people know that those who respond are not a representative sample of the entire audience, positive audience response brings a strong sense of personal satisfaction. One staffer indicated that

> we have a very active audience services department here, who sends out these things. ... They talk about how many phone calls came in for so and so, and how many letters they got, and what people usually thought, and they give quotes from letters, negative and positive. ... A letter from somebody or a call from somebody can have a lot of effect on a production piece—especially if it's something that criticizes something ... they really believed in or something, and somebody says, "Well, what about that?" So I think they're very affected by it. It's not so much affected by ... saying you got 20 percent more audience than last week. I mean, people think that's great and that's fine, but emotionally, I haven't seen that they're as much as an individual saying something about it.

This is clearly another form of "applause," and this kind of emotional lift may, in fact, be the primary effect that letters and phone calls have. One informant boasted of a recent program that had received 100 calls on the response line, all favorable. Another producer suggested that "those sheets come around, and it's thrilling when people like it. It's like you've sent something out into the void and it's hit an anchor."

Although production staff take great satisfaction from positive responses, there is little evidence that viewer responses serve as any kind of mechanism to help with future planning. One staffer, after suggesting that individual producers take audience response seriously, indicated that there is not "a conscious focus on what has happened in the past, to then decide on what will happen in the future, in terms of programming, from the audience response or the public response." Another noted, "I wouldn't say that comments that we get from that kind of thing are terribly important in focusing, changing what we might eventually do."

The public television workers I interviewed expressed more interest in, and show more respect for, their audience than did the network journalists Gans describes. Still, it is clear that public television workers, just like their colleagues at the networks, ultimately, in Gans's (1979: 230) words, "filmed and wrote for their superiors and themselves, assuming ... that what interested them would interest the audience."

There are other measures of success that are less viewer oriented. Reviews in major publications, especially the *New York Times,* serve as important determinants of success. One producer suggested that

> it comes down to the *New York Times* and the *Washington Post,* maybe the *L.A. Times.* And the first consideration is getting it favorably reviewed by the big national papers. ... This is a kind of Eastern view of things—it's only because I happen to be a slave to the *New York Times* myself that I—not just I personally—but that's a kind of Eastern elitist view, I suspect. But it's one that's held by the people who make programming decisions, too, so it's reinforced.

Another producer argued that "the single most important thing in public affairs tends to be the review in the *New York Times.* That, in some ways, defines the terms that the program is discussed on." The significance of the *New York Times* in particular, and reviews in major publications more generally, came up again and again. The importance of major dailies such as the *New York Times* highlights one of public television's principal contradictions. Public television, as we saw in Chapter 3, is ostensibly an alternative to commercial television, yet decisionmakers within the system perceive the *New York Times,* the paper that defines the journalistic mainstream, as an important judge of the quality and success of public television programs. There may be no ideological conflict here. PBS and the *Times* share a cultural space defined by its seriousness and absence of flair. But it should not then be surprising that public television is frequently criticized for its upscale, elitist sensibility. The *New York Times* symbolizes the abstract ideal of the realm in which public television seeks approval. In more concrete terms, it is precisely the readers of the *Times* and the elite circles it embodies that public television pursues as both viewers and supporters.

This relationship points out an interesting dilemma for public television: Is it an "insider" or an "outsider"? In its early years, there was, or so it appears in retrospect, a real sense that public television provided producers and viewers alike with an alternative. It existed on a very small budget with even smaller audiences than it now commands, and its programming had an outsider's sensibility. In the 1990s there are few remnants of this sensibility. But with acceptance in mainstream journals, such as the *New York Times* now serving as a central validating measure, it should not be surprising that public television no longer has the image, either internally or externally, of being an outsider.

Other measures of success provide the same kind of push toward a conventional notion of quality. For example, major television awards, Emmys in particular, rarely reward significant departures from convention. Furthermore, public television workers are concerned with acceptance within the mainstream academic community. Prominent academics, in fact, often play an important role in the preproduction and fundraising process. At the earliest stages, when proposals are being written, rewritten, and circulated, producers rely to a great extent on academics to find out the key issues and debates in the field. As I will discuss later, academics play an important role on advisory boards to programs, serving as content consultants during production and evaluating the finished product. Although the academic community may not reflect mainstream elite thinking to the same degree that the *New York Times* does, public television looks to it, particularly for historical documentaries, as a means of ensuring that programming articulates a consensus version of events—one that marginalizes alternative perspectives. As a result, less traditional interpretations are not likely to get much attention in these programs (cf. Cumings, 1992).

There are some producers who take little personal interest in either audience considerations or outside reviews by journalists and academics. These people argue that there are internal measures of quality programming that are more craft-oriented and take a professional eye to judge. One producer, for example, indicated that her/his professional sense of whether a program is "honest and tough and complete and moving and good story telling" determines the success of his/her own documentaries. In evaluating other people's work, s/he measures success by judging the work "in terms of … how compelling it is and how good of a film it is, how well it tells a story—at least intrinsically." Another producer suggested that s/he makes "a film I am interested in, and that the executive producer likes. That's the film I make. … I trust my judgment." Others indicated that colleagues in public television—other producers and television professionals—are most capable of judging a program's quality, and this is the prime measure of success for them. Still, even for those who argue that such internal measures are paramount, there remains a sense that the external measures, audience ratings, and reviews in prestigious publications are meaningful, if only because powerful players in the public television orbit define them as important.

Promotion, Participation, and Outreach

It is clear that public television professionals are concerned about the size of the audience. It is equally clear that they have concerns about its demographic makeup. One staffer indicated that the "PBS audience is more highly educated, wealthier than the general public, tends to be a little more culturally enlightened, whatever that means." Another longtime staffer suggested that the audience is "mostly upper income, or not poor anyway, except for maybe one or two shows. But in general, they are more white, who are more educated and more sort of okay financially." And a third dismissed PBS studies that indicate a diverse audience and argued that it is "basically an upper-middle-class medium. And it reaches a very small segment ... of the American public."

The challenge, then, as public television workers see it, is to "broaden" the audience. Others termed the same concept "attracting new audiences." This message also seems to be coming from above, particularly since PBS centralized programming decisions under the leadership of Jennifer Lawson, who stresses the need for a multicultural audience. But despite the genuine desire to broaden the audience, there was little sense among producers of how this can be done. The limitations posed by the adoption of a market-oriented ideology should not be understated. The notion that the public should somehow be more involved in public television never really emerged in my interviews, and solutions to the difficult issue of how to broaden viewership continued to depict the public as little more than a group of potential consumers of a product: PBS programming. One producer, who seemed genuinely concerned about the narrow audience, admitted, "I don't really know how you deal with [it]. I don't know how you get people to watch something." Ultimately, that is how producers conceptualize the problem: finding ways to get people to watch their programs.

An alternative conceptualization of the problem would focus on finding ways to involve people in public television as active participants, not simply as passive viewers. However, I rarely found even the smallest hint of such an idea in my interviews. One producer, noting the proliferation of video equipment in the United States, had been trying to pull together a program with a

> video "letter to the editors" section, in which we would encourage people to do their own little piece and send it in. Do their own—because there are two million of these things sold every year now. ... It's in a lot of homes now and every year there are more and more of them out there, and I thought this is a great way to harness some of this energy and get people to do their own little number in which they comment on something they see on television or a program or whatever, and send it in and we'd broadcast it.

But this was a rare exception, and even here, only a narrow segment of the audience would have the resources to make these videos. Moreover, this kind of involvement still identifies the public as an audience that simply responds to what it sees on television, albeit in a more creative fashion.

There are two other contexts in which some kind of public participation was raised: community advisory boards and outreach around programming. The Public Telecommunications Financing Act of 1978 required all local stations to establish a community advisory board to be eligible to receive funds from CPB.[2] However, it is not clear what role such boards play. Almost none of my informants had any knowledge of the WGBH community advisory board. Most had a vague sense that some such entity existed, but they had little interest in its composition or its work. Indeed, the community advisory board at WGBH has virtually nothing to do with the national programming produced there. It is, instead, a narrowly focused body with a limited potential to impact local programming. In particular, programs such as *Say Brother* and *La Plaza*—programs for and about Boston's African-American and Latino communities, respectively—are the domain of the community advisory board. When WGBH cancelled the *Ten O'Clock News* in May 1991, the board's attempt to pressure station management to renew the program ultimately did not meet with success.

To the extent that community boards are seen as functional, it is as surrogates for local audiences, with board meetings serving as a more formal outlet for feedback than audience response lines. They may also play a useful public relations role for the stations, which can at least make a symbolic effort at forging connections to the local community. (Commercial stations frequently have similar community advisory boards.) As a form of public participation in public television, however, community advisory boards play a very limited role.

Rather than working with citizen boards, national programs have expert advisory boards. These panels, as one producer put it, are "very carefully put together, of the best minds in the field." They provide assistance throughout the production process, although they seem to be most important at the proposal-writing, research, and fundraising stages, especially if they have contacts at such sources of funding as the National Endowment for the Humanities, the National Science Foundation, or private foundations. They are selected for their expertise, not to represent the public, and they are available as consultants throughout the production.

It is this expertise that makes them much more highly regarded than the community boards. One longtime staffer indicated that the expert boards are "much more influential and useful to us than community advisors. ... [Expert boards are] a bunch of true authorities in the fields. ... They never get involved in telling you what to do about any individual programming. They're a kind of sounding board as to whether you're doing well enough, giving you a report card." The legitimacy of these boards derives precisely from the fact that their members are not perceived as the audience. On the contrary, expert advisors are perceived more as colleagues or as professionals with access to a scarce resource: knowledge. There is substantial variance in how seriously individual producers take the comments of these experts, but for those doing documentaries the approval of the academic advisors is clearly important. Since the symbol used most frequently in my interviews to describe the culture of public television was a college campus, it should not be surprising that producers make such a sharp distinction between the academics who provide expert advice and the ordinary citizens who watch the programs.

Another means by which public television makes an effort to connect with the public is through outreach. Outreach grows out of the history of using PBS programming in the classroom. Telecourses for high school and college have traditionally been a part of public broadcasting and were a high priority for at least one major funder. The traditional telecourse is structured much like a regular course, with multiple parts that build on each other over a period of many weeks. As such, they can be used either in a classroom or by students in their own homes.

The notion of the telecourse has been expanded in recent years, and a variety of PBS productions have companion volumes that can be used along with the program in the classroom. *Vietnam,* for example, was structured for easy classroom use. And *Americas,* in production at the time of my interviews, was released with a companion volume for classroom use.

The kind of outreach that people in public television talk about today, however, has less to do with getting the program to the right educational institutions and more to do with the perceived need to broaden the audience. At least some public television workers seem to know that in order to broaden the audience, they must convince "new" viewers that the programming is relevant for them. This kind of outreach has the potential to develop new connections between public television and local communities. The *AIDS Quarterly,* for example, had an extensive outreach campaign in its first year. One staffer indicated that outreach

> was a major component of the program. Several people were working exclusively on that here, major appeals to all the target groups who were at risk for AIDS. And I think ... the expectations for that component of the series were maybe too unrealistic; it was a huge endeavor. But just the fact that that was pursued at all, and there were several series at WGBH who had some sort of outreach component.

But resource constraints severely limited the outreach program in the second, and final, year of the *AIDS Quarterly.*

On one level, outreach can be seen as a strategy to make useful material more available to people who can benefit from it. In essence, it is a means for public television to insert itself more actively into the community. But it is only a one-way street: Although outreach brings public television more actively into the community, it does not bring the community more actively into public television.

Despite the community-oriented nature of much outreach, within public television circles it is understood primarily as part of an effort to build the audience. This kind of outreach serves, perhaps most fundamentally, as a form of promotion. Many in public television see the lack of effective promotion as a prime reason that PBS has both lost audience share and been less influential than many producers would like. The implications of this view—and it may be emerging as the dominant one within public television circles—suggest a great deal about the future possibilities of greater public participation in public television.

Program promotion is something that network television does very effectively. With large promotion budgets, new programs receive a great deal of visibility well before they are broadcast for the first time. And the networks are organized in such a way that there can be a uniform national schedule, making promotion that much easier. Public television has small promotion budgets and does not have a uniform national schedule. Only in recent years did WGBH even take advantage of its own air time to promote upcoming programs. As one longtime staffer noted, "there's definitely been the viewpoint that people who are watching are interested. ... You're not grabbing them with gimmicks, necessarily. ... Before we didn't used to do teasers. ... We just never used to do those seven, eight, or nine years ago. And then we started doing them because they are a grabber, and they do get people in."

Distribution of PBS products through the Signals Catalog and LearningSmith stores is another promotion strategy that mirrors the kind of program/product connections used in commercial television. Still, the development of a national schedule and funding for major promotional campaigns are seen as the most important pieces of this new promotion effort. One producer noted that

> the whole idea of the showcase week and ... *The Civil War* for four or five nights and that kind of stuff is geared to trying to build up an audience. And I think they're putting more emphasis on publicity. ... We don't have a big promotion budget, ... and we try to get the audience to watch the reviews. But to take out a full-page ad ... in major markets takes money we don't have, and PBS has talked about earmarking a certain amount of money for promotion and I think they did that on *The Civil War*—General Motors, I guess, did it. You always try to get it, if you have a corporate underwriter, to get them to put money into promotion.

One of the principal lessons of *The Civil War*, the program that has had the most impact on recent thinking about the future of public television, is that a major publicity effort, coupled with packaging and scheduling to highlight a program, will bring a large audience. Of course, in order to hold that audience the program has to be well made and engaging. But it does not hurt when a promotional campaign makes programming appear to be of monumental significance.

Publicity will only be successful, however, if there is a uniform national schedule. One producer noted that the *AIDS Quarterly,* which was broadcast approximately every three months, was particularly difficult to promote because

> there's no centralization in scheduling, so people don't know when these programs are coming on, and they just happen to turn to it. I don't think that's an effective way to run a network or a station. And I think that's really part of the problem with promotion. ... I mean, it isn't always a quarterly, I mean it's not every third or fourth month; its when we get the show right. And then the times change depending upon, "Well, you know, so-and-so beat you to that slot, so you can't take it." It's really silly. It's very lax. And they really need to tighten up, because, for instance, with me, you call your friends up to say, "Oh, the show is coming on." "When?" "I don't know. Look in your local television guide or call your local PBS station." That's ridiculous.

Another producer noted, "When it comes to scheduling the program, people start suddenly thinking about the audience." PBS is now moving in the direction of a national schedule. Combined with more publicity, this new emphasis on promotion may indeed have an impact on the public television audience.

The Public as a Market

The growing sense that more aggressive promotion, rather than increased public participation, is a key to the future of public television indicates that public and network television operate within the same market-oriented paradigm. The contrast between *promotion* and *participation* is emblematic of the difference between a television system that relates to an *audience* and one that relates to a *public.* There may be, in fact, different underlying motives: one being to make profits, the other to provide a public service. But, as public television is currently organized, it shares commercial television's structural relationship to the public: as an audience. Perhaps the term "audience" is itself problematic, for there is a significant difference between an audience and a public. In order to understand public television in the United States, we need to turn Ang's concept of the audience-as-public on its head: In public television, the more appropriate term is public-as-audience. And this audience is ultimately little more than a market—perceived to have great buying power— for the consumption of public television and the messages of its sponsors.

Although the public television audience may be different from the network audience, the ideology of the market and the competition for the attention of the passive viewer still pervades public television. This market logic permits little or no room for the development of a new relationship to the public (as opposed to an audience), one that would be more collaborative. An intellectual culture that is more interested in *New York Times* reviews than public feedback only reinforces this market logic. It is as if the logic of commercial television has been adapted to public television, with important adjustments to fit the different capabilities of public television but without the kind of fundamental transformation necessary for the development of a television system with a broad commitment to democratic public life.

Notes

1. This data is from PBS Research, "National Audience Report," July 20, 1992.

2. The text of the act referring to community advisory boards (Public Law 95-567) reads as follows:

"(9) (A) Funds may not be distributed pursuant to this support to any public broadcast station unless such station establishes a community advisory board. Any such station shall undertake good faith efforts to assure that the composition of its advisory board reasonably reflects the diverse needs and interests of the communities served by such station.

"(B) The board shall be permitted to review the programming goals established by the station, the service provided by the station, and the significant policy decisions rendered by the station. The board may also be delegated any other responsibilities, as determined by the governing body of the station. The board shall advise the governing body of the station with respect to whether the programming and other policies of such station are meeting the specialized educational and cultural needs of the communities served by the station, and may make such recommendations as it considers appropriate to meet such needs.

"(C) The role of the board shall be solely advisory in nature, except to the extent other responsibilities are delegated to the board by the governing body of the station. In no case shall the board have any authority to exercise any control over the daily management or operation of the station."

CHAPTER SEVEN

— ■ —

Goal Ambiguity
and Organizational Survival

Chapter 3 suggested that a strong sense of mission accompanied the early development of public television. This mission focused on the need for an alternative to the least-common-denominator kind of television broadcast on the networks. It included a strong commitment to diversity and to the production and broadcasting of programming that either could not attract advertising dollars or would not necessarily attract a mass audience. The Carnegie Commission report, in particular, is charged with a sense of the great need for a public television system and of the important contribution that such a system could make to a democratic society.

The significance, in the early years, of a clear, passionate purpose for public television should not be underestimated. It may be one of the principal reasons that public television was able so quickly to attract talented and energetic journalists and filmmakers in the late 1960s. It is also unlikely that the federal government would have appropriated funds for public television without such a clearly defined purpose. Although the importance of organizational goals can be seen with the most clarity in the early years of public television, we should not assume that an organizational mission is no longer significant. At the most general level, a well-defined direction is an essential ingredient of any effective organization. This element may be even more critical for organizations, such as public television, with less than traditional goals. In commercial television the economic marketplace structures the goals; the networks operate much like other corporations, seeking to maximize profits. The not-for-profit nature of public television, however, means that its goals are not as straightforward. Public television does not exist simply to make money, to maximize profits, or to serve stockholders. On the contrary, public television was created for the express purpose of making television that would be independent of the economic market forces that constrain network television. We would expect public television's goals to be structured primarily by its public

137

service ethos rather than by profit maximization. Even with a general commitment to public service, however, public television exists within a broader market context. As we saw in Chapters 5 and 6, public television must compete for both financial resources and viewers. It exists within an environment that is defined largely by market-oriented values. The public service ethos, then, is constantly confronted by the culture of the economic marketplace.

In this context, it is particularly important for public television to clarify its mission, because the existence of a well-defined set of goals can serve as a partial counterbalance to the powerful, yet partially obscured, forces of the marketplace. For if public television is to remain a nonmarket institution and avoid the tendency to slide toward a more traditional, market-driven model, it will have to stay focused on its own reason for being. Although a public television mission was rather clearly articulated two decades ago, there is substantial ambiguity about public television's goals in the early 1990s.

Defining Public Television's Mission

There is little doubt that many of those who work in public television prefer a public service ethos to the culture of profit maximization. For more than half of my informants, the decision to enter the world of public television was a conscious career choice. That is, they were attracted by the programming, orientation, or possibilities that public television had to offer. In other words, the majority of my informants were attracted to public television by their perception, however vague, of its mission.

One producer, for example, indicated that s/he left the networks because "the work wasn't serious. ... I just wasn't interested. And the Vietnam series [on PBS] was interesting to me." Another noted that "there was one documentary I saw that gave me the idea that I wanted to work at PBS, and that was *Harlan County, USA.* ... It was fabulous! And when I saw that, I said, 'Boy, that's what I want to do.'" And another producer recalled, "The reason I applied to WGBH in the first place ... was because of *Upstairs, Downstairs.* I was studying history, and this was wonderful history come to life. And I ... thought, 'Jesus, I would love to work on something like that.'" Others had less specific stories but indicated that they were drawn to public television by either the programming possibilities or the general intellectual culture.

For most of these individuals, then, something particular about public television grabbed their attention. This was not the case for all of my informants; approximately one-quarter did not come to public television for any kind of philosophical reason. One producer even noted that s/he was working at WGBH *despite* the fact that it was part of the public television system, which s/he characterized as a slow-moving bureaucracy in comparison to the networks. Even among those who were not necessarily attracted by public television's mission, however, there was general agreement that public television had been created to serve a particular purpose. It was clear that public television stations were not just another undefined portion of the broadcasting landscape, that they existed to serve needs unmet by commercial television. Although there was a consensus that public television is supposed to be different from commercial television, the exact nature of that difference was elusive. In fact, it was much easier for my informants to define public television's mission in negative terms—as being different from commercial television—than it was to affirm what public television should be.

Asked to define public television's mission, informants were likely to take one of two roads. One response, slightly more common, was to suggest that mission questions were difficult, then give vague and uncertain descriptions. The second, and somewhat less common, answer was to respond enthusiastically to the question, to suggest that the issue is far too important to ignore, and to engage in lengthy, soul-searching monologues about public television's future.

These two types of response suggest that finding a suitable definition of mission and evaluating the success of public television on such grounds is very difficult. They also implicitly, and sometimes explicitly, indicate that the question of mission is not always high on the priority list of those who work in public television. Even those who were genuinely interested in the issue indicated that they have little time to think about it. Several respondents noted after our interviews that they were pleased to have had the opportunity to reflect upon the mission of public television. One producer even suggested that our interview served as a kind of surrogate for a more formal collective reflection that seldom happens in public television circles. In any case, it was clear that although the issue of mission was important to many of these public television workers and for some was an incentive for coming to WGBH in the first place, there was a great sense of confusion about just what the mission of public television ultimately is.

The one common thread that ran through a great many of these discussions was the conviction that public television is and must be different from commercial television. One producer made the point succinctly: "I think it [the mission] is to educate, engage, entertain, take people places that commercial stuff won't take them." Others made a similar point in much more detail. A producer, suggesting that public television needs a strong set of goals, argued:

> I think that to the extent that public television provides an alternative to the utterly crass, utterly dehumanizing content of commercial television, I think that's a good thing. I think most of the stuff on commercial television is dehumanizing. And I think probably public television is if nothing else a kinder, gentler kind of TV. ... It is stuff that affirms life more than it denigrates it.

Another producer noted that public television's own goals must be understood in relation to the shortcomings of commercial television. It is worth quoting him/her at length.

> I think [public television] serves the public interest by default, and then it's imperfect, maybe getting more imperfect every year now, but it's all we've got by way of an alternative to a system that doesn't serve the public interest at all, except incidentally and infrequently. And so the question is, how do you make it better, how do you make it do this better than it has? I think it has its moments. I went back and looked at a program that was done by the public broadcasting laboratory twenty years ago, now a defunct outfit, on the eve of the release of the Kerner Commission Report. And they did a 2-and-a-half hour program, prime time; it ran all over the country. It was quite expensive in its day. And it was really an extraordinary event; they got field reports from people like Jack Newfield, who went to Bedford Stuyvesant ... and they had a fiery interview with James Baldwin. And it was a very elaborate and expensive and quite impressive piece of work, which was shot all over the country, for what would be the equivalent of probably a million dollars today. I have no idea how sizeable an audience it had, probably not huge, but even a small audience is a million, 2 million, 3 million people. So we're talking, even at the very bottom, about a sizeable number of people, and a number of people who are, by self-selection, worth reaching—anybody who would take the time to sit down and watch this program was either a decision-maker or a thoughtful individual or somebody who's affected by whatever the issues are. ... And I thought this program served the public interest in a palpable and dramatic way. Anybody who saw this would have learned something about it; it happened at a moment where the cities were on fire, and there was a real sense of confusion and uncertainty about the future and nervousness about racial issues. And here was this very thoughtful and provocative and daring program which ventilated a lot of these issues, in which you heard people enraged, screaming, and it really got this all out in the open. And nobody else would have done that. Now that was twenty-some years ago, and hasn't happened very often since. But the fact is that public television is the sole remaining institution, not that it will never happen anyplace else, but it's the place most likely to turn up with that kind of program in that period, when it's needed.

In public television's short history, there have been several dramatic instances, such as the one recounted above, when the difference between commercial and public television became crystal clear. Such situations, although compelling, were infrequent; they highlighted the importance of public television's existence but still defined public television through its negative relationship to commercial television, not in affirmative terms that suggested what it should be. This type of definition may be the result of public television's position as the noncommercial outpost in a galaxy dominated by commercial broadcasting. Its reference point is commercial television, and its goals stem from this relationship. In such a situation, it is both easier and more compelling to define goals in negative terms, just as it is often easier for organizations to react than it is to act.

Beyond the general consensus that public television is not commercial television and can do things that commercial broadcasters will not do, there was a great sense of the uncertainty of the system's mission. Several respondents indicated that they had little knowledge of the official mission of public television. One producer noted, "I'm not even sure what the original mandate was. I just could sort of make it up, but I don't even know if it would be accurate." This was not an uncommon response. Another staffer, when asked about the mission of public television, replied "God, I don't know. I mean I don't know. I know there's a formal mission statement floating around." Yet another indicated that s/he had never read any material or had specific discussions about the mission of public television. As such, s/he said, "The idea that I haven't read [these materials] suggests something about the degree to which we're an ad hoc rather than a mission driven organization. I'm not sure exactly what it suggests, but it implies to me that the sense of mission doesn't necessarily permeate all the way." And another producer indicated that s/he once had a real sense of public television's mission but admitted, "I've just forgotten it. It's too bad because I had a very clear sense of what public television should have been all about. It's totally gone, totally gone."

At the other end of the spectrum, some repeated portions of the formal mission statement of WGBH, suggesting that all I needed to do was to get a copy for the exact language.[1] Yet even those who focused on the formal mission statement, referring to the need to educate the public by making programs that "inform, stimulate, and entertain,"[2] used such vague language that it was unclear what the mission meant to them in concrete terms. One longtime staffer, for example, argued that programming on public television needs to focus on being different. But s/he conceded that such an attitude did not say a great deal: "It's defining the difference that is the hard thing to do."

Perhaps one of the reasons there seemed to be an often undefined sense of a mission is that the goals of public television, however broadly or narrowly defined, are rarely discussed. One staff member noted that although s/he believes that there is a commitment to a concrete mission, "it hasn't been articulated a lot lately." And a producer indicated that the last time s/he "heard anything about mission is when [my boss] asked me and three or four other people to talk to [the] board of overseers. … They're fat cats, and we want to get them inspired and involved." Another indicated that the mission of public television is primarily discussed at fundraising time and is directed at the audience and potential funders, rather than the administrative and production staff.

With only infrequent and outward-directed articulations of public television's mission, it is not surprising that there is little sense among public television workers of a shared commitment to any specific, common goals. Few people have a clear idea of what public television's mission is in the first place, and there is no regular expression of it on a collective level. Many of my informants indicated that they did not really know whether they shared a set of goals with their colleagues. One producer's response was telling: "I should know the answer to that question, but I don't. I'm not sure I have a clue. We all operate pretty independently of each other, and I don't quite know what drives other people. I certainly don't think I have any greater missionary zeal than other people around here. I may have less for all I know." This was a typical response, particularly for producers, who are so focused on completing their own projects that they have little time to think about larger, less immediate issues. Perhaps this is one of the reasons that several of my informants were pleased to have had the opportunity, however brief, to explore these issues with me.

Although I found little to suggest that specific goals are shared, there was a feeling that people in public television do share some overall outlook. One producer explained, "It's like anything—you grow up in a family and there are certain articulated values, and then there are lots of things that are transmitted, and I think that that's the same here. There are articulated values and then there are just a lot of things that are in the air." Another indicated that there is an editorial mandate for his/her series but that "most people don't know it exists. I think part of the mandate is in the doing of it, rather than referring to a set of guidelines. ... And I think people are acting on them now on automatic."

What in fact are the values that are transmitted and that people have internalized at public television? In large part, these values are a reflection of the broader public service ethos that pervades the organization. They reaffirm the difference between public and commercial television, identifying public television as a less constrained forum for creative, talented people. As one producer put it, "we have a shared sense that public television, for all its frustrations and failures, is the best of the available choices for people who want to make television of a certain sort, which is relatively unpolluted and insulated from pressures external to the program-making. I think that's as far as I can go." This shared perspective may be, on one level, genuinely self-serving, for it provides an ideological justification for the career choices of those who work in public television. However, this would be an overly cynical interpretation. The shared commitment to making television that is *not* commercial, particularly in a field where most similar work is in the commercial sector, is one of the bonds that connects people working in public television. Although there is not a shared sense of a specific mission, there is at least some collective understanding that public television is, for these professionals, a preferable place to work than commercial television.

What makes public television preferable, however, is not entirely clear. The strongest differences in the minds of my informants, both the many who had experience in commercial television and those who had intentionally stayed away from it, is that the atmosphere of public television is less pressure-packed and more intellectual than that of commercial television. One producer, who felt very much at home at WGBH, noted that public television is "like an extension school. And I'm one of those people that enjoys learning and enjoyed my time in school, and this was sort of a way to continue that." The stereotype of the networks as ultra-fast-paced, bottom-line businesses that provide little room for creativity may be somewhat overdrawn. But it nevertheless provided many of my informants with a clear idea of what makes public television attractive. Ultimately, the distinct culture of public television—its slower pace and intellectual orientation—may be one of the principal grounds upon which public television workers distinguish their world from commercial television. It may be that the shared sense that they are not working in commercial television means precisely that—they do not have to endure the network culture.

Individual Goals

There is little evidence that public television workers share substantially more than a commitment to a work culture and a programming atmosphere that are not like commercial television's. By framing the question around the concept of shared goals, however, we might inadvertently be narrowing our focus so much that we overlook the phenomenon of *individual* goals that are in fact shared, but are not acknowledged as such. What are the goals that these public television workers set for themselves? What are their personal missions, other than staying out of commercial television? Are there underlying themes that link these individual goals together? Only one of my informants indicated that s/he had absolutely no sense of mission, that work was simply a paycheck. But s/he was quick to point out that this was atypical at WGBH, that most of her/his colleagues were in it for more than a weekly check.

Most of my informants had a much easier time articulating their individual missions, their own aspirations and goals, than discussing the larger goals of public television. It was in discussions of personal goals that these public television workers moved beyond the simple negation of commercial television and identified an affirmative sense of what they are trying to do. The sharp distinction between discussions of organizational and personal goals is in itself telling: It suggests that public television is perceived by many of my informants as a vehicle for the fulfillment of individual goals, rather than an institution with its own mission, to be collectively advanced. There is a dramatic difference between, on the one hand, a goal-oriented organization that attracts people committed to organizational goals and, on the other hand, an organization with vaguely defined goals that provides the opportunity for individuals to pursue their own personal objectives. One type of organization is not normatively "better" than the other. However, public television's posture and history suggest that it is the former type of organization, when in fact it is much more like the latter. It is not a goal-directed organization; it is more accurate to identify public television as an organization that is goal-ambiguous.

If individual goals and personal missions ultimately define the mission of the broader organization, what are these personal missions? Several people suggested that they were in public television specifically because they were committed to education. One producer, for example, indicated that his/her interest in public television "definitely wasn't an attraction to television. I don't really care about television. It was more an attraction to WGBH as an educational foundation, and the kind of product it makes. I was interested in being involved in educational material, something that would teach people something." Another indicated that s/he wanted her/his work "to have meaning" and was interested in public television because it served an "educational niche." And another suggested that s/he "came here basically looking to work in education."

One producer suggested that in terms of mission, "there's a kind of schizophrenia that's going on right now with public television because [it] doesn't know whether to be television or ... to be educational television." Indeed, historically many of the stations that are now PBS stations were once solely educational television stations. The underlying sensibility at many of these stations, including WGBH, was formed during these years of educational television. As I will argue later, however, educational and public television ultimately imply different choices and serve different missions.

Making programs that educate the public was only one among many personal goals. Others were more idiosyncratic. One producer suggested that s/he was "trying to develop programs that are, I hope, genuinely different, not always better than other people's programs, but I have for years tried to think about ways to make television that doesn't look like the rest of public television or the rest of what's on—and I've not succeeded to any dazzling degree, but I'm working at it, as are some other people." Another producer who makes historical documentaries indicated that the point is to "get it right." That is, rather than have money or time be the ultimate consideration, public television gives producers the opportunity to make sure that the film is done "correctly." This outlook implies a kind of journalistic objectivity, suggesting that there is a "right" and "wrong" way in documentary filmmaking, and it reflects the premise, examined in Chapter 5, that public television programs should make a definitive statement. Others suggested that they want to "raise public policy issues and try and explain in a way that's understandable," to tell "great stories [that] people should know about," and to "do the equivalent of Sunday morning television." For all of these individuals, public television, at least temporarily, offered them the best opportunity to pursue their own interests.

Many of my informants recognized that public television has changed over the years, and several longtime employees expressed a degree of cynicism about their experiences and their changing personal goals. One stated,

> I originally went into television to be able to make meaningful television shows and change the world. ... I guess that's what I always tell people. ... I feel as though, in the course of my career, I have had the opportunity to work on meaningful shows, and I don't know whether that changed the world, but I have had the opportunity to do things that I've thought would fulfill that goal. ... And I think the opportunity *might* still be there, if you go and hunt to find it. I don't know whether it is in public television. ... I've changed and public television has changed.

Another echoed that sentiment, suggesting that at a younger age s/he had

> much more a sense of mission. I felt that I needed to use media to change the world—that through media I could change the world. Through whatever kind of a radical form of presentation, that I could do the work that needed to be done. ... I sort of abandoned that really. I now feel like at least I'm not doing *Night Court*. The stuff that I work on doesn't hurt people, I hope.

A similar attitude—that a sense of personal mission used to be clearer and more exciting—pervaded many of my conversations. The notion that public television itself used to be more energized with a real purpose was also widely shared. For example, one producer indicated, "I really wish I'd been here in the early days, even ten or fifteen years ago, when it was still more grassroots. It sounded so interesting. And they did really, really interesting things." Perhaps this waning sense of purpose is a natural result of huge growth over the past two decades. As public television has developed it has become increasingly similar to other large organizations and lost some of the excitement and missionary zeal that accompanies new, experimental enterprises. One staffer indicated that goals have become less clear as public television has grown.

> There are people who take the mission seriously; I know that. I think they are in the minority. ... There is a sense of knowing that you're working on the best that's being done, and that the films that are being made are serious, and they're films that should be made, that are important films to make. That exists, and that's real. Those people are in the minority. One of the things that I despise as time goes on is how public television has become a growing system of bureaucracies and middle management and fundraising vehicles. And certainly there's a need for public television to make money, to fund programs. But I wonder at what cost that is being done. There's a steady commercialization of public television. ... I see public television going more and more toward a commercial operation, a commercial character. And I see a spreading bureaucracy which soaks up a lot of the money that this fundraising produces.

One of the consequences, albeit unintended, of public television's growth is its transformation from a mission-oriented organization to a survival-oriented one. Lashley (1992) concludes her analysis of public television by noting that "[m]ore than any other goal, managers of public television entities pursue organizational survival" (1992: 130). And one staffer suggested that the institutionalization of public television is the principal reason that there is no real shared mission.

> As anything gets successful it gets more funded and the stakes become higher. And I think what's happened is that public television has become a self-sustaining, self-interested bureaucracy that exists now primarily for its own survival. People have careers. People have worked in public television for twenty years now. And people are making big salaries, relatively big salaries. ... I think people's values change when that happens. I don't think people see themselves as missionaries. I don't think people who work in the system see themselves as reformers.

A producer made a similar point about the impact of public television's growth.

> I don't think certainly you would find the same conscious feeling of "We're all in the same small leaky boat" now that you would have found ten years ago, or much less twenty years ago. Public television has evolved into a different kind of creature now; it's much bigger, it's much more professional. There are people who come here from the networks because they want to make certain kinds of programs, and they've got a calling of sorts. But we're too big now really, we're not quite marginal enough to be "outsiders." ... Whatever remains of that attitude is probably diminishing. Maybe all this current crisis will help to clarify, and in the end it could be a good thing to have happen, and that'll force a lot of people to think about why we're doing this—and motivate us. But beyond a certain point, not that there isn't time to think about it, but there are too many other things looming up in front of you, and if you could just try to do them, try to make programs, find the money for them—you don't spend a lot of time thinking about why you're doing it.

On one level, then, the goals of public television are beside the point. The point is to keep going: keep raising money, making programming, building the audience, and increasing the prestige of the system. Concerns about what makes public television different or how to define its ultimate purpose become peripheral. As one producer put it, financial uncertainty means that there is not the "sense of security that would enable you to develop a sense that now I can worry about the overall mission. ... I think that pervades all the way up. Public television and WGBH, at the very top, I think they're thinking, 'Where's our next big money coming from?' Not 'What should our mission be?'" There will always be time to think about such issues after the next production is finished and the next budget is balanced—or so it seems.

Ultimately, the lack of a clear mission energizing the system as a whole may be functional for a large, bureaucratic system such as public television. Dimaggio (1987) suggests that goal ambiguity and heterogeneity are standard features of nonprofit cultural institutions: "Ambiguity of objectives plays a valuable role in masking goal dissensus so that participants can get on with their work and in sufficiently obscuring the nonprofit cultural organization's operating processes to afford it at least some insulation from its complex and demanding environment" (p. 212). For public television, goal ambiguity means that a wide range of personal goals, as well as differing visions of the system's mission, can coexist with relative comfort. In practical terms, producers, administrators, funders, and audiences may have vastly different views—even contradictory views—about the purposes of public television.

At the same time, goal ambiguity may allow public television more room to maneuver in a hostile economic environment. In a country where the mass media are predominantly market-based, public television occupies an awkward niche, and the existence of ambiguous goals may help to broaden its appeal to various constituencies. Furthermore, vague and heterogeneous objectives may make the system's public funding less controversial, for there is not a clearly defined set of points on which public television's opponents can criticize it. A decentralized system with heterogeneous goals does not provide the kind of easy target as a more centralized and goal-oriented system does. For both organizational and political reasons, the ambiguous nature of public television's purpose can be understood as protective, something that helps advance the ultimate goal of organizational survival.

Although goal ambiguity may serve various survival functions, it is not without drawbacks. Public television has attracted people who are motivated by a general sense of public television's mission but has done little to highlight or clarify this mission. Combined with the regular uphill battle to raise money and the ever-increasing demands of those who are providing the funding, the absence of a clear mission is a prime reason for the significant degree of cynicism within public television.

There are other tensions that come from goal ambiguity. Dimaggio suggests three resulting dilemmas in the nonprofit cultural arena: "tension between management and artistic professionals; tension between artists and management together and boards of trustees; and difficulties in evaluating managers and holding them accountable" (1987: 212). At least two of these tensions are ripe in public television. There is clearly friction between producers and administrators over such issues as money, control, and, perhaps most important, prestige. Producers with regular access to the airwaves are much less interested than administrators in the overall purpose of public television and are principally interested in making their own programs. (I should note, however, that producers who do not have regular access to the system are often very interested in the purpose of public television and argue, often persuasively, that PBS would serve its own mission by providing access to a wider range of talent.) Administrators, on the other hand, are likely to have a wider range of job possibilities outside of public television and are often more committed to the system and their perception of its goals than are individual producers.

The lack of clear goals also makes it difficult for the system, local stations, or individual managers to be held accountable to the public; there are often no clear guidelines on which to make judgments. Just as the lack of alternative measures of success heightens the importance of ratings, the absence of a clear sense of the purpose for public television can make more traditional goals, including the bottom line, important by default. In the long run, goal ambiguity is not likely to serve as an effective survival strategy; in the absence of clear goals—specifically, a commitment to producing a diverse alternative to commercial television—public television looks less and less different from its competition. Without a mission that defines organizational goals in a purposive sense—and the goal of providing a diverse alternative is anything but narrowly conceived—there is little to counteract the tendency to focus on maintenance goals and take the path of least resistance. However, as new technologies produce new television channels and the form, if not the substance, of increased choice, public television's viability will depend on its ability to demonstrate its difference. The ability to maintain this difference will only be ensured if public television can more sharply and effectively define its identity for both the people who produce the programming and for the general public.

Collective Identity

What is public television's identity? Is it even possible to speak of a public television identity? I have argued that, beyond survival, organizational goals are ambiguous. Stavitsky (1988) argues a similar point when he suggests that public television does not have a clear "rhetorical vision." In order to develop a sharper sense of mission, or rhetorical vision, public television needs first to build a stronger identity internally. Without a shared collective identity within public television, it will be difficult, if not impossible, to move beyond maintenance goals and focus on purposive goals. One producer noted that the time of our interview, the summer of 1990, was

> a moment of change and confusion and identity crisis, which is as pronounced as any that public television has experienced in its lifetime. And so it gets much harder to talk about the differences [between public and commercial television] today than it would have been a year ago. And I, like a lot of people, am watching to see what happens next, and will be affected by what happens next. But it all seems very murky to me and hard to speculate about where public television is going now.

The confusion about the future is fundamentally connected to the "identity crisis" facing public television. Without an identity, it is virtually impossible to envision the future, let alone formulate and articulate a mission.

The structure of public television, however, makes the construction of a collective identity highly problematic. One obstacle is the compartmentalized nature of the system. One staffer noted, "It's such an atomized organization, and the different programs, at least at the level that I'm at, really don't communicate with each other. There's no real sense of a cohesive whole of public television." A producer made a similar argument, noting that it is much like the structure of a university.

> People who are struggling for metaphors for what it's like to be here invariably come up with, "It's like a university." It really has the ethos of a university, where because people don't make enough money to use as the calculus of their worth, they argue about the turf kinds of questions that you argue about in the university. ... I mean that little sort of niggling competition that comes in a university setting. And the sort of aloofness of the university administration from the nuts and bolts of what goes on. And the fact that the sociology department may be located next to the physical anthropology department and they don't have anything to do with each other. It is essentially the same sort of big casbah; it's like a big tent where all these different people bring their—to mix the metaphor a little bit—bring their camels and just stay under the tent for a while. And then maybe they move on—but the variety, the lack of unity, the sort of infighting, but its not very intimate inside—the sort of atomized feel of it.

In this kind of atmosphere, it is not surprising that there is little sense of collective identity or collective goals.

Sociologists of social movements have paid particular attention to the importance of collective identity—its construction, maintenance, and importance for unified action (cf. Melucci, 1989; Cohen, 1985; Gamson, 1991, 1992). Borrowing from this literature will help us understand the obstacles to building a collective identity within public television and suggest why it will be important to overcome these obstacles. Gamson has pointed out that collective identity within social movements is not unidimensional; he suggests that "we think of it as three embedded layers: organizational, movement, and solidary" (1991: 40). These specific layers do not explain the various collective identities in public television. But Gamson does alert us to the fact that we need to see the multiple and potentially competing layers of collective identity and not assume that they are all necessarily complementary. My interviews with WGBH employees suggest that there are four layers of collective identity for these public television workers: craft, program, station, and system.

Some of these workers clearly identify themselves as craftspeople—television producers, filmmakers, or journalists. This type of identification does not necessarily imply any connection to the world of public television, simply an interest in PBS as an outlet for distributing their programming. PBS may, in fact, be seen as only one of several outlets that play a similar distribution role. More than one producer suggested that the same people are producing documentary films for PBS, the networks, and cable. To the extent that PBS is the principal broadcasting outlet for documentaries, there is a community of documentary filmmakers in and around public television. But for those who identify with their craft, there is no necessary connection to public television, nor is there a sense that administrators or other professionals are part of the same collective.

Others see themselves as part of a collective effort to produce a particular series or program. This is the case with many of those who work for ongoing projects such as *Frontline, American Experience,* and *Nova,* as well as those producing multipart programs such as *Columbus* or *Nixon.* The collective, in this case, includes all members of the program's staff, regardless of their specific position. Since the hours are often long and pay not always high, a strong feeling of working as part of a collective can be an important unifying factor. The relationship to public television in this case is variable, since public television may be the only outlet in the United States that would maintain such programs. However, commitment to a particular program does not necessarily imply commitment to the public television system, especially once a program has run its course. Much of the staff relates primarily with individuals working on the same program, with little day-to-day connection with staffers of other programs or with PBS. Particularly for the long-running series, in which a staff works together over a period of years, this program-oriented bond may be the strongest form of collective identity within public television.

Still others identify with WGBH, the Boston PBS station and a national production house. This particular station is so large, with over 640 full-time employees and a budget of close to $100 million in 1990, that it is a world in and of itself. Although labor-management negotiations caused tension at WGBH in the late 1980s, there was still a sense, across job categories, of a commitment to the station. To the extent that my informants praised the intellectually challenging work environment, they felt some sense of collegiality with their co-workers at the station. The station-based level of collective identity is less likely to appeal to producers than to administrators, who work for the station, not for a particular program.

The fourth level of collective identity—being part of a national public television system—is clearly the most peripheral. In many ways, public television as a national system, represented largely by PBS, is far from the minds of these public television workers. To the extent that individuals are major players in the system—either as administrators or high-level producers—they are more likely to identify with PBS. But most of my informants had little relationship to PBS outside of bureaucratic paperwork, and many thought there was little connection between their own work and a national public television system.

Many of my informants may have held several layers of collective identity. It is clear that the least common form of identity was to the larger system. Because WGBH is such a large organization and is one of the principal producers of programming for the system, a station-oriented identity and a system-oriented identity may have overlapped substantially. One would expect that the situation is different at smaller local stations that do not produce national programming. Nevertheless, it was striking that so few of my informants believed that they had any connection to public television as a system. This sense was clearly reflected in the fact that so few were capable of articulating the mission or purpose of a national public television system.

My data do not allow me to rigorously evaluate the ways in which these multiple forms of identity overlap. But they do suggest that collective identity in public television is problematic. People are pulled by several different identities, and that of a nationwide public television system seems to have the least pull on these producers of national public television programming.

The consequences of the weak system-based identity are not immediately obvious. But social movement theorists who are interested in how organizations with purposive goals mobilize resources effectively—a process not dissimilar from the task for public television—have persuasively argued that the construction of a collective identity is central to the task of building an effective organization that will endure (see Gamson, 1991). Unless a movement has a sense of "who" it is, its ability to map goals, forge commitment, and build strategy will always be confused. The same can be said for public television: If it lacks a sense of what it is, again other than a self-sustaining bureaucracy, there is little likelihood that goals will be specified, let alone reached. Ultimately, a strong collective identity, one that explicitly identifies the collective as a public television system, is integral to the future of public television in this age of privatization. Those in leadership positions need to do the hard work of building a collective identity within public television, one that focuses on and specifies the mission of producing a diverse alternative to commercial television. A process of identity-construction cannot occur in a vacuum, as if various individuals do not have other identities. It will need to build on already existing identities at the levels of craft, program, and station and forge links, already nascent, between these narrower identities and the public television collective. Such a process of identity building can also clarify for members of the public the goals of public television and provide a clearer picture of the public's role within the system.

Two Dilemmas

From the beginning, public television has faced a set of choices about both the character of its programming and the nature of the public it serves. If public television is to clarify its mission and define a corresponding set of goals, one of the first steps will be to resolve two long-standing dilemmas: Is this a *public* or an *educational* television system? Is the goal the production of *quality* programming or *alternative* programming?

Educational or Public Television?

The Carnegie Commission coined the term "public television" in its 1967 report. In so doing, it argued that the United States needed more than simply an educational television system, which it had originally been charged with studying; the nation needed a "public" television system. Central to this change in terminology was a sense that educational television was too narrowly focused.

There remains, however, a strong sense within public television circles that the system should be, first and foremost, educational. The two traits may not be contradictory—educational television exists on public television today, primarily in the form of telecourses—but they certainly highlight different kinds of programming. The most important difference is the underlying sensibility. Public television, at least when the term was coined in 1967, implied a notion of television as a cultural medium of immense power. Viewing it as educational, in the narrow sense of instructional, did not do justice to its potential for expression. Public television was envisioned as a site for controversy rather than as a strictly educational tool, a place where neglected ideas could be heard, a forum for debate.

As an underlying philosophy, educational television stresses consensus over controversy; it is this orientation that makes producers of documentaries believe that they have to make the "definitive" statement on a subject. Since programs are seen as teaching, producers feel that they have to get the story "right." And programs that do not meet the standards of "objectivity" are clearly identified as such, in order to differentiate the "truth" from a subjective account. For example, PBS's *P.O.V.* ("Point of View"), which carries some of public television's most innovative programming, is titled to suggest this very difference.

An orientation more in line with the earlier notion of public television would see each program as an attempt to raise issues and further debate rather than as the final word—one that would be perfect for high school and college classes. It would be less concerned about making a rigid distinction between "objective" and "subjective" programs, recognizing that all programming contains varying degrees of subjectivity. And it would celebrate controversy and challenges to orthodoxy and stress asking questions over providing answers. Rather than teaching, producers would be engaged in an ongoing dialogue with the public, defined broadly to include those who are generally ignored by commercial television.

Sooner or later, public television will have to decide whether it is in the business of public or educational broadcasting. National Public Radio, although it certainly has its own shortcomings (cf. Ryan, 1993), clearly has decided on a "public" radio sensibility. It may be that external pressures, funding in particular, provide incentives for public television to maintain a commitment to educational programs and a corresponding philosophy. The educational dimension of public television may be one of the principal grounds on which my informants see their work as a public service. But this perspective acts to reproduce the notion of the public as an audience, an audience that is taught—rather than simply sold products—by the television. A broader notion of public television would still provide the public with resources with which to learn, but learning would occur in the context of debate and controversy that more actively engages the public.

Quality or Alternative?

Throughout my interviews, my informants indicated that public television is in the business of making what was referred to variously as "quality," "serious," "intelligent," or "meaningful" television. I suspect that the specific meanings of these terms have some degree of variability, depending on the context and the informant, yet they all seem to suggest the same general attitude. Public television makes programming that does not use a least-common-denominator formula to simply attract a large audience. In fact, although many of the producers I interviewed did not want to appear too critical of network television and almost half had worked in it, there was a general sense that public television could broadcast what the networks could not—primarily for audience reasons. The term "quality television," then, is something producers use to distinguish their programs from commercial television. From this perspective, commercial television is concerned with attracting audiences, public television with producing quality.

This definition of public television, much like the broader definition of its goals, highlights its opposition to commercial television. However, it does little to explicitly identify what, in fact, quality television is. By digging below the surface, we can begin to uncover what this term means and why it has such wide currency. Those who produce programs for public television believe they are making programs that would have little chance of surviving at the networks. For many, this distinction is principally an issue of form or style; the long-form documentary and the repackaged British import, for example, are now clearly part of the public television niche. What makes these programs different from network offerings is that they are more than simple entertainment.

These "quality" programs are heralded because they are considered more intellectual than network material. Even if they border on being stuffy, they certainly are more serious and care more about ideas than most network fare. For many, this is the principal virtue of much of public television programming: It encourages people to think. Several of my informants suggested that this was both the strength and weakness of public television: Programs can be thought-provoking and informative, but they also may be hard work to watch. It is likely that the highly educated producers who make the programs, the academics who advise the programs (and study the system), the audience members who have the income to contribute to local stations, and the local elites who sit on the boards of local stations will find much of this programming satisfying.

"Quality" television, then, is the kind of programming that appeals to highly educated people. It differs from commercial television not because there is no concern for the audience but rather because it appeals to a different, more select audience. Essentially, the term "quality television" has become a code for elitist, highbrow programs. Such quality programs are, not coincidentally, also the kinds of programs that are perceived to be "safe"—they contain a minimal amount of controversy and they appeal to corporate funders, well-off members of the public, and prestigious critics. These kinds of quality programs serve the interests and reflect the tastes of important people within the public television orbit. At the same time, they clearly differentiate public television from commercial television—largely along class lines. This narrow definition of quality programming excludes a whole range of programs that do not fit the traditional notion of "high culture." Such challenging programs as *Tongues Untied*, Marlon Riggs's documentary about African-American gay male life, do not easily fit into this limited notion of quality television. It is no wonder, given the underlying definition of quality programming, that public television is concerned about attracting "new" audiences.

Public television is an alternative, then, to the extent that it produces a particular brand of quality programming. Alternative content—as in different perspectives on the world, perspectives that are neglected by commercial media—is not part of this definition. One producer made this point quite clearly. S/he suggested that people at public television "see themselves as an alternative. But, I think a lot of people perceive the alternative as being simply higher quality. It's kind of a more refined, rarefied worldview, as opposed to any sort of political difference." And the notion that televised texts should be produced by diverse authors is only beginning to emerge. Ultimately, there is a very narrow definition of "alternative" among public television workers, one that is much narrower than in the early years of public television: Public television is different because of its quality. It is, most fundamentally, alternative because it is "better" television—although the definition of quality is defined in large part by the type of people that are watching. A more inclusive notion of alternativeness—one that highlights the inclusion of neglected voices and unheard perspectives, as only a noncommercial system is capable of doing on a regular basis—exists only on the fringes of public television.

Mission Versus the Market

The consequences of the absence of a clear mission stressing the alternative nature of public television are far-reaching. Without a commitment to an alternative set of goals, public television will increasingly feel the pressures of the more immediate need to survive, particularly if the political and economic climate become more hostile. Blau and Meyer (1971: 123), in their study of bureaucracy, argue that "when organizational objectives are uncertain, there is a tendency to determine goals and activities according to the resources available." This tendency illuminates a great deal about the situation at public television. In the absence of a clear organizational mission, a mission defined by inclusiveness, not rigidity, the availability of resources becomes a central determinant of public television's goals. That is, the immediate tasks associated with raising funds to continue the system's operation can obscure the apparently less immediate questions of the reason for the existence of a public television system. As a result, questions about the mission of public television, and its future direction, become increasingly less relevant, and the ability of public broadcasters to resist the market environment decreases as well.

Organizational theorists have noted that the larger environment can have a powerful impact on organizations (cf. Aldrich and Pfeffer, 1976; Meyer and Rowan, 1977). In the case of public television, the broader market environment exerts pressures—both economic and ideological. The environment, however, does not determine how an organization will evolve. At the most, it makes certain outcomes more likely than others, and there are strategies by which organizations can resist the pressures imposed by their environment. One of these strategies is to articulate, collectively reinforce, and codify a mission that defines a clear set of goals, a task at which public television has had little success.

The underdeveloped collective mission may allow for a smoother day-to-day operation of public television, and it may help provide the resources for the continual growth of the system. At the same time, though, it facilitates the advance of market pressures on an ostensibly nonmarket institution. The increasing competition for resources will likely increase the confusion about public television's mission and the power of market forces in the coming years.

Notes

1. Perrow (1961) suggests that we need to differentiate between "official" and "operative" goals, arguing that operative goals "tell us what the organization actually is trying to do, regardless of what the official goals say are the aims" (p. 855). I was less interested in discussing the formal mission statement of WGBH and more interested in how my informants perceived the mission themselves and how this mission operated on a day-to-day basis.

2. WGBH's Formal Mission Statement reads as follows: "The purpose of the corporation is to promote, through broadcasting or other means, the general education of the public by offering programs that inform, stimulate and entertain, so that persons of all ages, origins and beliefs may be encouraged, in an atmosphere of artistic freedom, to learn and appreciate the history, the sciences, the humanities, the fine arts, the practical arts, the music, the politics, the economics, and other significant aspects of the world they live in, and thereby to enrich and improve their own lives."

CHAPTER EIGHT

■

Democracy and the
Future of Public Television

The preceding chapters have suggested that after more than twenty-five years our public television system is far from the ideal-type identified in Chapter 3. In particular, I have argued that the funding process puts subtle but very real constraints on programming; that public television has little or no relationship to citizens as a public, but instead sees that public as a passive audience; and that goal ambiguity only reinforces the importance of resource considerations in decisionmaking. The argument that public television does not meet ideal-typical criteria, however, is only a starting point; the content of the differences, not the simple existence of difference, is what we need to examine. The comparison between the ideal-type and the concrete form of public television highlights a recurring theme: the intrusion of the market on public television. The funding process, the transformation of the public into an audience, and the consequences of goal ambiguity suggest that the market, as both a material and an ideological force, is at the center of an explanation of the limitations of public television. Conversely, it suggests that insulation from market forces (and the ideology of market television) will be central to formulating strategies for constructing a more democratic public television.

In some respects, the argument that market insulation is at the center of a strategy for building a democratic television system is counterintuitive, for it goes against the grain of American political culture, which combines reverence for the market and suspicion of the state. As this book has shown, and as early proponents of public media foresaw, democratic discourse is not advanced by mass media systems that cater to the interests of their financial patrons and produce programs to attract a mass audience of potential consumers. There are, of course, alternatives to the organization of media along commercial lines.

One of the central premises of this book is that television can play a positive role in the construction and maintenance of a democratic society. In the

157

United States in the 1990s, public television's particular structure makes it the site that is most likely to serve such a role. Ultimately, then, the point of this book is to understand how public television can play a more central role in the regeneration of an active public sphere, one that is needed for a healthy democracy to flourish.

If the 1990s are a time in which privatization proceeds apace and reverence for the market grows accordingly, it would seem difficult to even open a discussion about either the importance of a strong public sector or the particular structure of a public television system. Of course, it is in just such a climate that I am arguing for the need to find new ways to insulate public television from the very market forces that are so widely revered as a prerequisite for democracy. However, the end of the cold war and the corresponding close of the historic ideological battle between the forces of capitalism and state socialism are, most fundamentally, opportunities to rethink ideas and reenvision the future. International geopolitical changes, as well as developments in the global economy, raise a whole series of questions about the future of democracy, the nation-state, the public sector, and mass communication. Although policymakers and political insiders have largely defended tradition and maintained the supremacy of current arrangements, it is incumbent upon scholars to move the discussion beyond political expedience. Political changes signaled by the end of the cold war, coupled with the end of the Reagan/Bush era, present a new opportunity for critical assessment of our economic, political, and cultural institutions. At the same time, economic stagnation, political apathy, and technological developments suggest that there is a great need for this kind of critical reassessment.

Whether the United States is entering a new era, as pundits on both Left and Right have argued, will ultimately depend only partially on the changing of the guard at the White House or the breakup of the Soviet Union. Such changes may provide openings, but the opportunity will only be realized if we can muster the political and intellectual courage to critically examine our beliefs and provide room for the emergence of new ideas. The future of the public sector will depend, at least in part, on the outcome of this emerging battle of ideas.

Public television, having entered its second quarter-century in 1992, is an institution whose future has been challenged several times in its short life. As we saw in Chapter 1, partisans of the Right have already opened the contest by arguing for the total privatization of public television. This position has not been matched, in either political or scholarly circles, by a systematic attempt to articulate a justification for reinforcing the public nature of public television. Certainly public television has had its share of defenders—including members of Congress, public television executives, and viewers. However, there has been little effort by those committed to the public sector to rethink the structure of public television. This chapter begins to lay the framework for a vision of a new, more *public* public television, offering both principles upon which such an institution should be based and policies that begin to move in that direction. This framework draws on recent work, also hastened by global changes, in critical social theory that reexamines the relationship between the market, the public sector, and democracy.

Critics, of course, will charge that an effort to envision a future public television without taking stock of the political feasibility of the specific proposals is shortsighted. We should keep in mind, however, that part of the very process of making change is laying out a vision. It is shortsighted, I would argue, to allow short-term versions of "realism" to inhibit the development of an alternative conception of public television. In fact, paying homage to "responsible" opinion is one of the principal shortcomings of the U.S. mass media, for it closes off the very possibility that new ideas will ever emerge. It is ultimately counterproductive to stifle the discussion of a new public television system before even articulating that vision.

We should also recognize the incomplete and uneven manner in which the banner of realism is used to discredit ideas. Conservative activists, in their critiques of public television, have pushed beyond the boundaries of what was once considered reasonable and have opened up an entirely new discussion about completely privatizing public television. Although opponents of the conservative position are in no short supply, little criticism focuses on the proposal's political feasibility, or lack thereof. Advocates of the total cessation of government funding for public television are not castigated for the "unrealistic" nature of their proposal. Of course, such impracticable proposals from the Right are bolstered by support from allies in the national media and well-funded Washington think tanks. Such support can make even the most seemingly unworkable proposals worthy of serious discussion. Proposals from the Left, which lacks such powerful allies, are generally not afforded such treatment. They are routinely dismissed as unrealistic, and claims that they lack short-term political feasibility help to discredit them before they are even discussed. Scholars whose work could open debate to a new set of perspectives often are ignored or, in response to routine exclusion from political discourse, retreat to abstract theorizing in scientific journals, making little effort to bring their ideas to a broader public.

In the case of public television, the sides of the debate have been drawn very narrowly: those who want to eliminate public broadcasting versus those who defend it.[1] There are, of course, other perspectives in this debate; the discussion about the future of public broadcasting can only benefit from the inclusion of new ideas, regardless of their short-term practicability. Moreover, as events of the late 1980s indicated, calculations of political feasibility can change rapidly; citizen activism, in particular, can quickly alter the political climate. It is the responsibility of scholars to move beyond the narrow limits imposed by considerations of political feasibility and articulate a vision of the possible. The eminent sociologist Robert S. Lynd made this argument with great clarity in 1939.

> [S]ocial science is confined neither to practical politics nor to things whose practicality is demonstrable this afternoon or tomorrow morning. Nor is its role merely to stand by, describe, and generalize, like a seismologist watching a volcano. There is no other agency in our culture whose role it is to ask long-range and, if need be, abruptly irreverent questions with research and the systematic charting of the way ahead. The responsibility is to keep everlastingly challenging the present with the question: But what is it that we human beings want, and what things would have to be done, in what ways and in what sequence, in order to change the present so as to achieve it? (Lynd, 1967 [1939]: 250)

In the case of public television, we need to rethink how the institution can best contribute to the construction of a democratic public sphere.

The Technology of Television

Am I asking too much of television, even a public television system? Is it absurd to think that television can serve democracy? Since the early days of television, there has been a growing sense that this technology may be inimical to democracy. Critics have argued, often persuasively, that the medium encourages passivity, causes isolation and alienation, and helps to create a nation of "couch potatoes." And popular discourse includes such terms as "idiot box" and "boob tube," which suggest the stupefying consequences of watching too much television. At their most articulate, these arguments often ring true to scholars concerned about the impact of television, critics troubled by the lack of political participation in the United States, and activists trying to mobilize people for collective action. It is not uncommon to hear commentators on both left and right suggest that television causes or exacerbates a variety of social problems.

Mander's (1978) is the most polemical argument for the elimination of television. He suggests that television is dangerous to both individuals and society and is not reformable. He also makes clear that he is talking not simply about American television or network television but about the technology of television. Mander argues that "[t]elevision technology is inherently antidemocratic. ... Television freewayizes, suburbanizes and commoditizes human beings, who are then easier to control. Meanwhile, those who control television consolidate their power" (1978: 349). Television is, in short, a technology that is not compatible with a democratic society.

Neil Postman (1985) also presents a well-known case, albeit in less polemical terms, that television poses a threat to democracy. He suggests that television is fundamentally about entertainment and that it has created a public discourse that has little substance. For Postman, "'serious television' is a contradiction in terms" (1985: 80). And although he is not particularly concerned about the "junk" that populates the airwaves, Postman argues that "television is at its most trivial and, therefore, most dangerous when its aspirations are high, when it presents itself as a carrier of important cultural conversations" (1985: 16). In short, when television tries to cross the boundary between entertainment and information, it blurs the line and cheapens public life at the same time.

Sennett's (1976) discussion of the decline of public life in the United States locates the impact of television in a larger context. Sennett suggests that electronic media, and television in particular, discourage public life by rendering actual contact unnecessary. "Experience of diversity and experience in a region of society at a distance from the intimate circle; the 'media' contravene both these principles of publicness" (1976: 282). However, Sennett is not unaware of the paradox of television: "The mass media infinitely heighten the knowledge people have of what transpires in the society, and they infinitely inhibit the capacity of people to convert that knowledge into political action" (1976: 283). This inhibition takes place because television is, for Sennett as for Postman, something that we watch, generally in our own homes, with no way to "talk back to the TV." It is therefore something that substitutes for human interaction, creating atomized individuals—such as Chance the gardener from Jerzy Kosinski's novel *Being There* (1971)—who become accustomed to watching rather than doing.

I have little argument with significant portions of the critiques offered by Mander, Postman, and Sennett. Television viewing can be a fundamentally isolating experience, one that gives the illusion of contact with the world while discouraging actual human interaction. And it is difficult to argue that television did not play a part in the degradation of public life in the 1980s. Although the arguments advanced by Mander and Postman, in particular, may have gained wide currency in popular discourse, there is by no means a consensus within scholarly circles that television viewing is so passive and inherently antidemocratic. European scholars, in particular, have argued, as Stuart Hall (1986: 8–9) notes, that

> television viewing, the choices which shape it and the many social uses to which we put it, now turn out to be irrevocably active and social processes. People don't passively absorb subliminal "inputs" from the screen. They discursively "make sense" of or produce "readings" of what they see. ... Viewing is almost always accompanied by argument, comment, debate and discussion. Programmes are surrounded, if not totally submerged, by an incessant flow of other activity and talk, only some of it television-related.

This perspective, shared by a range of scholars in media and cultural studies, suggests that the type of argument advanced by Mander and Postman is fundamentally problematic, for it ignores the actual experiences of viewers in diverse settings. If emerging theories provide a powerful critique of the perspective offered by Mander and Postman, they have no monopoly on such criticism. I am troubled by the argument, made most explicitly by Mander but implied by both Postman and Sennett, that the *technology* of television is inherently problematic.[2] The underlying message is that television discourages public life because it is *television*. Although there is no need to minimize the shortcomings, nor uncritically glamorize the possibilities, of television or other new communications media, the principal flaw in the critique of television as a technology is that it does not separate the technology from its dominant organization and use. Neuman makes a similar point succinctly: "One must recognize that to a degree, the development of a new technology ... follows its own scientific logic. But the direction of research funding, the control of design and implementation, and the pace of development of any new technology are highly constrained by the values and priorities of the host culture" (1991: 19). He concludes, as if in response to Mander and Postman, that "to identify technology as evil is to ignore the variability of its design and use" (1991: 19).

It is possible to appreciate the shortcomings of the current role of television without slipping into a technologically determinist argument. Television, as it is currently organized in the United States, does little to contribute to public life. Those who lament its impact on American politics and culture have identified an important problem. But the problem is not with the technology per se. Technologies themselves do not have inherent social properties; they cannot be classified as either liberating or oppressive outside of their specific social context. It is their concrete use that determines their social and political roles. In the case of television, as I suggested in Chapter 2, the economic organization of the technology is where we need to focus our attention.

American television is ruled by the market. This reality is far more important for assessing the current state of American television than is the specific capacity of the technology. Public television is not immune to the power of the market; the market is one of the principal threats to the ability of public television to contribute to a democratic public sphere. However, state-dominated television is no alternative to the market orientation that is so constraining. If we are to move the discussion of television and democracy forward at all, we have to move beyond the simple market/state dichotomy.

Market, State, and Civil Society

Traditional mass communication discourse suggests that mass media can be organized along the lines of either state control or market "freedom." This view, particularly in the post–cold war world, needs to be discarded. The choices are not limited to market or state; and we abandon the possibility of constructing a more democratic media system by restricting the future to such choices. In other words, a critique of market-based media and, in this particular case, of the intrusion of the market on public television does not imply that state-centered television is the only viable option. Wolfe (1989), among others, argues that there is an alternative to either market or state, what he refers to as "civil society." For Wolfe, civil society "is the proper subject matter of sociology, but civil society viewed as the process by which individuals construct together with others the social meanings through which they interpret reality" (1989: 208). The kind of democratic public sphere that I have suggested television can help construct is an integral part of civil society. In fact, a vibrant public sphere is a prerequisite for the kind of civil society that Wolfe envisions.

What is the relationship between this civil society and the market and state? For Wolfe, civil society is not completely separate from either one, it "exists as a sphere alongside the market and the state, [and] it contributes to the more effective working of both of them" (1989: 258). Although I find Wolfe's analysis useful, the concept, and importance, of civil society remain fuzzy. This vagueness may be one of the reasons it has become so fashionable in academic discourse in the early 1990s; it can have a range of meanings, depending on the author and the context.

Cohen and Arato (1992), in their impressive effort to reintroduce the concept of civil society into modern political theory, also suggest that we need to see civil society as a sphere separate from both the market and the state.[3] After examining the use of the term "civil society" and the demands associated with it in such diverse settings as Poland, France, Germany, and Latin America, Cohen and Arato conclude that civil society is

> a normative model of a societal realm different from the state and the economy and having the following components: (1) *Plurality:* families, informal groups, and voluntary associations whose plurality and autonomy allow for a variety of forms of life; (2) *Publicity:* institutions of culture and communication; (3) *Privacy:* a domain of individual self-development and moral choice; and (4) *Legality:* structures of general laws and basic rights needed to demarcate plurality, privacy, and publicity from at least the state and, tendentially, the economy.

Contemporary forms of mass media, as the principal institutions of communication, are a central part of this definition of civil society. Mass media are a site for public discussion, the introduction of new ideas, and the airing of grievances. Civil society depends, to a great degree, on the existence of spaces for such public discussion and debate. Cohen and Arato argue that "the two sets of rights most fundamental to the institutional existence of a fully developed civil society are those that secure integrity, autonomy, and personality of the person and those having to do with free communication" (1992: 403).

Much of the discussion of civil society remains on an abstract theoretical level. At its most concrete, it points to the existence of social movements, vol-

untary associations, and spaces for public discussion as signs of an independent "civil" sphere. The recent literature on civil society sets forth the notion
that democracies need autonomous public spaces—spaces that are neither
fully commercialized nor simply state-controlled—in which genuine public
discussion and debate can take place. This is why the mass media are such an
important piece of civil society. Eastern Europeans, who were early promoters
of the idea of civil society, have heralded the rise of a new free press, separate
from the state, as an important sign of the rebirth of civil society. In the
United States, we need to focus on the other side of the coin and develop
forms of mass media that are not subject to the severe market constraints outlined in Chapter 2. This is where public television enters the picture. It is one
of the few national media that has the possibility to be part of this autonomous sphere: It is already at least partially removed from both market constraints and state control. The task ahead, then, is to move public television
further in this direction, structuring ways to insulate it from both the market
and the state.

Having identified the importance of constructing autonomous media organizations, I want to return to the difficult question of television's relationship
to democracy. I have already argued that the technology of television does not
contain an inherent ability either to serve or undermine democracy. But I
want to amplify this position to suggest that media in general, and television
in particular, not only do not have intrinsic positions on democracy but are essentially paradoxical in this regard. That is, television carries with it tendencies
toward both democratization and social control. When we focus on the technology of television, then, we need to be aware of this paradox. And when we
construct social policy, we need to bear in mind the contradictory nature of
mass media.

Habermas, in his *Theory of Communicative Action,* suggests that it is impossible to remove one side of this paradox from the other. He notes that
mass media

> hierarchize and at the same time remove restrictions on the horizon of possible
> communication. The one aspect cannot be separated from the other—and
> therein lies their ambivalent potential. Insofar as mass media one-sidedly channel
> communication flows in a centralized network—from the center to the periphery
> or from above to below—they considerably strengthen the efficacy of social con-
> trols. But tapping this authoritarian potential is always precarious because there is
> a counterweight of emancipatory potential built into communication structures
> themselves (1987: 390).

This paradox explains why it is so difficult to make judgments about the political impact of television. It also makes it difficult for either theorists or policymakers, were they so inclined, to construct a democratic communications system.

Given that the nature of television (and other mass media) is contradictory, we need to do more than simply lament its degradation of public life or celebrate its great potential. We need to do the hard work of identifying the principles of a democratic communications system, locating those existing structures that are most likely to contribute to it and clarifying the obstacles to the realization of such a system. To do so, we will need both theoretical work to indicate what these principles are and empirical research to understand the nature of current media structures and their future potential.

This is the direction in which media sociologists need to move. That is, we need to move from critique, of which there is an abundance of useful work, to a level that incorporates the insights of this critique into a theory of a more emancipatory media. This work will be done in bits and pieces and has already begun in both the scholarly and activist world. Keane's (1991) piece is one of the more useful in this regard. In his critique of both market and state media, he outlines a new model.

> This new model of public service communications has profound implications for the ways in which we have thought about the media and democracy. It acknowledges the point that in large-scale societies representative structures of communication cannot be bypassed; and that—analogous to representative government—the dangers of irresponsible communication permanently threaten democratic societies. … [A] revised public service model also requires the development of a plurality of non-state and non-market media that function as permanent thorns in the side of state power, and serve as the primary means of communication for citizens living within a diverse and horizontally organized civil society (1991: xii).

Implicit in my analysis throughout this book is the notion that public television, already partially removed from both market and state and with a rhetorical commitment to more than simply selling products, is a key site in the struggle for a reinvigorated public sphere and a more healthy civil society. Moreover, I have suggested that, contrary to most "public" institutions, public television is principally constrained not by the state but the market. In fact, the privatization of public television is one of the more alarming signs of the general trend toward the privatization of public spaces and the deepening of market forces.

The Privatization of Culture?

Schiller (1989) argues that the trend toward privatization in the United States is fundamentally antidemocratic. Perhaps we are witnessing another phase in the structural transformation of the public sphere, as Habermas called it thirty years ago. But this may be more than simply a transformation: The public sphere, it would appear, is losing its public character as it becomes increasingly privatized. New marketing techniques have brought commercial television into the public school classroom. Large bookstore chains dominate the book-selling market, carrying titles almost exclusively from major corporate presses. Billboards hawking beer and cigarettes pollute the urban landscape. Independent movie houses are almost nonexistent. New computer technologies have allowed for private information networks that only money can buy. Now, more than ever, culture has become an industry ruled by the principles of marketing.

I do not want to paint a picture that is too bleak. The privatization of culture has not been all-encompassing. Theorists of popular culture remind us that there is an ongoing struggle between people and the culture industry. Fiske (1989), for example, notes that "the study of popular culture requires the study not only of the cultural commodities out of which it is made, but also of the ways that people use them. The latter are far more creative and varied than the former" (1989: 15). As an example, Fiske describes the process by which manufacturers began to market torn jeans in response to the style preferred by youths. He suggests, however, that youths simply found new ways to tear or disfigure their jeans, rather than accepting the factory-made torn jeans.

Such examples should alert us to the fact that the privatization of culture is not a done deal. In the realm of media, there remain noncorporate voices that struggle to survive. Alternative publications, independent presses, public access television, and college radio stations are all examples of small openings carved out in the increasingly closed public sphere. Still, such outlets have comparatively little reach to the broader public, and little access to the resources that would allow for a broader reach. That is why the arena of mass media, of which public television is an integral part, is so important. Despite, or perhaps because of, the warnings of critics such as Schiller, public spaces will never be completely privatized. Still, the existence of a healthy national public sphere is in jeopardy, and if democracy is to retain any substantive meaning, the public sphere will have to be recreated.

In arguing that the public sphere has been eroded, however, there is no room for nostalgia about the old days of the public salon, when men (and it was almost exclusively men) sat in cafes and discussed the important issues of the day. Nor is it necessary to assert that open public discussion produces some absolute, unchanging truth. As Habermas has reminded us, decisions reached through a process of public discussion are always negotiable. The process of negotiation and renegotiation—an ongoing dialogue—is the essence of a healthy public sphere and critical to the existence of democratic decisionmaking. As Wolfe suggests in his discussion of moral obligation, "allowing people to be wrong may be less risky overall than insisting on rules by which they may be right, if so doing permits them to keep vibrant a place in which they can cultivate their social capacities to act as moral agencies" (1989: 247). An open public sphere and a mass media that will nourish it allow people to "be wrong"; it is this ongoing process of discussion, agreement, and disagreement that forms the core of a democratic public sphere.

Public television, most fundamentally, ought to contribute to a vigorous public sphere. But to do so, the system must be removed as much as possible from the forces of the market and the power of the state. This public television system would play a dual role in reinvigorating public life. First, it would broaden the horizons of public discourse simply by serving as an electronic platform for perspectives and ideas that are largely unheard in commercial media. Second, by providing citizens with access to a wide range of ideas and structuring viewer participation into the system, a reinvigorated public television would help prepare citizens to become more active in other arenas of public life. In short, a public television driven by the principle of free and open discussion could be an integral part of a healthy democracy.

Thus far, the discussion about the role of public television in the public sphere has remained largely abstract. I have suggested that we need to construct a mass media that is neither driven by the market nor constrained by the state. In the remainder of this chapter, I will articulate the basic principles of a new public television system. Before moving forward, however, it is worth noting why public television is integral to any discussion of the relationship between media and democracy. First, it is clear that public television is already partially removed from both market and state constraints (although the power of market intrusion is not widely recognized). Second, the creation of public television only one-quarter of a century ago must be seen in light of the various other democratic openings of the 1960s. Although public television may not have been the direct result of a demand for the democratization of the mass media, its early proponents were certainly influenced by the broader movement for the democratization of American institutions. The work of democratizing the mass media must be pursued on several fronts; it certainly will not be completed overnight. Rather than focusing solely on the building of new institutions, those concerned with constructing a more democratic media need to see the 1967 creation of public television as a significant early step in an ongoing process. In important respects, particularly its partial removal from market forces and the early articulation of its commitment to diversity, our current system of public television provides a concrete example of both the vast potential and the increasing necessity of a more democratic mass media.

Principles of a Democratic Public Television

Young (1985) suggests that a democratic communication system needs to be information rich, interaction rich, and oriented to the construction of a public sphere. He also notes that "the technology for a democratic communication exists. The resources to assemble a democratic communication exist. The political necessity for a democratic communication increases continuously. Only private ownership and/or party control of the media interferes with democratically organized communication" (1985: 72). This is a useful starting point, for it identifies the principal obstacles to democratic media (market and state) and suggests basic principles for restructuring the media. However, it only takes us part of the way, for Young posits a highly abstract vision of a new structure, focusing more on the need for change and less on the specific content of the proposed changes.

In the context of the analysis of public television presented here, I want to suggest five general principles of a democratic media and elaborate how they can be incorporated into our public television system. These principles—social ownership, diversity, participation, interaction, and criticism—may appear to have little relevance for much of our current commercial media. Without changes in the ownership structure of commercial television, it is unlikely that any vision of a democratic communication system will ever fully emerge. But these principles still have immediate relevance for the current system of public television, some more than others. I will also suggest concrete proposals with which to begin the process of implementing these principles.

Social Ownership

The first principle is social ownership. This may be the most crucial of the five principles, for it facilitates the implementation of the others. Public television may not be far from having a structure of social ownership. The Corporation for Public Broadcasting and the Public Broadcasting Service are non-state, nonprofit organizations. However, their governance is intimately connected to the state (CPB board members are appointed by the president), and the funding of public television is, as I have argued previously, intimately intertwined with the market. I will return to the issue of system (and station) governance in the discussion of participation. The question of financing, however, is central to our discussion of social ownership. A socially owned television system needs to have a plan for adequate long-term funding in order that powerful forces from either market or state (in this case, most likely the market) do not intervene to subvert the very purpose of the ownership structure.

In order, then, for public television to exist as a socially owned entity, it must be more than simply a nonprofit organization that is not officially part of the state sector. It must be financially independent of both market forces and state intervention. The Carnegie Commission understood this point, as I have suggested earlier, and it recommended a then–politically unacceptable plan for ensuring financial independence. (It also noted that the entire proposal for the creation of a public television system would be inadvisable without the creation of what it called the Corporation for Public Television to insulate the new system.) The commission's plan, a tax on the purchase of television sets to be placed in a trust fund for the exclusive use of public broadcasters, would have divorced the public broadcasting system from the politics of the federal budget appropriations process. It also would have allowed public television to avoid the pressures of the private funding market. In short, it would have given the system much greater independence.

Is it possible to return twenty-five years later to the notion of a tax on television sets? Even if it is deemed politically feasible, is it desirable? And should we understand such a tax as regressive? These questions do not present simple answers, but the struggle over the financing of public television for the past two decades has made them only part of a larger puzzle. The real issue is: How can we shape a strategy for raising a reliable supply of funds for public television without demanding more from an increasingly overburdened and deficit-ridden state or turning wholesale to commercial sources of revenue? Those enamored with the free market and its ability to encourage innovation will suggest that public television has to more aggressively integrate itself into the market, in the spirit of American entrepreneurship. Conversely, those who fear the homogenizing influence of the market will argue that public television is an important public good that needs to be supported by the state; as a result, it must engage even more forcefully in the fight for government resources.

There are problems, however, with both of these perspectives. On the one hand, as I have suggested, the free market is a principal inhibitor of public television. On the other hand, although I have sympathy for the idea of more state funding, I find it ultimately problematic. First, the 1990s, despite the end of the cold war, are unlikely to be a time of growth in the state sector. Regardless of the strength of the argument that public television is an institution worth state support, it is likely that policymakers and citizens feeling the crunch of economic changes, the loss of other state services and increases in local and state taxes will not support a dramatic increase in appropriations for public television. But this is only part of the reason that simple reliance on the state is problematic. Further state funding will, in all likelihood, lead to further attempts by the state to intervene in public television. (Witness, for example, recent efforts by the federal government to interfere in grant making by the National Endowment for the Arts.) In fact, the Public Telecommunications Act of 1992, which authorized federal funding for public broadcasting for the fiscal years 1994 through 1996, included strong language about the content of public broadcasting programming. In response to pressure from congressional conservatives, the legislation stipulated that the CPB board must review public broadcasting programming on a regular basis for, among other things, objectivity and balance; the results of these reviews are to be submitted annually to the president and to Congress. This is a textbook example of how political pressure increases as state resources increase. To the extent that public television becomes more closely connected to the state, it will be less likely (and less able) to contribute to an autonomous public sphere. Ultimately, then, there are good political and theoretical reasons to be wary of the argument that public broadcasters should focus their attention on increasing their share of the federal budget.

So where does this leave us? One direction, in recognition of the proliferation of television sets and television-related products, is to return to the original Carnegie Commission plan and propose a revised version of the television tax. This approach would highlight the fact that almost every American household owns a television set and that middle- and upper-income families are likely to own several sets. At the same time, the majority of households now own videocassette recorders, and millions of Americans own video cameras. Rather than just television sets, all television-related items could be taxed a small amount, perhaps 1 percent, with the revenue going directly into a trust fund for public television. As a means of counteracting the regressive nature of any flat sales tax, a threshold, similar to those that are part of so-called "luxury" taxes, could be established, with the first $200, for example, deemed not taxable.

There are, of course, strengths and weaknesses to this kind of plan. On one hand, a tax on television-related goods would indicate that the constituency of public television includes all citizens who use television—virtually everyone—rather than only those individuals and corporations that choose to contribute. By clarifying and expanding the public television constituency, the tax may generate more interest among a diverse range of citizens in local and national public television. On the other hand, the introduction of any new tax, even those for such essentials as education and health care, would likely be resisted by the very citizens who, in order to make public television more public, would have to support it. Furthermore, the plan does not address the fact that there are identifiable individuals and organizations that derive profits specifically from the use of the public airwaves who may be a more appropriate source of revenue than citizens who purchase television-related equipment.

One alternative, then, is to impose a tax on the advertisers and television station owners who reap such large profits from commercial television. Versions of this proposal have bounced around the edges of mainstream political discourse for some time. In 1987 a modest version of this idea was introduced as a bill in the U.S. Senate. The Communications Transfer Fee Act of 1987 would have assessed a tax of 2 percent of the sale price (to be paid by the seller) on the transfer of television and radio station licenses. If the license had been held for less than three years, the tax would be 4 percent of the sale price to discourage trafficking in broadcast licenses. The act also called for the creation of a "Public Broadcasting Trust Fund," into which revenue from the tax would be deposited. Although the proposal was a modest one, only taxing the sales of stations, it met firm resistance from broadcasters. In response to heavy lobbying by the broadcast industry, the bill was defeated in a one-sided vote, although Senator Fritz Hollings claimed that there was initially broad support for the measure.

Opposition from broadcasters is, of course, a major obstacle for any legislation of the sort defeated in 1987. But the broadcast industry is not omnipotent: Measures that it opposes should not automatically be relegated to the dustbin. On a theoretical level, as Senator Hollings noted in 1987, the rationale for taxing broadcast license owners is that those who profit from the commercial use of the television airwaves—major corporate advertisers, local station owners, and (increasingly less) the television networks—should foot the bill for a television system that is oriented more to the creation of a public sphere than the selling of goods.

We need to move the discussion of financing public television beyond the parameters of the 1987 bill. Although more thorough financial analysis will be needed, the basic principle should be clear: A socially owned public television would draw its funding precisely from those who make money from the current organization of the television industry. Major advertisers, who have used the networks as a national sales force, would be taxed a percentage of the amount they spend on commercials, a tax to be split with the broadcasters who receive the payments. Profits from both local stations, which can run as high as 20 percent annually, and the national networks would also be taxed a small amount, as would the sale of broadcast licenses. This revenue would be placed in a specific trust fund, in line with the 1987 bill, in order to insulate public broadcasting from the politically charged federal government appropriations process. Under this kind of plan, strict limitations would also be placed on corporate underwriting of public television programming, with the goal of dramatically scaling back, if not entirely eliminating, this form of funding.

It is likely that the costs of such a tax would, at least in part, be passed from advertisers to consumers in the form of higher prices. This possibility may make the concept somewhat more palatable to the corporate community, but it will leave consumers paying at least some of the costs of the public television system. It is, however, a small price to pay for a more healthy public sphere. The very process of imposing such a tax will certainly face major opposition in the corporate community. The payoff, however, will be more than increased stability in the funding of public television. It will once again clarify that the airwaves are owned by the public and that the commercial use of them is but one construction of a television system.

Diversity

The second principle is diversity. I have suggested throughout the book, particularly in the discussion of the *MacNeil/Lehrer NewsHour* in Chapter 4, that a public television system needs to maintain a commitment to providing a variety of perspectives. It is worth noting that it has become fashionable in the

1990s to criticize those who champion diversity, with the most virulent attacks suggesting that advocates of diversity are totalitarian. In spite of this climate, however, I want to reiterate the significance of diversity as a value in itself. In the context of creating a vibrant public sphere, diversity must be understood as a high priority.

Diversity, in the broadest sense of the word, is in fact central to a democratic society. For democracy is not simply about ratifying decisions made by elites or even going to the voting booth every November. It is about having a society in which citizens participate in wide-ranging discussions that help to shape the decisionmaking process. It is not an easy process, nor does it always run smoothly. In fact, it seems to me that disagreement, rather than consensus, is always at a premium in a democratic society. Keane, discussing Habermas's work, makes this point clearly:

> Habermas' implied model of democratic, public life ... recognizes no fantastic futures, in which existence would become free, easy and ridden of division. Future public life, he infers, would openly recognize, indeed encourage, a plurality of groups and political divisions. Under "post-modern" conditions, the real antagonist of democratic, public life would not be the presence of particularities—competing claims, political quarrels and disputes—but, rather, the denial of their legitimacy (Keane, 1982: 28).

Democracy, then, is about diversity. Democratic public spheres are sites where a multiplicity of ideas from a variety of perspectives can be aired. A democratic public television system needs to take the charge of diversity seriously. It needs to move beyond a simple equation of diversity with multiculturalism (although this is certainly an important first step) and understand the need to seek out dissent and controversy[4]—often the very antithesis of current public television (as well as commercial television) attitudes. Public television will contribute to a healthy public sphere to the extent that it serves as an arena for the airing of different perspectives, particularly those that are outside the boundaries of the established consensus. Doing so certainly will differentiate it from commercial television, which rarely, if ever, strays from the mainstream. It also will make public television a place where new ideas can emerge and be subjected to debate and challenge and where old ideas can be subjected to rigorous scrutiny. With a focus on a diversity that encourages disagreement and dissent, a public television system can make a significant contribution to democratic public life.

Participation

The third principle is participation. A public television system committed to democratic public life needs to develop structures for active citizen involvement. Contemporary democratic theorists have pointed out that participation in one realm can facilitate participation in others. Pateman (1970), for example, argues that workplace participation prepares and empowers people for broader political participation. She notes that "[t]he major function of participation in the theory of participatory democracy is ... an educative one, educative in the very widest sense, including both the psychological aspect and the gaining of practice in democratic skills and procedures" (1970: 42). She concludes that participation in areas of life other than the narrowly defined political arena "would enable the individual better to appreciate the connection between the public and the private spheres. ... In the context of a participatory society the significance of his [sic] vote to the individual would have changed; as well as being a private individual he would have multiple opportunities to become an educated, public citizen" (1970: 110). In short, participation can serve as the key to breaking the barriers between the private and the public realm and reinvigorate democratic public life.

A variety of critics have suggested that the mass media do not adequately prepare citizens in the United States for political participation (cf. Entman, 1989; Kellner, 1990; Bennett, 1988). Even within mainstream American journalism, there is regular commentary about the shortcomings of media coverage of politics and of presidential elections. I do not deny that there is, in fact, a significant lack of substance in much mass media coverage of elections. Nor do I disagree with the broader argument that television often does little to prepare citizens for participation in national political discussion. However, critics who have focused exclusively on the content of the news have overlooked a central point about the nature of political participation. Citizens will not become politically active simply because the news becomes more substantive. It will also take practice in participation, which can be learned through experience in other arenas of society. At the same time, participation in multiple arenas helps to create a democratic public sphere in which citizens are heavily involved in decisionmaking.

Democratic media structures need to create spaces for citizen participation at all levels of the enterprise. In the case of public television, citizen participation can help turn the audience into an active public that is more than simply a market to be targeted. The private ownership of mass media makes the general adoption of a participatory media system impossible. Therefore, public television has the extra responsibility, as well as the opportunity, to begin to develop a more participatory system. As a public institution, public television should be accessible to citizens at both the national and local levels. In decisions ranging from funding to programming, citizens can play a central role. At the national level, both CPB and PBS can make their decisionmaking processes clearer to the public by, in particular, publicizing and opening meetings to interested citizens. The CPB's 1993 plan to hold a series of local meetings with citizens about programming is at least a start; such meetings need to become a permanent feature of public television. More formal structures of participation can also be developed: An arrangement along the lines of that used in Germany, where government, business, labor, and other organized sectors collectively govern public television, has promise for increasing input by those outside the narrow circles that now operate public television at the national level.

Given the largely decentralized nature of the system, increased participation in public television is more feasible, and perhaps more needed, at the local level. Boards of directors of local stations need to become more reflective of their communities, comprising a diverse set of community members rather than simply local elites. By opening boards to citizens and including representatives from diverse constituencies, public stations can move beyond asking for advice and provide the public with a voice in the broader decisionmaking process. The development of these kinds of structures will both strengthen public television's connections to local communities and provide avenues for bringing new constituencies into its orbit.

Public television can also encourage the active involvement of citizens in the creation of programming. Granting access to public television would be a large step toward making the airwaves truly public. Kellner (1990), noting the important role of public access television for a democratic communication system, suggests that "where there are operative public access systems, individuals have a promising, though not sufficiently explored, opportunity to produce and cablecast their own television programs" (1990: 208). Public access stations not only offer an outlet for citizens to make their own programs but also provide training in the use of video equipment, helping to demystify the technology that we spend so much time watching. The growth of public access television, however, has not signaled any change in our public television system. Yet public access television provides an important clue for how to develop a more participatory public television system. As a step in that direction, public television should begin to retake some of the ground that public access has pioneered. Blocks of time could be made available on a regular basis for the broadcasting of programming made by members of the community. Perhaps the Dutch model, based on the principle that "airtime should be available to independent organizations in relation to proven support given to each of them" (Abramson et al., 1988: 202), is a useful reference point. In this case, local organizations that meet certain membership requirements would be given routine access to the airwaves. Additionally, public television should make a commitment to training citizens in the use of video equipment. This kind of education in television literacy is a means by which local stations can build bridges to the public. A television literacy program would both increase the likelihood that citizens would be capable of producing programming and provide citizens with resources for making sense of what they watch. The combination of this kind of hands-on educational program, particularly when public schools lack the resources to develop them, with the possibility of local broadcast will make local public television stations more vibrant community institutions.

Public television should look on increased citizen participation as a great opportunity. Since it is the only broadcast operation with the structural capability to develop such a participatory system, it will be one important way to differentiate public television from the competition. And what better way to build a loyal public following, one that will provide the essential popular support, than to provide avenues for real participation? Ultimately, a more participatory structure will make public television a more vital institution in public life and serve to prepare citizens for participatory roles in other arenas of society.

Interaction

Closely related to participation is a fourth principle, interaction. That is, democratic public television has to allow for more than simply one-way communication. A more participatory system, one that permits citizens to make their own programming, will go a long way toward making television two-way. But such a system will still only provide access to a small percentage of the population. We also need to find ways to make the everyday experience of television less passive and more interactive. In short, we need to develop structures so that people can talk back to the television.

This may seem at first to be a somewhat absurd suggestion; only people who are a little odd would actually talk back to a monitor in their homes. New technologies, however, make interactive television a real possibility in the not-too-distant future. We should not underestimate the powerful forces that will push these technologies in the direction of product promotion and marketing rather than development of a more interactive television system (cf. Neuman, 1991). At the same time, we should recognize that interactive technologies have the capacity to widen the scope of political discussion. Abramson and his colleagues suggest that new communications technologies can help restore democracy by creating an "electronic commonwealth." This "electronic commonwealth harks back to the old democratic ideal of congregating the people together. The contribution of new communications technologies is not to change or update that ideal. It is simply to use electronics to practice the lost democratic arts" (1988: 31). Interactive technologies make a new version of town meetings (which Tocqueville saw as so central to democracy in the United States) possible at the regional and national levels as well. Such programs as National Public Radio's *Talk of the Nation,* and C-Span's call-in shows have begun to provide the kind of electronic, nationwide discussions that commercial broadcasting has largely ignored. The wider application of such technologies provides possibilities for significantly broadening the range of dialogue and debate in the United States.

Other developments include such systems as Warner-Amex's QUBE, which allowed viewers to interact with programmers simply by pushing buttons on a keypad attached to their television sets (cf. Abramson et al., 1988; Rogers, 1986). Although QUBE was used largely for such purposes as home shopping, interactive technologies, in Barber's words, "have a great potential for equalizing access to information, stimulating participatory debate across regions, and encouraging multichoice polling and voting informed by information, discussion, and debate" (1984: 276).

Still, it is important to separate the futuristic hopes for a society run by instant referendum from the use of new technologies to widen debate and discussion. Pushing buttons on a television set, even if it is to signal one's policy preferences, is not equivalent to engaging in a democratic discussion. Arterton, after studying thirteen experiments that used communications technologies to enhance political participation, argued that there is little hope that the new technologies can create a direct democracy—a "teledemocracy"—run by electronic plebiscite. He did, however, find that "technology can make teledemocracy, in the sense of pluralist dialogues, possible" (1987: 200).

Without the pressure to sell products that burdens commercial television, public television has an opportunity to begin to develop interactive technologies for the purpose of enhancing public life. It is likely that there will be only small short-term payoffs but potentially great long-term benefits. Public television is best positioned to take advantage of the new technologies for democratic purposes. It would not be difficult for public television to marshal these technologies for the development of local and national interactive discussion programs, thereby taking back some of the terrain that such cable services as C-Span have usurped.

At the same time, viewers need to think of ways to organize themselves as a means of talking back to those who produce public television. Interactive technologies are not required for citizens to form local or national monitoring associations that provide a structure for collective response to public television. In some communities, such organizations already exist. In the short run, public television, at a minimum, needs to articulate more clearly the importance of feedback from the public and encourage citizens to actively engage both local stations and the national public television system.

Criticism

The fifth principle of a democratic public television system is criticism. The essence of a democratic television system is the ability to critically examine and interrogate major American institutions rather than simply glorify them. During the Gulf War, for example, the principle shortcoming with most media coverage was its celebratory tone (cf. Kellner, 1992). Major media presented themselves as part of the same team as the military and went out of their way to commemorate or salute the military victory. There is certainly a role in all societies for this kind of jubilation. However, it is clearly not the function of a democratic media to play such a prominent role in cheerleading.

A democratic public television needs to make criticism a principal goal. Such criticism need not be partisan in the strict sense of the word; it should be multiperspectival, to use Gans's (1979) term. That is, critical analysis should come from a variety of political viewpoints, from both "expert" analysts and laypeople, and should be seen as part of an ongoing process of criticism and discussion. If we are to become a nation of "critical thinkers," as so much literature in the field of education suggests, we need to begin to find ways to use television to stimulate such thinking. In particular, it will be important for public television to develop strategies for critically analyzing the medium of television itself. The development of a more self-consciously critical approach, with a special emphasis on television criticism, is an achievable short-term goal for public television.

Moving Toward a New Public Television

The road ahead will not be easy. Powerful obstacles, including the forces of the free market and an ideology that separates television producers from the citizenry, will stand in the way of making public television a more public institution. Moreover, the reinvigoration of the public sphere will not be accomplished simply by reforming our public television system. Public television is, nevertheless, a necessary site in which to take this challenge. It is surprising that public television has been ignored by sophisticated analysts who have called for reforming the mass media. Barber's (1984) thoughtful argument for the creation of a "strong democracy," for example, calls for the development of a Civic Communications Cooperative but makes no mention of public television. Abramson and his colleagues (1988) make a good case that new media technologies can help create an "electronic commonwealth" but have little to say about the role of public television. Despite such omissions, it is clear that any serious discussion of democracy and the media in the United States, especially discussions that are policy oriented, must include public television as a central focus.

My own conclusion is that the first step toward reforming public television is to change the funding structure to further insulate it from both the market and the state. This reform would create stable, long-term funding that comes neither from private corporations nor the regular (and highly politicized) appropriations process of the federal government. Perhaps the best place to start is to resurrect a version of the Communications Transfer Fee Act of 1987 and pass national legislation to restructure the funding of public television.

National legislation, although a key starting point, is only part of the picture. If the point of reform is the construction of a democratic public sphere, the process must involve more than simply the passage of new laws. Others, both inside and outside the system, will have to play a role. For example, PBS and local stations will have to become more open to the participation of citizens and develop structures to facilitate such participation. Access to the airwaves will have to be expanded to the broader public, perhaps on the model of *P.O.V.,* the PBS series that broadcasts a wide range of independently produced documentaries each season. And the system will need to begin to experiment with interactive technologies to see if there are ways to use public television to expand local, regional, and national discussion.

With powerful forces aligned against such changes, it is clear that public television will not be restructured in the immediate future. We can, however, begin to examine the conditions under which change is possible and identify signs that suggest that change is occurring. First, and perhaps most important, is the need for a renewed grassroots movement as the carrier of a vision for change. There are indications that social movements have begun to focus more attention on the importance of the mass media. Ryan (1991) showed how various movements have identified the mass media as an arena in which symbolic contests are waged. As a result, reform groups have begun to develop a set of strategies for gaining access to mass media and shaping media coverage. Beyond issue-specific movements, social movement organizations that focus their activism primarily on mass media have also emerged. The campaigns in 1990 to preserve the *Ten O'Clock News* on Boston's public television station and to pressure PBS for discussions of the Gulf War suggest that there is a sense of the importance of public television. Citizen activism, however, has to move beyond a focus on the content of coverage and take on the larger project of restructuring the mass media. Public television, as the most accessible and most reformable segment of the major media, will have to become the major focus of a broad-based grassroots campaign.

It is not inconceivable that such a movement will emerge in the not-too-distant future. Already, citizens with a wide range of political and ideological commitments are unhappy with the media. With most of the anger directed at the commercial media, public television could emerge as the focus of a movement attempting to "save" the airwaves from naked commercialism. The national anticensorship organization FAIR (Fairness & Accuracy In Reporting) has identified public television as a central focus. Independent film producers have made a major effort to broaden access to public television, and they have found allies in Washington and among journalists and filmmakers within public television. A movement focused on the need to further insulate public television from both the market and the state, particularly one calling for a new, long-term funding structure, will find strong supporters at all levels of the public television bureaucracy. And alliances built around the need to reform the funding structure will be instrumental in the development of a more participatory and interactive public television.

Renewed grassroots activism alone will not immediately change public television. Other conditions, which certainly will be facilitated by renewed activism, are necessary as well. The Clinton administration, which is clearly more sympathetic to public television and to nonmarket institutions in general than its predecessors, may be a significant factor. One concrete result of a more sympathetic president will be a change in the makeup of the FCC. A new FCC, less committed to a deregulatory, market-oriented philosophy, could play an important role in facilitating the restructuring of public television.

There are signs that suggest movement in the direction outlined above. The fact that a bill to establish a new public television financing mechanism was introduced in the U.S. Senate, a bill that was strongly supported by public broadcasters, indicates that a new funding arrangement is at least on the agenda. Discussions about such issues as multiculturalism within PBS, including a workshop on multiculturalism for producers at the 1990 annual PBS meeting in Dallas, indicate a growing sensitivity about the importance of diversity. The PBS program *The 90s*, which broadcast activist and experimental video, was at least a small sign that there is room for a more active public in public television (Oullette, 1992). There are also indications that some local community advisory boards have become interested in taking a more active stance toward their local stations.

We should not discount the strong political and economic forces that will provide obstacles to changing public television. The first step, reorganizing the funding structure, is opposed by a powerful and well-organized commercial broadcasting industry. In the 1990s, conservative opponents of PBS have had more resources and better organization than those forces calling for the further insulation of public television. Additionally, a professional culture that identifies the public as an audience will likely make many within public television uncomfortable about a more participatory system. The existence of such obstacles, however, does not guarantee that change is impossible. In a decade that celebrates the expansion of the market into new arenas of social life, it can be difficult to remember the enthusiasm that accompanied the creation of public television in 1967. Conditions for the wholesale restructuring of public television clearly do not exist today; but the forces that could begin to change the political climate, including a broad-based grassroots movement, may not be that far away.

Change at public television is part of a larger project that envisions the construction of a healthy public sphere. Public television is only one site among many. Future research needs to examine the media more generally and begin to envision a larger communications system that enhances public life. At the same time, democratic theorists need to bring the mass media more clearly into the center of their analysis. Such work needs to move beyond a simple recitation of the Bill of Rights as the key to understanding the role of the media in a democratic society. Certainly, protection from state censorship is crucial to a democratic society, but it is only part of the picture. The scholarly literature on the mass media has pointed out the powerful censoring effect of the market, which the Bill of Rights does not address. As this study has suggested, market forces remain a powerful constraint, even in our public television system.

Mass media are an increasingly important part of American culture and society. In this context, the democratization of the media is a crucial part of the ongoing work of defending and extending sites of democratic participation. It is not beyond our capacity to construct a more vigorous public sphere. Given the stakes, it is surprising that many of us are comfortable leaving the media to the forces of the free market. There are, of course, choices to be made; television can be used to enhance public life, not simply to divert our attention or to sell products. A more "public" public television can be an important model on the road to this democratic public life.

Notes

1. In the midst of the 1992 controversy, ABC's *Nightline* (May 12, 1992) presented this narrow two-sided discussion, with conservative columnist George Will criticizing PBS and public television's Bill Moyers defending it. Critics from the Left, particularly those who argue that corporations wield too much influence on public television, were excluded even from the taped report that preceded the Will-Moyers debate. However, comments from such conservative critics as Laurence Jarvik of the Heritage Foundation, Brent Bozell of the Media Research Center, and conservative Senator Jesse Helms were included in the taped segment.

2. Neither Postman nor Sennett make this argument directly, and both make qualifying remarks about the impact of television. Sennett notes that the decline of public life began well before electronic communication; Postman notes that it is ridiculous to think that television can be eliminated. Still, Postman's argument in particular implies that the fundamental problem is with the technology.

3. Cohen and Arato point out that their conception is different from the Hegelian version, which identified civil society as being in opposition to the state. "Beyond the antinomies of state and market, public and private, Gesellschaft and Gemeinschaft, and ... reform and revolution, the idea of the defense and democratization of civil society is the best way to characterize the really new, common strand of contemporary forms of self-organization and self-constitution" (1992: 30).

4. See Croteau and Hoynes (1990) for a discussion of the importance of diversity on television news. They suggest four types of diversity: demographic, substantive political, national, and topical.

Methodological Appendix

In-depth interviews served as the principal research method for this study. Following such studies of commercial news organizations as Epstein (1973), Tuchman (1978), and Gans (1979), as well as Powell and Friedkin's (1983, 1986) study of public television, it was clear that a qualitative research strategy was most appropriate for this project. In particular, I wanted to get "inside" public television to examine the constraints facing those who work in the system and to understand how economic, organizational, and audience "considerations," to use Gans's term, influence the process of producing public television programming. This kind of approach, based on in-depth interviews, is also a useful addition to the existing body of literature on public television, which focuses almost exclusively on content analysis of programming but pays little attention to the internal dynamic of our public television system. (See the literature review in Chapter 3 for further discussion.)

Interviews also allowed me to explore sensitive issues regarding the pressures faced by these public television workers, which a large scale survey would have likely overlooked. In particular, in-depth interviews allowed me to rephrase questions, pose them from different vantage points, and allow informants to pursue their own line of reasoning at length. Interviews were structured but flexible enough to allow for slight changes in emphasis in different interviews, depending on the particular experiences of each informant. When particular stories or examples appeared, I was able to explore them in detail and draw my informants out further.

The face-to-face interaction was also helpful, as I was able to build a strong rapport with twenty-four of the twenty-five informants. In the one difficult case, I dealt with the tension immediately, restored a sense of mutual trust, and continued with an interview that produced interesting and useful data. Finally, interviewing allowed me to weave my informants' words throughout the empirical chapters of this book. This approach provides the reader with a more personal glimpse of these real-life public television workers, whom I often discuss in more abstract terms.

Chapters 5 through 7 are based primarily on in-depth qualitative analysis of these interviews. Between June and December 1990 I interviewed twenty-five individuals who work at Boston's WGBH in the production of national, nonfiction programming for PBS. I used a snowball sample, starting with two individuals at WGBH, to identify potential informants. At the end of each interview, I asked my subject for the names of three more individuals who might be willing to be interviewed. I also requested that the subject allow me to use his or her name in making contact with potential informants. In almost every case, this method provided me with new sources and access to these individuals. In only one interview did an informant refuse to provide me with new names, citing a concern about bothering already overburdened colleagues. In all of the remaining interviews, informants provided at least one further source (although it was not always a new one), and the vast majority agreed that I should use their name in making initial contact. Many even alerted potential informants in advance of my formal letter. The snowball sample provided both a large pool of names and avenues for making contact with these potential informants.

I made use of the principles of "theoretical sampling" outlined by Glaser and Strauss (1967; Strauss, 1987) to help select the specific individuals to interview from this larger pool. This strategy does not seek a sample that is strictly representative of the entire population. Instead, theoretical sampling is a method qualitative researchers use to protect against drawing conclusions too quickly based upon very small samples. Theoretical sampling entails constantly reexamining data, looking for new data, and completing the interview process when new data is no longer emerging. In more concrete terms, I sought out a wide variety of individuals at WGBH, including producers, other production personnel, and administrative staff. As I neared the end of the interview process, I interviewed several free-lancers, all of whom had a great deal of experience at WGBH but did not work for WGBH exclusively. My informants, though not representative in the statistical sense, did represent a variety of occupational categories and, perhaps more important, had a diverse set of experiences at WGBH. The use of two starting points for the snowball also helped to ensure that I would not draw a sample from any one clique within WGBH.

Potential informants initially were contacted by mail. Some responded to my letter requesting an interview; in other cases I followed up the letter with a phone call to schedule. I had a good deal of success recruiting informants; more than three-quarters of those that I initially contacted agreed to be interviewed. Those who would not consent to the interviews provided a wide range of reasons, including a lack of time, a lack of interest, concern about confidentiality, and concern about how one's superiors would respond. In several cases, I did not interview individuals with whom I had made initial contact because it became clear that they were very similar to previous informants. With limited resources, I did not want to spend time duplicating interviews. All informants were assured that interviews were anonymous. The majority of potential informants indicated that anonymity was a condition of the interview. As such, I have not identified any of my informants by name, position, name of program, or gender.

Since my sample is not representative, I present no quantitative data from the interviews. This, it seems to me, is the best approach when using such small sample sizes, for quantitative data would do little more than describe the characteristics of my small sample. Qualitative research is, however, an entirely different matter. In this book, I do not attempt to lay out a formal model of public television, nor do I make direct causal statements or suggest that I am describing the attitudes of people who work inside public television. Large scale surveys with representative samples are much more appropriate for these kinds of issues. This project makes use of a qualitative approach to explore the various economic and organizational pressures faced by public television workers, as well as the meanings these workers attach to such constraints. For this project, then, the question of sample representativeness was less important than such issues as the quality of the data that such interviews were producing, rapport and trust between investigator and informants, candor of informants, and access to a wide range of informants. Given the fact that the literature on public television is focused almost exclusively on content, with little work examining the forces that drive public television, a qualitative approach that focuses on exploring phenomenon, generating hypotheses, and proposing explanations was more appropriate, even for the social scientist, than a project that sought to elaborate a causal model.

Interviews averaged slightly more than one hour and ranged from a low of fifty minutes to a high of two hours. All interviews were audio taped and transcribed. Nineteen of the twenty-five interviews took place at the offices of WGBH, five at the home of the informant, and one at my home. Prior to the interview, each informant was provided, either by phone or by mail, with a general overview of the plan for the interview. This same overview was reiterated immediately before the beginning of each interview. The interview schedule focused on seven issues: personal background of informant, the similarities and differences between commercial and public television, the funding of public television, the organization of public television, the role of and relationship to the public, the mission of public television, and the future of public television. I tried to remain flexible enough to allow my informants to develop their own perspectives and to permit probing in discussions of sensitive issues.

In line with the principles of theoretical sampling, during the stage of identifying potential respondents I made an effort to contact a variety of people. Of the twenty-five respondents, eleven were women and fourteen were men. Twelve were producers, nine were production staff, and four were administrators. I also wanted the perspectives of people who entered the system at different times. Of the twenty-five informants, eight were relative newcomers with less than five years of experience in public television; ten were veterans with between five and ten years in the system; and seven were old-timers with more than ten years in public television.

My effort to interview a range of people who work on national, nonfiction programming suggested that I be alert to several other issues. A great many public television producers have previous experience in commercial television. In my sample, twelve informants had experience in commercial television and thirteen did not. As I neared the end of my interview process, I made a particular effort to interview several people who had recent experience in both commercial and public television production.

Informants had experience working on a wide-range of PBS programs, including *Frontline, American Experience, Nova, AIDS Quarterly, Americas, Vietnam: A Television History, War and Peace in the Nuclear Age, Living Against the Odds, Eyes on the Prize, Crisis in Central America, Columbus and the Age of Discovery, Nixon, Korea: The Unknown War, Inside Gorbachev's USSR, Enterprise,* and *The Advocates,* among many others.

Printed transcripts of these interviews served as the primary data source. After transcription, interviews were coded thematically; these themes, in many instances, became the basis for sections of chapters, often denoted by subheadings, within the empirical chapters of this book. I also wrote field notes immediately after each interview. These notes served as an important supplemental source of data, particularly throughout the recruitment and interview process. Field notes were helpful in preparing for future interviews, sharpening my ability to conduct the interviews, helping me to develop and rethink preliminary interpretations, and helping to select future informants.

In addition to these interviews, I conducted a case study of the *MacNeil/Lehrer NewsHour,* the principal news program on public television. The case study compared *MacNeil/Lehrer* with a comparable hour of ABC News (both *World News Tonight* and *Nightline*) over a six-month period, from February 6, 1989, through August 4, 1989. Every edition of both *MacNeil/Lehrer* and *Nightline* during this period was included, along with all weekday editions of *World News Tonight*—a total of 130 editions per program. Analysis of *MacNeil/Lehrer* and *Nightline* was based on printed transcripts of the 130 programs. Analysis of *World News Tonight* was based on the abstracts to the Vanderbilt Television News Archive, which are published in *Television News Index and Abstracts.*

Stories on each of the three programs were coded by topic. For *MacNeil/Lehrer,* all stories other than the brief news update were included. For *World News Tonight,* all stories lasting one minute or longer were included. All guests appearing on either *MacNeil/Lehrer* or *Nightline* were coded on a variety of dimensions, including race, gender, nationality, occupation, and institutional affiliation. Only those individuals who were actual guests on the two programs—that is, who appeared in the studio, via satellite, or by telephone in an interview or discussion segment—were included in this analysis. Those quoted in the *Nightline* background segments or in the lengthy taped reports on *MacNeil/Lehrer* were not coded as guests. Four major issues during the six-month period—the environment, the economy, China, and Central America—were also subject to more in-depth qualitative analysis as a means of further comparing the *NewsHour* and *Nightline*. All relevant segments, whether interview, discussion, or taped report, were included in these four case studies.

These data allowed for the comparison between *MacNeil/Lehrer* and *ABC News* to focus on three areas that suggest a great deal about the content of the programming. The comparison of story topic on the *NewsHour* and *World News Tonight* is suggestive of the range of coverage on the two programs. The quantitative analysis of the guest lists of *MacNeil/Lehrer* and *Nightline* tells us a great deal about the political content of the programs, since both programs rely on guests for their discussions and debates of current issues. The format of both *MacNeil/Lehrer* and *Nightline* allows substantial room for guests to present their personal interpretation of issues. As a result, the choice of guests is crucial to the content of the program. Finally, the case studies allowed for a more in-depth comparison of coverage of specific issues. Since television news programs address a wide range of stories, comparative analysis is most fruitful with the case study approach.

There are several relevant issues for public television—and for a media sociology interested in the relationship between media and democracy—that these methods have not highlighted. Future research on public television needs to examine local public television stations more fully, particularly small stations that are not involved in national production, as is WGBH. It is likely that the dynamics I discuss in this book, as well as questions for the future, are different at smaller stations. Longitudinal content analysis of public television programming would also be helpful, as it would suggest a good deal about the changing nature of public television over the past quarter-century. Analysis of the activities of community advisory boards in various cities, as well as the meaning of station "membership" for those individuals who contribute to public television, would further develop our understanding of the current and potential relationship between public television and various publics. Research at the national level on the nature of the Public Broadcasting Service and the Corporation for Public Broadcasting will also help to fill out our picture of how public television works. In particular, Lashley's (1992) analysis of CPB and its relationship to the federal government suggests that the political pressures faced by these national organizations is an area that is ripe for future research. With such a short supply of recent research on public television and with a growing debate about the utility of noncommercial television, research on a wide range of issues, making use of both qualitative and quantitative approaches, is needed in the coming years.

References

Abercrombie, Nicholas, Stephen Hill, and Bryan S. Turner. 1988. *The Penguin Dictionary of Sociology*, 2nd edition. London: Penguin.

Abramson, Jeffrey B. 1990. "Four Criticisms of Press Ethics," in Judith Lichtenberg, ed., *Democracy and the Mass Media*. Cambridge: Cambridge University Press.

Abramson, Jeffrey B., F. Christopher Arterton, and Gary R. Orren. 1988. *The Electronic Commonwealth*. New York: Basic Books.

Agostino, Don. 1980. "Cable Television's Impact on the Audience of Public Television." *Journal of Broadcasting* 24 (3): 347–365.

Aldrich, Howard E., and Jeffrey Pfeffer. 1976. "Environments of Organizations." *Annual Review of Sociology* 2: 79–105.

Ang, Ien. 1991. *Desperately Seeking the Audience*. New York: Routledge.

Angus, Ian, and Sut Jhally, eds. 1989. *Cultural Politics in Contemporary America*. New York/London: Routledge.

Arterton, F. Christopher. 1987. *Teledemocracy: Can Technology Protect Democracy?* Beverly Hills: Sage.

Aufderheide, Patricia. 1991. "Public Television and the Public Sphere." *Critical Studies in Mass Communication* 8 (June), 168–183.

_____ . 1989. "Are Private Interests Ruling Public Television?" *Business and Society Review* 69: 16–19.

_____ . 1988. "The Corporatization of Public TV: Why Labor's Voice Is Seldom Heard on PBS." *Extra!* November/December, pp. 12–14.

Auletta, Ken. 1991. *Three Blind Mice: How the TV Networks Lost Their Way*. New York: Random House.

Avery, R., and R. Pepper. 1980. "An Institutional History of Public Broadcasting." *Journal of Communication* 30 (3): 126–138.

Bagdikian, Ben. 1990. *The Media Monopoly*, 3rd edition. Boston: Beacon Press.

Barber, Benjamin R. 1984. *Strong Democracy*. Berkeley: University of California Press.

Barnouw, Erik. 1990. *Tube of Plenty*. New York: Oxford.

_____ . 1978. *The Sponsor: Notes on a Modern Potentate*. New York: Oxford University Press.

Baughman, James L. 1985. *Television's Guardians: The FCC and the Politics of Programming 1958–1967*. Knoxville: University of Tennessee Press.

Bellah, Robert N., Richard Madsen, William M. Sullivan, Ann Swidler, and Steven M. Tipton. 1985. *Habits of the Heart*. Berkeley: University of California Press.

Bellah, Robert N., Richard Madsen, William M. Sullivan, Ann Swidler, and Steven M. Tipton. 1991. *The Good Society*. New York: Knopf.

187

Bennett, W. Lance. 1988. *News: The Politics of Illusion*, 2nd edition. New York: Longman.

Berkman, David. 1980. "Minorities in Public Broadcasting." *Journal of Communication* 30 (3): 179–188.

Beville, Hugh Malcolm, Jr. 1985. *Audience Ratings: Radio, Television, Cable*. Hillsdale, NJ: Lawrence Erlbaum Associates.

Blakely, Robert J. 1971. *The People's Instrument: A Philosophy of Programming for Public Television*. Washington, DC: Public Affairs Press.

Blau, Peter M. and Marshall W. Meyer. 1971. *Bureaucracy in Modern Society*, 2nd edition. New York: Random House.

Bourdieu, Pierre. 1984. *Distinction: A Social Critique of the Judgement of Taste*. Translated by Richard Nice. Cambridge: Harvard University Press.

Branscomb, Anne W. 1976. "A Crisis of Identity: Reflections on the Future of Public Broadcasting," in Cater and Nyhan, eds. *The Future of Public Broadcasting*. New York: Praeger.

Brown, Les. 1971. *Television: The Business Behind the Box*. New York: Harcourt Brace Jovanovich.

Burger, Thomas. 1976. *Max Weber's Theory of Concept Formation: History, Laws, and Ideal Types*. Durham, NC: Duke University Press.

Campbell, David C. and Joyce B. Campbell. 1978. "Public Television as a Public Good." *Journal of Communication* 28: 52–62.

Cantor, Muriel G. 1978. "Where are the Women in Public Broadcasting?" in G. Tuchman, A. K. Daniels, and J. Benet, eds., *Hearth and Home: Images of Women in the Mass Media*. New York: Oxford.

Carey, John. "Public Broadcasting and Federal Policy," in Paula R. Newberg, ed., *New Directions in Telecommunications Policy*, Volume 1. Durham: Duke University Press, 1989.

Carnegie Commission on Educational Television. 1967. *Public Television: A Program For Action*. New York: Bantam.

Carnegie Commission on the Future of Public Broadcasting. 1979. *A Public Trust*. New York: Bantam.

Cohen, Jean L. 1985. "Strategy of Identity: New Theoretical Paradigms and Contemporary Social Movements." *Social Research* 52: 663–716.

Cohen, Jean L. and Andrew Arato. 1992. *Civil Society and Political Theory*. Cambridge: MIT Press.

Cole, Barry, and Mal Oettinger. 1978. *Reluctant Regulators: The FCC and the Broadcast Audience*. Reading, MA: Addision-Wesley.

Collins, Richard, Nicholas Garnham, and Gareth Locksley. 1988. *The Economics of Television: The UK Case*. London: Sage.

Communications Transfer Fee Act of 1987. [S. 1935]

Coontz, Stephanie. 1992. *The Way We Never Were: American Families and the Nostalgia Trap*. New York: Basic Books.

Corporation for Public Broadcasting. 1992. *Public Broadcasting and You*. Washington, DC: CPB.

———. 1991. *1991 Annual Report: From Wasteland to Oasis: A Quarter Century of Sterling Programming*. Washington, DC: CPB.

Corporation for Public Broadcasting, Task Force on Public Participation in Public Broadcasting. 1978. "Public Participation in Public Broadcasting." Washington: CPB.

Croteau, David, and William Hoynes. 1990. "Democracy, Diversity, and Television News." *Television Quarterly*, Fall.

Cumings, Bruce. *War and Television*. London/NY: Verso. 1992.

CUNY Committee for Cultural Studies. 1990. "PBS and the American Worker." Unpublished report.

Daniel, Josh. 1992. "Uncivil Wars: The Conservative Assault on Public Broadcasting." *The Independent*, August/September.

Dates, Jannette L. 1990. "Public Television," in J. L. Dates and W. Barlow, eds., *Split Image: African Americans in the Mass Media*. Washington: Howard University Press.

Dimaggio, Paul. 1987. "Nonprofit Organizations in the Production and Distribution of Culture," in Walter W. Powell, ed., *The Nonprofit Sector*. New Haven: Yale University Press.

Edelman, Murray J. 1988. *Constructing the Political Spectacle*. Chicago: University of Chicago Press.

Elliott, Phillip. 1982. "Intellectuals, the 'Information Society' and the Disappearance of the Public Sphere." *Media, Culture and Society* 4: 243–253.

Emerson, Steven. 1989. "The System That Brought You *Days of Rage*." *Columbia Journalism Review*, November/December, pp. 25–30.

Entman, Robert. 1989. *Democracy Without Citizens*. New York: Oxford.

Epstein, Edward J. 1973. *News From Nowhere*. New York: Vintage.

Ermann, M. David. 1978. "The Operative Goals of Corporate Philanthropy: Contributions to the Public Broadcasting Service, 1972–1976." *Social Problems* 25: 504–514.

Fairness and Accuracy In Reporting. 1992. "PBS' Missing Voices." *Extra!* June.

Fiske, John. 1989. *Understanding Popular Culture*. Boston: Unwin Hyman.

———. 1987. *Television Culture*. London/New York: Routledge.

Fletcher, James E. 1977. "Commercial Versus Public Television Audiences: Public Activities and the Watergate Hearings." *Communication Quarterly* 25 (4): 13–16.

Frank, Ronald E., and Marshall G. Greenberg. 1982. *Audiences for Public Television*. Beverly Hills: Sage.

Frank, Ronald E., and Marshall G. Greenberg. 1980. *The Public's Use of Television: Who Watches and Why*. Beverly Hills: Sage.

Gamson, William A. 1992. *Talking Politics*. Cambridge: Cambridge University Press.

———. 1991. "Commitment and Agency in Social Movements." *Sociological Forum* 6: 27–50.

Gamson, William A., David Croteau, William Hoynes, and Theodore Sasson. 1992. "Media Images and the Social Construction of Reality." *Annual Review of Sociology* 18: 373–393.

Gamson, William A., and Andre Modigliani. 1989. "Media Discourse and Public Opinion on Nuclear Power: A Constructionist Approach." *American Journal of Sociology* 95 (1): 1–37.

Gans, Herbert. 1988. *Middle American Individualism*. New York: Free Press.

———. 1979. *Deciding What's News*. New York: Vintage.

Garnham, Nicholas. 1990. *Capitalism and Communication: Global Culture and the Economics of Information*. London: Sage.

———. 1986. "The Media and the Public Sphere," in Golding, Murdock, and Schlesinger, eds., *Communicating Politics*. New York: Holmes and Meier.

———. 1983. "Public Service Versus the Market." *Screen* 24:1 (January/February).

———. 1978. *Structures of Television*. London: British Film Institute.

Gerth, Hans, and C. Wright Mills, eds. 1946. *From Max Weber: Essays in Sociology*. New York: Oxford University Press.

Giddens, Anthony. 1971. *Capitalism and Modern Social Theory*. Cambridge: Cambridge University Press.

Giroux, Henry A. 1988. *Schooling and the Struggle for Public Life*. Minneapolis: University of Minnesota Press.

Gitlin, Todd. 1985. *Inside Prime Time*. New York: Pantheon.

———. 1980. *The Whole World Is Watching*. Berkeley: University of California Press.

Glazer, Barney G., and Anselm L. Strauss. 1967. *The Discovery of Grounded Theory*. New York: Aldine de Gruyter.

Greider, William. 1992. *Who Will Tell the People*. New York: Simon and Schuster.

Grossman, Lawrence K. 1992. "PBS Funding Mix Helps Keep It Uniquely Free." *Boston Sunday Globe*, May 17, p. 84.

Habermas, Jurgen. 1987 [1981]. *The Theory of Communicative Action: Volume 2. Lifeworld and System: A Critique of Functionalist Reason*. Boston: Beacon Press.

———. 1989 [1962]. *The Structural Transformation of the Public Sphere*. Cambridge: MIT Press.

Hacket, Robert A. 1984. "Decline of a Paradigm? Bias and Objectivity in News Media Studies." *Critical Studies in Mass Communication* 1 (3): 229–259.

Hall, Stuart. 1986. "Introduction," in D. Morley, *Family Television*. London: Comedia.

Herman, Edward, and Noam Chomsky. 1988. *Manufacturing Consent*. New York: Pantheon.

Hertsgaard, Mark. 1988. *On Bended Knee*. New York: Schocken Books.

———. 1989. "Covering the World: Ignoring the Earth." *Rolling Stone*, November 16, pp. 47–49.

Himmelstein, Jerome L. 1990. *To the Right: The Transformation of American Conservatism*. Berkeley: University of California Press.

Holtz-Bacha, Christina. 1991. "From Public Monopoly to a Dual Broadcasting System in Germany." *European Journal of Communication* 6: 223–233.

Hood, Stuart. 1986. "Broadcasting and the Public Interest: From Consensus to Crisis," in Golding, Murdock, and Schlesinger, eds., *Communicating Politics*. New York: Holmes & Meier.

Horowitz, David. 1991. "The Politics of Public Television." *Commentary* 92 (December): 25–32.

Hoynes, William. 1991. "War as Video Game: Media, Activism, and the Gulf War," in Cynthia Peters, ed., *Collateral Damage: The 'New World Order' at Home and Abroad*. Boston: South End Press.

Hoynes, William, and David Croteau. 1990. "All the Usual Suspects: *MacNeil/Lehrer* and *Nightline*." New York: FAIR.

Hurwitz, Donald. 1984. "Broadcast Ratings: The Missing Dimension." *Critical Studies in Mass Communication* 1 (2): 205–215.

Isber, Caroline, and Muriel Cantor. 1975. *Report of the Task Force on Women in Public Broadcasting.* Washington: CPB.

Ivers, Susan C. 1989. "Congress, the Corporation for Public Broadcasting, and Independent Producers: Agenda Setting and Policy Making in Public Television." Paper presented to the Broadcasting Education Association, Annual Convention, Las Vegas, Nevada.

Ivers, Susan C., and Charles E. Clift. 1989. "A Decade of Quiet: The Failure of Academic Research to Explore Public Broadcasting in the United States in the 1980s." Unpublished paper presented to the International Communication Association, San Francisco, California.

Iyengar, Shanto, and Donald R. Kinder. 1987. *News That Matters: Television and American Opinion.* Chicago: University of Chicago Press.

Jamieson, K. H. 1984. *Packaging the Presidency.* New York: Oxford University Press.

Jarvik, Laurence. 1992a. "Making Public Television Public." Washington, DC: The Heritage Foundation.

———. 1992b. "What Price PBS?" *Boston Sunday Globe,* May 10, p. 73.

Jhally, Sut. 1990. *The Codes of Advertising.* New York: Routledge.

———. 1989. "The Political Economy of Culture," in I. Angus and S. Jhally, eds., *Cultural Politics in Contemporary America.* New York/London: Routledge.

Kahn, Frank J. 1978. *Documents of American Broadcasting,* 3rd edition. Englewood Cliffs, NJ: Prentice-Hall.

Katz, Helen. 1989. "The Future of Public Broadcasting in the US." *Media, Culture and Society* 11: 195–205.

Keane, John. 1991. *The Media and Democracy.* London: Polity Press.

———. 1984. *Public Life and Late Capitalism.* Cambridge: Cambridge University Press.

———. 1982. "Elements of a Radical Theory of Public Life: From Tonnies to Habermas and Beyond." *Canadian Journal of Political and Social Theory* 6 (3): 11–49.

Kellner, Douglas. 1992. *The Persian Gulf TV War.* Boulder, CO: Westview Press.

———. 1990. *Television and the Crisis of Democracy.* Boulder, CO: Westview Press.

Kosinski, Jerzy. 1971. *Being There.* New York: Bantam Books.

Krugman, Dean M., and Leonard N. Reid. 1980. "The 'Public Interest' as Defined by FCC Policy Makers." *Journal of Broadcasting* 24 (3): 311–321.

Lashley, Marilyn. 1992. *Public Television: Panacea, Pork Barrel, or Public Trust?* New York: Greenwood Press.

Lashner, Marilyn A. 1977. "The Role of Foundations in Public Broadcasting, II: The Ford Foundation." *Journal of Broadcasting* 21 (2): 235–253.

———. 1976. "The Role of Foundations in Public Broadcasting, Part I: Development and Trends." *Journal of Broadcasting* 20 (4): 529–547.

Lee, Martin A., and Norman Solomon. 1990. *Unreliable Sources.* New York: Lyle Stuart.

Lewis, Justin. 1991. *The Ideological Octopus.* New York: Routledge.

Lichter, S. Robert, Daniel Amundson, and Linda S. Lichter. 1992. *Balance and Diversity in PBS Documentaries.* Washington, DC: Center for Media and Public Affairs.

Lynd, Robert S. 1967 [1939]. *Knowledge for What?* Princeton: Princeton University Press.

MacDonald, J. Fred. 1990. *One Nation Under Television.* New York: Pantheon.

Macy, John W., Jr. 1974. *To Irrigate a Wasteland.* Berkeley: University of California Press.

Mander, Jerry. 1978. *Four Arguments for the Elimination of Television.* New York: Quill.

Matelski, Marilyn J. 1985. "Image and Influence: Women in Public Television." *Journalism Quarterly* (Spring) 147–150.

McCombs, Maxwell E. 1988. "Concentration, Monopoly, and Content," in Picard, Winter, McCombs, and Lacy, eds., *Press Concentration and Monopoly: New Perspectives on Newspaper Ownership and Operation.* Norwood, NJ: Ablex Publishing.

McDonnell, James, ed. 1991. *Public Service Broadcasting: A Reader.* London/New York: Routledge.

McQuail, Denis. 1987. *Mass Communication Theory: An Introduction,* 2nd edition. London: Sage.

Meehan, Eileen R. 1990. "Why We Don't Count: The Commodity Audience," in Patricia Mellencamp, ed., *Logics of Television.* Bloomington: Indiana University Press.

Melucci, Alberto. 1989. *Nomads of the Present.* Philadelphia: Temple University Press.

Meyer, John W., and Brian Rowan. 1977. "Institutionalized Organizations: Formal Structure as Myth and Ceremony." *American Journal of Sociology* 83: 340–363.

Millard, Steve. 1976. "Specialized Audiences: A Scaled-Down Dream?" D. Cater and M. J. Nyhan, eds., *The Future of Public Broadcasting.* New York: Praeger.

Miller, Marc Crispin, ed. 1990. *Seeing Through Movies.* New York: Pantheon.

Morley, David. 1986. *Family Television.* London: Comedia.

Mowlana, Hamid, George Gerbner, and Herbert I. Schiller, eds. 1992. *Triumph of the Image: The Media's War in the Persian Gulf, A Global Perspective.* Boulder, CO: Westview Press.

Murdock, Graham. 1992. "Citizens, Consumers, and Public Culture," in M. Skovmand and K. C. Schrøder, eds., *Media Cultures: Reappraising Transnational Media,* pp. 17–41. London/New York: Routledge.

Naureckas, Jim. 1992. "Study of Bias or Biased Study?: The Lichter Method and the Attack on PBS Documentaries." FAIR Research Memo, May 14. New York: FAIR.

Neuman, W. Russell. 1991. *The Future of the Mass Audience.* New York: Cambridge University Press.

Neuman, W. Russell, Marion R. Just, and Ann N. Crigler. 1992. *Common Knowledge.* Chicago: University of Chicago Press.

Nimmo, Dan, and James E. Combs. 1990. *Mediated Political Realities,* 2nd edition. New York: Longman.

Noll, Roger G., Merton J. Peck, and John J. McGowan. 1973. *Economic Aspects of Television Regulation.* Washington, DC: The Brookings Institution.

Ouellette, Laurie. 1992. "The (Video) Revolution Will Be Televised." *Utne Reader* 50 (March/April), pp. 20–22.

_____ . 1991. "Right Wing vs. Public TV." *MediaCulture Review* 1: 1.

Paletz, David L., and Robert M. Entman. 1981. *Media, Power, Politics.* New York: Free Press.

Pateman, Carole. 1970. *Participation and Democratic Theory.* Cambridge: Cambridge University Press.

Pearce, Jone L., and Judy Rosener. 1985. "Advisory Board Performance: Managing Ambiguity and Limited Commitment in Public Television." *Journal of Voluntary Action Research* 14 (4): 36–47.

Pepper, Robert M. 1979. *The Formation of the Public Broadcasting Service.* New York: Arno Press.

Perrow, Charles. 1961. "The Analysis of Goals in Complex Organizations." *American Sociological Review* 26: 854–866.

Philo, Greg. 1990. *Seeing and Believing: The Influence of Television.* London/New York: Routledge.

Picard, Robert G., James P. Winter, Maxwell E. McCombs, and Stephen Lacy, eds. 1988. *Press Concentration and Monopoly: New Perspectives on Newspaper Ownership.* Norwood, NJ: Ablex Publishing Corporation.

Postman, Neil. 1985. *Amusing Ourselves to Death.* New York: Viking.

Powell, Walter W. 1987. "The Blockbuster Decade: The Media as Big Business," in Lazere, Donald, ed., *American Media and Mass Culture: Left Perspectives.* Berkeley: University of California Press.

Powell, Walter W., ed. 1987. *The Nonprofit Sector.* New Haven: Yale University Press.

Powell, Walter W., and Rebecca Friedkin. 1986. "Politics and Programs: Organizational Factors in Public Television Decision Making," in P. Dimaggio, ed., *Nonprofit Enterprise in the Arts.* New York: Oxford University Press.

Powell, Walter W., and Rebecca Friedkin. 1983. "Political and Organizational Influences on Public Television Programming." *Mass Communication Review Yearbook* 4: 413–438.

Press, Andrea L. 1991. *Women Watching Television.* Philadelphia: University of Pennsylvania Press.

Public Broadcasting Act of 1967. [Public Law 90-129]

Public Broadcasting Service. 1985. *Who Watches Public Television?* Alexandria, VA: PBS Research.

Public Telecommunications Financing Act of 1978. [Public Law 95-567]

Public Telecommunications Act of 1992. [Public Law 102-356]

Rapping, Elayne. 1987. *The Looking Glass World of Nonfiction Television.* Boston: South End Press.

Reed, Craig, Steve Sherman, and Pearl Smith. 1992. *National Audience Report.* Alexandria, VA: PBS Research.

Reeves, Michael G., and Tom W. Hoffer. 1976. "The Safe, Cheap and Known: A Content Analysis of the First (1974) PBS Program Cooperative." *Journal of Broadcasting* 20 (4): 549–565.

Reinarman, Craig. 1987. *American States of Mind.* New Haven, CT: Yale University Press.

Rogers, Everett M. 1986. *Communication Technology.* New York: Free Press.

Rowland, Willard D., Jr. 1986. "Continuing Crisis in Public Broadcasting: A History of Disenfranchisement." *Journal of Broadcasting and Electronic Media* 30 (3): 251–274.

――――. 1980. "The Federal Regulatory and Policymaking Process." *Journal of Communication* 30 (3): 139–149.

――――. 1976. "Public Involvement: The Anatomy of a Myth," in Cater and Nyhan, eds., *The Future of Public Broadcasting.* New York: Praeger.

Ryan, Charlotte. 1993. "NPR: Tilting Center." New York: FAIR.

――――. 1991. *Prime Time Activism.* Boston: South End Press.

Scannell, Paddy. 1990. "Public Service Broadcasting: the History of a Concept," in A. Goodwin and G. Whannel, eds., *Understanding Television.* London/New York: Routledge.

――――. 1989. "Public Service Broadcasting and Modern Public Life." *Media, Culture and Society* 11: 135–166.

Schiller, D. 1986. "Transformations of News in the U.S. Information Market," in Golding, Murdock, and Schlesinger., eds., *Communicating Politics.* New York: Holmes and Meier.

Schiller, Herbert I. 1989. *Culture, Inc.* New York: Oxford.

Schone, Mark. 1992. "The Jarvik Mart." *Village Voice,* February 25, pp. 46–47.

Sennett, Richard. 1974. *The Fall of Public Man.* New York: Vintage.

Slade, Joseph W. and Leonard J. Barchak. 1989. "Public Broadcasting in Finland: Inventing a National Television Programming Policy." *Journal of Broadcasting and Electronic Media* 33 (4): 355–373.

Spigel, Lynn. 1992. *Make Room for TV.* Chicago: University of Chicago Press.

Stavitsky, Alan G. 1988. "Toward a Rhetorical Vision of Public Television." Unpublished paper.

Steinem, Gloria. 1990. "Sex, Lies, and Advertising." *Ms.* July/August: 18–28.

Stone, David M. 1985. *Nixon and the Politics of Public Television.* New York/London: Garland Publishing, Inc.

Strauss, Anselm L. 1987. *Qualitative Analysis for Social Scientists.* Cambridge: Cambridge University Press.

Syvertsen, Trine. 1991. "Public Television in Crisis: Critiques Compared in Norway and Britain." *European Journal of Communication* 6: 95–114.

Tocqueville, Alexis de. 1945 [1835]. *Democracy in America.* New York: Vintage.

Traub, James. 1985. "That [too long?] One-Hour News Show." *Columbia Journalism Review,* January/February, pp. 41–43.

Tuchman, Gaye. 1978. *Making News.* New York: The Free Press.

Weber, Max. 1949. *The Methodology of the Social Sciences.* Translated and edited by Edward A. Shils and Henry A. Finch. New York: The Free Press.

Wenner, Lawrence A. 1975. "Citizen Involvement in Public Television." University of Iowa: Unpublished paper.

Westin, Av. 1982. *Newswatch.* New York: Simon and Schuster.

Wicklein, John. 1986. "The Assault on Public Television." *Columbia Journalism Review,* January/February, pp. 27–34.

Williams, Gilbert A. 1985. "Public Television's Black Pioneer: WHMM TV/32." *Phylon* XLVI (4): 363–371.

Witherspoon, John, and Roselle Kovitz. 1987. *The History of Public Broadcasting.* Washington, DC: Current.

Wolfe, Alan. 1989. *Whose Keeper? Social Science and Moral Obligation.* Berkeley: University of California Press.

Young, T. R. 1985. "The Structure of Democratic Communications." *Mid-American Review of Sociology* 10 (2): 55–76.

About the Book and Author

Public television is uniquely positioned in our country to contribute to the invigoration of democratic public life because, ostensibly, it is neither driven by the market nor dominated by the state. In this comprehensive analysis of the forces that shape our public television system, sociologist William Hoynes finds that public television increasingly is falling prey to privatization.

Taking note of the 1992 conservative campaign to end federal funding of public television, Hoynes examines the nature of public television's funding structure and its impact on programming, the relationship between public television and the public that it is intended to serve, and the consequences of the absence of shared goals within public television. He shows that the forces of the economic market are imposing increasingly severe constraints on this supposedly "independent" television system.

Hoynes offers a fascinating comparison of the *MacNeil/Lehrer NewsHour* to ABC's *Nightline* (the most comparable news program to be found on commercial television) on issues ranging from China to the environment to the economy to Central America. His findings will be startling to most of us.

In his final chapter, Hoynes outlines the principles of a nonmarket, nonstate public television system and assesses the forces capable of reforming public television to maintain its independent voice. Fundamentally, this is a book about the relationship between media and democracy, as well as an examination of the kind of system needed to help sustain a democratic society.

William Hoynes is assistant professor of sociology at Vassar College.

Index

as obsolete, 8
as outsider, 128–129, 146
ownership, 168–171
and presidential administrations, 22(n3)
and ratings, 117–129
reform of, 177–179
success in, 125–129
workers in, 143–148. *See also* Producers
See also Corporation for Public
  Broadcasting; Funding; Local stations;
  Public Broadcasting Service
Public utilities, 38, 41. *See also* Public
  service model

QUBE, 176

Race to Save the Planet, 78
Racial issues, 140
Radio, 13, 38–39, 41, 44(n12), 51, 152–
  153, 166, 170, 175
Radio Act of 1927, 38
Rain forests, 78
Ratings, 16, 17(fig.), 33–37, 68, 85, 94,
  129
  cume ratings, 17, 18(fig.)
  as democratic mechanism, 33, 34–37
  meters for, 44(n11)
  as price-setting mechanism, 34, 35
  in public television, 117–129
  stability in, 119
  and success, 125–129
Rawl, Lawrence, 79
Raymond, Lee, 80
Reagan, Ronald, 4, 28, 114
Reeves, Michael G., 61
Reforms, 177, 178, 179
Regulation/deregulation, 4, 28, 32, 38,
  40
Reilly, William, 79
Research, 10, 25, 48, 55–63, 131, 165,
  179
Reviews, 128, 129, 135
Revolving door, 40
Riggs, Marlon, 154
Risk-taking, 23(n7), 61. *See also under*
  Funding
Robinson, Randall, 107
Rowland, Willard D., Jr., 58–59, 60

Ryan, Charlotte, 178

Say Brother, 131
Scannell, Paddy, 42
Schiller, D., 32
Schiller, Herbert, 32, 165
Self-censorship, 109–112
Seniors, 62
Sennett, Richard, 161, 162, 180(n2)
Signals Catalog, 133
Social control, 164
Social problems, 160
Social science/sociology, 10, 22, 35, 48,
  149, 160, 163, 165
Social theory, 159
Solomon, Norman, 57
South Africa Now, 106–107
Soviet Union, 5
SPC. *See* Station Program Cooperative
State control. *See* Political/state control
State government, 12, 90, 100
Station Program Cooperative (SPC), 4,
  23(n7), 61, 95
Stavitsky, Alan G., 60, 148
Steinem, Gloria, 30
Subscribers, 15, 90, 92, 92(table), 94,
  100, 112–113

Talk of the Nation, 175
Taxation, 170–171. *See also* Excise taxes
Technology, 160–162, 174, 180(n2). *See
  also* Mass media, new technologies
Telecommunications Financing Act of
  1978, 59, 131
Television channels, 39, 44(n13)
Ten O'Clock News (WGBH/Boston), 68,
  131, 178
The 90s, 179
Theory of Communicative Action
  (Habermas), 164
Think tanks, 76, 159
Tiananmen Square, 76–78
Time magazine, 31, 69
Tinker, Grant, 89
Tisch, Laurence, 67
To Irrigate a Wasteland (Macy), 50
Tongues Untied, 154
TransAfrica, 107